Eco Bible

VOLUME ONE
An Ecological Commentary
on Genesis and Exodus

Rabbi Yonatan Neril *&* Rabbi Leo Dee
EDITORS AND LEAD CONTRIBUTORS

First Edition
Printed according to ecological standards.
Library of Congress Control Number: 2020912653

ISBN 978-1-7353388-0-4

Cover design by Austin Rubben
Set in Arno Pro and Hoefler Requiem
by Raphaël Freeman MISTD, Renana Typesetting
Cover image by Tien Vu from Pixabay

Permissions: Content from Canfei Nesharim articles have been reprinted by permission of Canfei Nesharim, a branch of Grow Torah.

About 500 verses have been reprinted from the *Tanakh: The Holy Scriptures* by permission of the University of Nebraska Press. Copyright 1985 by The Jewish Publication Society, Philadelphia.

Translations of the Babylonian Talmud have been reprinted by permission of Koren Publishers from The William Davidson Digital Edition of the Koren Noé Talmud.

Praise for Eco Bible

"What faith communities need from the Bible in such a time as this are dialogue and direction. *Eco Bible* offers a rich repository of insights, drawing from both ancient rabbinic commentary and current ecological insights, for people of faith to move forward with wisdom, inspiration, and hope, all for the sake of God's good creation."

– Professor Bill Brown, Professor of Old Testament,
Columbia Theological Seminary, Georgia

"Every generation reads the Hebrew Bible with its own eyes and its own concerns. Rabbi Neril and Rabbi Dee's special lens allows us to discover in the Hebrew Bible continuing inspiration in our battle to expand our consciousness and to include all of creation in the vision and message of the Hebrew Bible. This is a wonderful tool for garnering new insights into the Hebrew Bible and to increasingly sensitize us to a broader message that the Hebrew Bible can deliver, concerning human responsibility, stewardship, and unity with all of creation. Well done!"

– Rabbi Dr. Alon Goshen-Gottstein, Director,
The Elijah Interfaith Institute

"Imagine a gathering of some of Judaism's sages reading the Bible through their love for the earth. Imagine listening in during a period of great urgency, a time when the very sustainability of life was on the line. Imagine finding the timeless/timely wisdom to address that crisis, allowing the teachings of the Hebrew Bible to mobilize us as allies of our embattled planet and all living things. Well, imagine no longer. This book is that gathering, that call to action!"

– Rabbi Dr. Bradley Artson, Dean,
Ziegler School of Rabbinic Studies of AJU

"Rabbi Judah Lowe of Prague taught that to truly love the Creator as we are commanded means to love His works as well. Taking care of the creation is a manifestation of our love of the Creator. Moreover, only when we take care of creation does it take care of us. The importance of this truth is more evident today than ever before when we face existential environmental crises. We accordingly owe a deep debt of gratitude to Rabbis Neril and Dee who, in publishing this ecological commentary on the Hebrew Bible, have provided us with an invaluable resource and inspiration drawn from a vast cross-section of Jewish sources and commentaries, to enable us to live up to the Biblical mandate to love the Creator and His creation."

– Rabbi David Rosen KSG CBE,
International Director of Interreligious Affairs, AJC

"Grounded equally in religious thought and environmental science, *Eco Bible* provides inspiration and guidance on how we can and must repair our world in these urgent times. It offers powerful fodder for personal reflection and group discussion. It serves as an unparalleled resource guide for all who feel a spiritual responsibility for our irreplaceable planet and its life-sustaining biodiversity."

– Jessica Sachs, author of *Good Germs, Bad Germs*

Table of Contents

Book of Exodus

To my wife, Shana
and our children,
Shacharya Ohr and Hallel Moriya –
may God bless you with joy and good health!
– YN

To my wife, Lucy
and our children,
Maia, Keren, Tali, Rina, and Yehuda –
you are all my inspiration!
– LD

Acknowledgments

We are grateful for those supporters who have helped enable the publication and distribution of *Eco Bible*. First and foremost, we thank Marilyn and Jerry Burke and The Julia Burke Foundation, for providing instrumental support for our efforts over the past decade, including with publishing and distributing this book. We also thank Marcia and Bruce Sklare, the Sinton Family Fund, Opaline Fund, David and Edna Miron Wapner, Richard and Lois Gunther Family Trust, Andi and David Amovitz, Marla and Gidon Stein, Fred Nicholas, Chad and Jessica Haller Fund, Morton and Marilyn Neril, Michael and Victoria Neril, Gewurz Family Fund, Carole Kaminsky, and Wiliam and Leah Molle Fund.

Deborah Rose provided in-depth editorial comments that significantly strengthened this book, for which we express our appreciation. We are grateful for Dr. Alon Tal, whose thorough review and suggestions improved the book, especially the scientific aspects. We appreciate the contribution of Jessica Sachs, who offered thorough edits of the full manuscript. We thank Sorelle Weinstein and Rachel Meghnagi for careful copy-editing of the manuscript.

We express our appreciation to Faygle Train for her editing and work on the action items and endnotes, and to Andrei Borokhovich and Eliana Koehler for reviewing the entire manuscript. We also gratefully acknowledge Sarah Kudishevich, Quinn McVeigh, Rabbi Mattisyahu Brown, Professor Bill Brown, Rabbi Alon Goshen-Gottstein, Marilyn Neril, Rabbi Simcha Daniel Burstyn, and Rabbi Baruch Rock for reviewing parts of the manuscript. We are grateful for all of the contemporary authors who provided commentary for this volume.

We thank our parents for their love and support.

In 2008 Yonatan Neril co-edited a collection of 54 essays on the Hebrew Bible and ecology, which was published by Canfei Nesharim, now a branch of Grow Torah. In 2012, he and Evonne Marzouk co-edited: *Uplifting People and Planet: 18 Essential Jewish Teachings on the Environment.* It was published by Canfei Nesharim, a branch of Grow Torah. Some of the content of these two books is incorporated with permission into this present volume, updated and in shortened form. We thank Yosef Gillers, director of Grow Torah, for granting permission to use this content.

We praise God, the Source of all life, for enabling the publication of this book.

Yonatan Neril and Leo Dee
4 Sivan, 5780 / May 27, 2020

Introduction

"Rabbi Amorai asked: 'Where is the Garden of Eden?' He replied: 'It is on earth.'" [1]

Rabbi Jonathan Sacks writes, "Hope is a human virtue, but one with religious underpinnings. At its ultimate it is the belief… [that God] is mindful of our aspirations, with us in our fumbling efforts, that He has given us the means to save us from ourselves; that we are not wrong to dream, wish and work for a better world. Hope is the knowledge that we can choose; that we can learn from our mistakes and act differently next time." [2]

Many people fear that humans have irrevocably destroyed the ecology of "Eden" on earth. But God created the world out of love for life on earth. This new, unique *Eco Bible* explores the deep inspiration we can find in the Hebrew Bible for fulfilling the blessing of all life, for changing course to preserve God's creation, and for sustaining human life in harmony with nature and all of God's creatures.

The Hebrew Bible is also called the Torah, the Five Books of Moses, or the Pentateuch (and also refers to the Prophets and Writings, which are not addressed in this commentary). How does the Hebrew Bible relate deeply to living in balance with God's creation, through a lifestyle that is not only aware of but protects the natural world? Is concern for environmental stewardship external to the Hebrew Bible, or a central message embedded within it? *Eco Bible*'s commentaries on the Hebrew Bible reveal a spiritually grounded vision for both long-term sustainability and immediate environmental mindfulness and action.

Some people believe religion is separate and distinct from ecology or care for God's creation. Most Hebrew Bible study, teaching, and preaching occur without addressing the ecological crisis, the greatest crisis facing humanity. *Eco Bible* applies an ecological perspective to reveal how the Hebrew Bible itself, and thousands of years of Biblical teaching by Jewish rabbis, indeed *embrace* care for God's creation as a fundamental message. An ancient Jewish commentary on the Hebrew Bible, the Midrash, teaches that "God gazed into the Hebrew Bible and created the world."[3] The Divine teaching is a blueprint for all of creation and instructs us about living sustainably in the world God created.

Were it not for the receiving of the Hebrew Bible on Mt. Sinai, the Midrash teaches, God would have returned the world to chaos and void.[4] Rabbi Samson Raphael Hirsch writes that the ideal of the Hebrew Bible "awaits the generation which will finally have become matured for its ideals to be made into a reality."[5] Applying the teachings of the Hebrew Bible to stewardship of God's creation is not just an idea for today, but essential for a future in which we achieve a balanced, worldwide ecosystem and thrive on a planet viable for all life.

Eco Bible quotes over 100 rabbis and other great Jewish thinkers commenting on verses from the Hebrew Bible. Until now, their ecological insights could be found scattered in hundreds of books but might only be noticed by a Bible scholar also focused on ecology. *Eco Bible* gathers and connects these insights for anyone studying the Hebrew Bible – insights which relate even more critically to our time than any before. *Eco Bible*, including Volume I, Genesis and Exodus, and Volume II, Leviticus, Numbers, and Deuteronomy, is being published during a time of accelerating environmental challenges, a worldwide coronavirus pandemic, and widespread protests for racial justice. Ecological disasters and COVID-19's devastating spread are causing the tragic loss of so many lives as well as a profound disruption of natural ecosystems, families, communities, cultures, and the populations of entire nations. Pollution disproportionately impacts people of color and calls for environmental justice are growing.

These interconnected crises are signals to humanity of the need for restoring balance between people and nature. The Hebrew Bible's Divine wisdom can provide important messages for striving to find this balance. Some of the Hebrew Bible's verses – which first "spoke" to people in ancient times when the Bible was given – may seem cryptic, obscure, or irrelevant to our modern times or lives. The chief function of contemporary commentaries like *Eco Bible*, as with all rabbinic commentaries that have strived to enlighten, is to make the holy book relevant in our own generation and those to come.

Eco Bible explores how the Hebrew Bible and traditional commentaries relate to a range of critical, contemporary ecological challenges, such as preserving animal and plant biodiversity, ensuring clean air, land, and water, and showing compassion to both domestic and wild animals. The book not only focuses on about 500 Hebrew Bible verses – to reveal how the 3,500-year-old Jewish tradition offers profound ecological insights – but suggests many achievable action items. The editors of *Eco Bible* encourage people also to create their own action items. Reading the Hebrew Bible can be a deeply personal process, and so can repairing the world. Each of us can take many different kinds of actions that sustain the world and sustain our souls. "Study is not the most important thing, but action,"[6] Rabbi Shimon ben Gamliel says.

The Bible is by far the most-read, most-purchased book in the world, with more than five billion copies sold in the past 200 years[7] and 40 million sold each year in the US.[8] "Simply put, the Bible is the most influential book of all-time… The Bible has done more to shape literature, history, entertainment and culture than any book ever written. Its influence on world history is unparalleled, and shows no signs of abating,"[9] writes author David Van Biema in *Time* magazine.

So why do we need yet another commentary? At a time of ecological and spiritual crisis, how the Bible is understood can have a profound impact on human behavior, since billions of people in religions worldwide consider it a holy book. In US Christian congregations, 61 percent of sermons quote verses from the Hebrew Bible, according to a 2020 Pew finding.[10] *The Washington Post* cites a survey showing that 44 percent of Bible readers admit needing help with interpretation.[11] We hope this *Eco Bible* will speak to all those who relate deeply to the Hebrew Bible and deeply care about the health and survival of our planet.

THE NEED FOR AN ECOLOGICAL
COMMENTARY ON THE HEBREW BIBLE

The Ark, which held the Tablets God gave Moses on Mt. Sinai, physically moved with the Israelites during their 40 years in the desert.[12] The word of God contained in the Ark is a revolutionary teaching; to remain dynamic and alive, it has to keep moving with human concerns or it will become reactionary, static, fixed. Commentaries on the Bible must move forward too. This new *Eco Bible* commentary is extremely timely – both grounded in millennia of rabbinic thought and speaking to the greatest challenges facing humanity in the twenty-first century.

Rabbi Abraham Isaac Kook, the first chief rabbi of Israel before its statehood in 1948, spoke of learning the Hebrew Bible "for its sake," where the teachings "become more and more expansive."[13] Rabbi Daniel Kohn understands this to mean that the Hebrew Bible becomes ever more multifaceted, expressive, variegated, and beautified.[14] *Eco Bible* attempts to unfold and reveal the profound Divine teachings of the Hebrew Bible from an ecological perspective, among what Rabbi Shlomo ben Aderet recognizes as "the ever-increasing number of fresh understandings of the Bible's verses."[15]

Gus Speth, former dean of the Yale School of Forestry and Environmental Studies, says, "I used to think that top global environmental problems were biodiversity loss, ecosystem collapse and climate change. I thought that with 30 years of good science, we could address these problems, but I was wrong. The top environmental problems are selfishness, greed, and apathy, and to deal with these we need a spiritual and cultural transformation. And we scientists don't know how to do that."[16]

Scientific research has powerfully revealed the widespread degradation of nature, yet scientists' ability to motivate society toward ecological change is limited. Religious belief and understanding have the potential to move many more people worldwide to environmental action than science has done. The Pew Research Center's Forum on Religion and Public Life estimates that 84 percent of the 2010 world population are affiliated with a religion.[17] More than 76 percent of Americans are religiously affiliated, according to a 2014 Pew study.[18] Nonetheless, religions have so far failed to substantially integrate scientific and ecological findings into their preaching, teaching, and living.

In the US, a survey by the Public Religion Research Institute and the American Academy of Religion found that "most Americans who attend religious services at least once or twice a month hear little from their clergy leaders about the issue of climate change."[19] Could the low incidence of American clergy addressing climate change be playing a role in the US having the world's highest historical carbon emissions? While governments individually and collectively seek to address global environmental challenges, current approaches have yet to catalyze a collective global response that will truly meet these challenges. Part of the reason is failure to engage those people with possibly the greatest potential to inspire behavior change – faith leaders, clergy, and religious teachers.

Religion has been a channel for moral and ethical instruction across the ages and the world. Faith can and should help us to address the roots of our planet's ecological crisis. Rabbi Dov Berkowitz says in regard to the Hebrew Bible, "How do we utilize 3,500 years of spiritual consciousness for the betterment of our contemporary society?"[20] When we are faced with the compelling, sustained insights of religious thought and tradition, we can come to see our current life choices in a different and more ecological light.

ADDRESSING THE SPIRITUAL ROOTS OF THE ECOLOGICAL CRISIS

What on earth are we doing to creation? We have disrupted the ecological balance of all God created on earth, and we owe it to God, to each other, and to all species to restore the balance. This is the greatest physical and spiritual challenge humanity has ever faced together. Caring for creation is key to receiving the full blessings of the Creator. Awareness of the Infinite opens us up to protecting the immediate – the very planet on which we live.

As a fundamental part of many people's lives, religion can be a key motivator by shaping values. Religion appeals not just to our intellect but to our soul – and this is where change is most needed. When God is at the center of our environmental awareness, it becomes much more powerful. At this moment in history, we need a major infusion of energy specifically to help faith groups inspire behavioral change for sustainable living.

We offer this book to accelerate the awakening religious and spiritual process, so humanity can keep moving fast enough to avert irreversible environmental deterioration of our only home. The environmental movement has failed to effect transformational change in the past 50 years partly because fear of the darkness of ecological collapse has driven the movement. The light of spirituality can spark a more hopeful approach with deeper and broader effect. Here are three reasons why.

First, religion can persuade people to consume in moderation as they find true satisfaction in spirituality, community, and family. Spiritual living should bring consciousness to our consumption. To rise to this ultimate challenge for human civilization, we have to raise our spiritual awareness and maturity. A person can exist at varying levels of soul awareness, but a sustainable planet will require that we learn to live and thrive at higher levels of spiritual consciousness.

Second, religious teachings help instill foresight and long-term thinking. The rabbis of the Talmud taught about 1,500 years ago: "Who is the wise person? The person who can see the effect of their actions."[21] We must put both the present and future of our children and grandchildren first, above expanding our own standard of living. Spiritual awareness can help us recognize the link between our actions and the larger problem, while cultivating foresight, concern, and change.

Finally, and perhaps most importantly, religion embodies hope. Some people – out of terror, anger, or depression – despair of our ever returning to personal and planetary balance and sustainability. Yet, to reiterate Rabbi Sacks' words, "Hope is a human virtue, but one with religious underpinnings."[22]

Billions of people equally respect the scientific view of the universe and the spiritual view. *Eco Bible* draws on the wisdom of many generations of Jewish sages, contemporary rabbis, and scientific sources to connect religion and science. E.O. Wilson, famed biological scientist and educator, writes in his book *The Creation: An Appeal to Save Life on Earth*, "Religion and science are the two most powerful forces in the world today... If there is any moral precept shared by people of all beliefs, it is that we owe ourselves – and future generations – a beautiful, rich and healthful environment."[23]

DRILLING ON SHIPS

According to an 1,800-year-old Jewish commentary on the Hebrew Bible, Rabbi Shimon bar Yochai describes a group of people traveling in a boat. One of them takes a drill and begins to bore a hole. The others ask, "Why are you doing this?" The person replies, "Why are you concerned? Am I not drilling under my own place?" The rest reply, "But you will flood the boat for all of us!"[24]

Imagine being a passenger on this boat. One person, without concern for others, jeopardizes your safety and security. The person drilling may have compelling reasons. Perhaps they are hungry and want to drop a fishing line, or hot and want to cool their feet in the water. Maybe the boat is on fresh water, and they are thirsty. But no matter how compelling the reason, drilling a hole in a boat to fulfill one person's desires threatens everyone.

Rabbi Shimon's story warns us of the destructive power of letting our selfish desires overtake all other considerations. Today's environmental challenges are *not* about "whatever floats your boat." Everyone on the boat (or planet) needs to work together to ensure such behavior doesn't continue. The person drilling is dangerous, but the rest of us ignoring the threat they pose is equally dangerous. If the boat sinks, the fault is both the driller's and those who stood idly by.

THE EARTH IS OUR COLLECTIVE SHIP

We have one home. With close to eight billion people and around eight million species, the earth is our collective ship. Jumping ship is out of the question. Some of the most profound ecological lessons come from people on a ship, from Noah to today's polar researchers, on a ship trapped in Arctic ice to study climate change. Something about being surrounded by water heightens our awareness of vulnerability, and of personal and collective safety. People on a ship can feel more compelled to act when someone behaves recklessly, because they see how directly another's damage can endanger their and others' lives. The ship metaphor sharply conveys the paradigm of responsibility, stewardship, and respect that we need for sharing and steering our planet.

In our times, the indirectness and "invisibility" of the planetary damage we cause poses a major challenge. Even when we are very aware of our role in the problem, we don't see the effect of our actions on a daily basis. The earth is so big and complex. Turning on a car engine, a light switch, or an air-conditioner doesn't suddenly raise the outside temperature or trigger an extreme storm. But we are essentially drilling holes without fully grasping the consequences of our action. If we did fully grasp them, could we look our children in the eye and admit to them that our lifestyle will jeopardize their future?

Perhaps we are ecologically passive because our current lifestyle gives us so much pleasure and comfort. We are bombarded, tantalized, and too often influenced toward increased consumption by advertising mottoes like "Makes me happy" and "I'm lovin' it!" The Ba'al Shem Tov teaches that when the soul lacks spiritual pleasure, it compensates by pursuing the pleasures of this world and its excesses.[25] What do we truly care about most? We must face the collective reality that we cannot simultaneously expand our consumer behaviors and live sustainably.

Our actions are the true indication of our commitments. In 1992, the world's governments committed to curbing climate change and reducing emissions of greenhouse gases, yet every year since, humanity's emissions have risen. Emissions of CO_2 in 2020 have doubled since 1990. Clearly, we are not sufficiently committed to the announced goal. Since 1992, billions of people have continued to source their food unsustainably from across the planet, collectively taken millions of plane flights and driven billions of miles, and eaten a tremendous amount of food cultivated through unsustainable and even dangerous processes. These trends show no sign of reversing. What can shift our direction, to care and work more diligently toward what is most important – a thriving, spiritually aware, and sustainable humanity – and to live in ways that can actually achieve this?

NOAH'S ARK AND THE TITANIC[26]

According to Jewish oral tradition, God gave humans 120 years before unleashing the Flood. God chose Noah as a messenger to build the Ark as a sign to the people that the flood would come unless they changed their actions.[27] Noah said to the people, "Return from your evil ways and deeds."[28] They did not. What led God ultimately to carry out the most serious environmental catastrophe in human history and, through flood, wipe away virtually all living creatures?

The judgment was sealed because of the sin of lawlessness, robbery, or wrongdoing (*chamas*). The rabbis of the Talmud teach that "a person would put out a market stall full of beans, and each person would come and take less than a penny's worth so that they could not be prosecuted by the law."[29] Rabbi Samson Raphael Hirsch teaches that "*chamas* is a wrong that is too petty to be caught by human justice, but if committed continuously can gradually ruin your fellow person."[30]

God said, "You are not playing by the book, so I too will not play by the book."[31] God responded by bringing a single drop of rain and then another. Just as the people took one bean and then another, without looking at the consequences of their combined actions, so God punished them drop by drop, culminating in the Flood.

We can see parallels in our modern times. In 1896, Swedish Nobel chemist Svante Arrhenius was recognized for his theory of climate change.[32] Nearly a century later, the UN created the 1988 Intergovernmental Panel on Climate Change "to provide the governments of the world with a clear scientific view of what is happening to the world's climate."[33] The world has largely ignored the panel's warnings. Even concerned nations struggle to significantly change the actions of their governments and populations.

It has been 120 years since Arrhenius' climate change theory, and massive floods now repeatedly threaten even the most developed countries. After Hurricane Harvey in 2017, *The New York Times* quoted Maya Wadler, a teenager in Houston, Texas, as she recalled the moments her family's home flooded. "I usually just trust my parents that everything is going to be okay. But I looked up, and I saw that my dad was closing his eyes, the water was getting in his eyes. And I just thought: He has absolutely no idea where we are going to go."[34] In 2019, Houston flooded for the third time in three years.

Many such devastating events have arrived sooner and more intensely than predicted.[35] We are ill-prepared. With eight billion people sharing our planet, the greatest risk again comes from seemingly inconsequential actions of individuals, combining in their impact. This age is even called the Anthropocene, including the human-caused sixth great extinction event on earth.[36] *For the first time, humans can now destroy or radically alter virtually **all** life on earth – a power so great it could once only be ascribed to God.*

Our current reality has striking similarities to the Titanic, whose captain received many warnings of icebergs from other ships but chose to ignore them. He believed that his ship – the largest ever built – was stronger than nature, unsinkable. By the time the crew spotted the fatal iceberg, it was too late to turn the ship away from its cataclysmic collision course.

Today, we are on an ecological collision course of our own making and are bearing full steam ahead. But there is still time to act like Noah instead of the Titanic's captain. Our ship carries all of humanity and all species. By uniting and striving to live in balance with creation, and with God's help, we can steer toward a future that ensures the survival and thriving of everyone and every thing on board.

Rabbi Yonatan Neril
Jerusalem, 5780/2020

Part One
Commentary on the Book of Genesis

Torah portion of Bereishit

❧ CARING FOR CREATION ❧

Genesis 1:1 – In the beginning, God created the heavens and the earth.

Rabbi Samson Raphael Hirsch makes the first verse in Genesis personal and proactive. He writes that the words teach us "to think of the world as God's world and ourselves as creatures of God...We must not destroy the world, but preserve it – every single creature, every insect, every plant is part of God's world. Woe to those that disturb His world! Hail to those that preserve His world!"[37]

Rabbis throughout the ages make clear that God tasks humanity with caring for creation. "When God created Adam, He took him and showed him all the trees of the Garden of Eden and said to him...Be careful not to spoil or destroy my world – for if you do, there will be nobody after you to repair it,"[38] teaches the Midrash, a major rabbinic commentary on the Hebrew Bible.

Rabbi Shlomo Eiger, a distinguished intellectual who became a Hasid (spiritual and pious person), was asked what he learned from his first visit with the hasidic Rabbi Menachem Mendel of Kotzk. Rabbi Eiger answered simply, "In the beginning, God created." The questioner pressed him: "Did a renowned scholar have to travel to a hasidic rabbi to learn the first verse of the Bible?" Rabbi Eiger responded: "I learned that God created only the beginning; everything else is up to human beings."[39]

Rabbi David Rosen explains the ecological impact of the Bible's opening verse: "If you believe that this world is the creation of a Divine Power, therefore creation itself manifests the Divine Presence, as it says in Psalms, 'The heavens declare the glory of God and the firmament declares the work of His hands.'[40] If you are a Divinely sensitive person, whether you want to define that as religious or spiritual, then the wellbeing, the health of the environment, and of creation, is a religious imperative."[41]

❧ SUSTAINABILITY AND SPIRITUAL AWARENESS ❧

Genesis 1:3 – God said, "Let there be light"; and there was light.

Since the sun was not created until the fourth day (see Genesis chapter 1, verse 16), the light God created on the first day of creation was not a physical light but a spiritual one. Rabbi Sholom Berezovsky teaches that "without this holy light there is no merit in sustaining creation."[42] Those who seek God perceive this spiritual light. The sustainability of creation therefore depends on the spiritual awareness of humanity.

❧ PREVIOUS AND CURRENT EXTINCTION EVENTS ❧

Genesis 1:5 – God called the light Day, and the darkness He called Night. And there was evening and there was morning, a first day.

The Midrash asks why this verse reads *"And* there was evening" rather than just "There was evening" – implying that there was something else before. The Midrash answers, "…time existed before this…God created and destroyed worlds until this one…when it says, 'God saw everything He had made and behold it was very good,'[43] that teaches us that the previous ones were not."[44]

This explanation suggests that cataclysmic extinction events once occurred, and that sustained existence on this planet is not guaranteed. Scientists understand that five extinction events occurred in the last 500 million years, and humans are causing a sixth one at the current time.[45] The previous extinction events were caused by "acts of God," like comets and massive volcanic eruptions. But the current one is caused by people on a creation that God declared "very good."

❧ WATER AND DRY LAND ❧

Genesis 1:9 – God said, "Let the water below the sky be gathered into one area, that the dry land may appear." And it was so.

The Midrash states: "In human experience, a person empties a full vessel into an empty one; does one ever empty a full vessel into a full vessel?

Now the world was full of water, yet it says [that God gathered the water], 'into one area'! From this we learn that the little held a lot."[46]

Water separated from the earth by draining into the seas and by forming ice on the land. For most people who do not live near a glacier, the amount of earth's water held as ice may seem small compared to all the water in lakes and oceans. In fact, roughly 68 percent of the world's freshwater is locked in ice caps, glaciers, and permanent snow.[47] Due to human-caused climate change, however, ice melting of Antarctica has increased from 40 gigatons per year in the 1980s to 252 gigatons per year over the 2010s. All that ice melting into the ocean has raised global sea levels.[48] In some coastal areas, sea level rise is beginning to regularly flood whole towns and low-lying parts of major cities. God said that dry land should appear from the water, yet by humanity's actions, more and more water is covering land.

❧ EDIBLE TREES ☙

Genesis 1:11–12 – And God said, "Let the earth sprout vegetation: seed-bearing plants, fruit trees of every kind on earth that bear fruit with the seed in it." And it was so. The earth brought forth vegetation: seed-bearing plants of every kind, and trees of every kind bearing fruit with the seed in it. And God saw that this was good.

As Ba'al HaTurim (Rabbi Jacob ben Asher) points out, God commanded the earth to produce "fruit trees that bear fruit," meaning trees whose bark could be eaten as well as their fruit. However, he notes that the earth produced trees (whose bark is not eaten) that produce fruit in order that the trees themselves would not be devoured.[49]

Long ago, and today, we have come to understand that trees – in addition to the fruit they produce – have broader value including providing homes for animals large and small, and retaining soil to prevent erosion and catastrophic mudslides.

❧ GOD BLESSES FISH AND BIRDS ☙

Genesis 1:22 – God blessed them [fish and birds], saying, "Be fertile and increase, fill the waters in the seas, and let the birds increase on the earth."

Radak (Rabbi David Kimchi) explains that God's blessing to fish to "be fertile" is to have the potential to create new generations, while the blessing to "increase" is to thrive in numbers.[50]

Worldwide, humans are now depleting the planet's fish stocks through overfishing and plastic use. A UN report indicates that one-third of marine fish stocks were being harvested at unsustainable levels in 2015.[51] Extensive plastic pollution kills fish, marine mammals, seabirds, and other wildlife, and reduces their ability to give birth, rear their young, and sustain their species.[52] In regard to birds, a 2019 Cornell University study "finds steep, long-term losses across virtually all groups of birds in the US and Canada. It reveals across-the-board declines that scientists call 'staggering.' All told, the North American bird population is down by 2.9 billion breeding adults."[53]

God desires abundant sea life to fill the ocean and healthy bird populations. Should we not, therefore, be strong advocates for sustainable fishing, ending ocean pollution, and protecting both land birds and sea birds?

❧ ON EATING ANIMALS ❧

Genesis 1:26 – And God said, "Let Us make man in Our image, after Our likeness. They shall rule the fish of the sea, the birds of the sky, the cattle, the whole earth, and all the creeping things that creep on earth."

This verse states God intends for people to rule over fish, birds, and animals. Yet in Genesis 1:29, God states that human beings are only permitted a plant-based diet. Rabbi Isaac Karo explains that "ruling" over creatures mentioned in the verse clearly does not involve killing them for human food.[54] Rabbi Gil Marks notes:

> ...historically, meat, when consumed, was usually a flavoring agent and, as a rule, a component in a dish reserved for special occasions. Only in the past century has animal flesh assumed such a prominent role in the diet, with meat frequently being served once, sometimes twice, or even three times, a day. On the contrary, throughout most of history, cattle and sheep were not regarded as sources of food, but rather sheep were prized for their milk and wool, and cows were valued for plowing, turning the wheels that drew water from rivers and canals, hauling heavy materials, trodding grain for winnowing, powering the millstones for grinding grain, and turning the stone wheel for pressing olives. Flocks and herds served as the principal

source of clothing, wealth, and security for our ancestors, something that would have been squandered if eaten. Meat was the exception, not the rule.[55]

❧ WILL HUMANS RULE, OR ANIMALS?[56]

Genesis 1:28 – God blessed them and God said to them, "Be fertile and increase, fill the earth and master it; and rule the fish of the sea, the birds of the sky, and all the living things that creep on earth."

On the surface, the words of this verse appear to give people license to degrade and subdue the earth, but the rabbis over the millennia for the most part do not read them this way. The rabbinic commentaries reveal much about these verses beyond the simple reading and make clear that a wholly different message is being conveyed.

Verse 26 states, God said, "Let Us make man in Our image, after Our likeness. They shall rule [*ve-yir-du*] the fish of the sea, the birds of the sky, the cattle, the whole earth, and all the creeping things that creep on earth."[57] Verse 28 uses a command verb form, with God saying, "Rule [*u-re-du*] the fish of the sea, the birds of the sky, and all the living things that creep on earth.'"[58]

The Midrash commentary here is based on a play on words in Hebrew, in which the root of the word "to rule" is the same root as the word "to be taken down." Rabbi Chanina interpreted the Midrash to say: "If humankind is worthy, God says '*u-re-du*' [you rule!]; while if humankind is not worthy, God says, '*yé-ra-du*' – he will be taken down (or let others [the animals] rule over him)."[59]

Based on the Midrash, Rashi (Rabbi Shlomo ben Yitzchak) agrees that if we are not worthy, we will be ruled by animals.[60] In this vein, H. Freedman and Maurice Simon comment, "Man is entitled to pre-eminence only as long as he cultivates his God-like qualities; when he voluntarily abandons them he is even lower than the brute creation."[61]

Can humans be ruled by animals today? At first, we may think human beings are so powerful, we are immune to these predictions. Yet, for example, insect infestations around the world have caused tremendous havoc in human life, from grasshoppers in Africa to bed bugs in North America. Insect-borne diseases such as malaria, dengue fever, West

Nile virus, and Zika virus have spread to more northern latitudes, as human-induced climate change expands the range of certain mosquito species.[62] The most recent case of tiny organisms antagonizing people is the coronavirus pandemic. Some research indicates that the virus likely spread from bats to pangolins (a spiny anteater) to people.[63]

One key message from the Midrash is that God's blessing to rule over other creatures depends on our living as righteous people. If humanity becomes worthy by living in a righteous way, then humans shall rule over nature. But if humans do not merit dominion, because they do not act in an upright fashion, then humanity will descend and not be granted rulership over nature. The rabbis learn this from the juxtaposition of God saying that humans will be created in God's image immediately before saying that humans will rule over other creatures.[64]

Rabbi David Sears writes that ruling "comprises a form of stewardship for which humanity is answerable to God. Both Talmudic and kabbalistic sources state that it is forbidden to kill any creature unnecessarily, or to engage in wanton destruction of the earth's resources. All forms of life are precious by virtue of the Divine wisdom that brings them into existence, whatever rung they may occupy in the hierarchy of creation ... The Divine mandate for man to dominate the natural world is a sacred trust, not a carte blanche for destructiveness."[65]

❧ A PLANT-BASED DIET FOR PEOPLE ❧

Genesis 1:29 – God said, "See, I give you every seed-bearing plant that is upon all the earth, and every tree that has seed-bearing fruit; they shall be yours for food."

One of the only statements God made to people when they were created is to eat a plant-based diet. "It is altogether impossible to conceive of the Blessed Ruler of all creation ... imposing upon this most excellent creation an eternal decree such as this: that the human race would maintain its existence by going against its moral sensibilities through the shedding of blood, albeit the blood of animals," Rabbi Abraham Isaac Kook writes. "Is it possible to conceive that a highly valued moral virtue, which had already existed as a part of the human legacy, should be lost forever?"[66] Rabbi Kook wrote in the early 1900s that in a "brighter era," people will return to a plant-based diet and "God shall cause us to make great spiritual strides, and thus extricate us from this complex question."[67]

Rabbi Elchanan Samet teaches: "What is the content of God's first statements to man? They do not contain commandments and prohibitions related to man's relationship to God. Rather, these initial statements are intended to mold people's relationship with creation. In current times, this question has become crucial, owing to the ecological crisis threatening the world and all its inhabitants. Human beings, having 'filled the world and conquered it, and ruling' over all its elements (animal, vegetable, mineral), have brought our generation to this crisis, which already threatens our world and places a question mark over the future of the generations to come."[68] Indeed, our own survival depends on the health and thriving of creation.

❧ VEGAN CROCODILES ❧

Genesis 1:30 – "And to all the animals on land, to all the birds of the sky, and to everything that creeps on earth, in which there is the breath of life, [I give] all the green plants for food." And it was so.

Rashi teaches us: "God equated cattle and the animals to them [to people] regarding the food [that they were permitted to eat]. God did not permit Adam and his wife to kill a creature and to eat its flesh; only every green vegetation they were all permitted to eat equally."[69] Animals were also created to be vegan.

Contemporary science researchers have discovered that the early ancestors of crocodiles, for example, had herbivore teeth, suggesting that they were vegan at some point early in their evolution.[70]

❧ CREATION WAS "VERY GOOD"

Genesis 1:31 – And God saw all that He had made and found it very good. And there was evening and there was morning, the sixth day.

Nachmanides (Rabbi Moshe ben Nachman) asks what was very good on the sixth day and suggests that it was the wholeness of creation, not any individual species.[71]

From an ecological standpoint, the sixth day was "very good" because people and animals were eating a plant-based diet, and there was no killing of sentient beings in order for other creatures to survive. There was to be no violence by humans toward animals, animals toward animals, or animals toward people on planet earth. In the words of the prophet Isaiah, "the wolf will dwell with the lamb."[72]

❧ PRAYING FOR CREATION ❧

Genesis 2:5 – When no shrub of the field was yet on earth and no grasses of the field had yet sprouted, because the Lord God had not sent rain upon the earth and there was no man to till the soil.

Rashi asks, based on the Midrash, "And what is the reason that God had not caused it to rain? Because there was no person to till the ground and no one to recognize the utility of rain. When Adam came, however, and realized that rain was necessary for the world, he prayed for it and it fell, so that trees and plants sprang forth."[73]

Based on this, Rabbi Daniel Kohn explains that the human being's first appearance was as one who cared about creation – the person is that same earth, made of dust and water, a clod of dirt with a soul that prays. The Midrash teaches that plants did not grow until the first human showed concern for creation, and the prayer for rain and plant growth is what makes plants grow. Hence the primary role of a person is to recognize God and to pray. "Adam" is from the Hebrew word *adama*, meaning earth. This suggests that to pray is to summon the essential "clod of dirt" within us, to pray on behalf of the entire planet.[74]

❧ RE-CREATING PARADISE ❧

Genesis 2:8 – The Lord God planted a garden in Eden, in the east, and placed there the man whom He had formed.

Rabbi Kook writes, "Our sense is yearning to re-create Eden: the social and environmental harmony, peace, absence of conflict, absence of competition, absence of environmental problems. Our purpose on earth is to re-create paradise."[75]

❧ THE STEWARDSHIP PARADIGM ❧

by Rabbi Lord Jonathan Sacks[76]

Genesis 2:15 – The Lord God took the man and placed him in the garden of Eden, to till it and tend it.

Genesis chapter 1 is only one side of the complex Biblical equation. It is balanced by the narrative of Genesis chapter 2, which features a second creation narrative that focuses on humans and their place in the Garden of Eden. The first person is set in the Garden "to work it and take care of it."[77] The two Hebrew verbs used here are significant. The first – *le'ovdah* – literally means "to serve it." The human being is thus both master and servant of nature. The second – *le'shomrah* – means "to guard it." This is the verb used in later Biblical legislation to describe the responsibilities of a guardian of property that belongs to someone else. This guardian must exercise vigilance while protecting and is personally liable for losses that occur through negligence. This is perhaps the best short definition of humanity's responsibility for nature as the Bible conceives it.

We do not own nature. "The earth is the Lord's and the fullness thereof."[78] We are its stewards on behalf of God, who created and owns everything, and we are duty-bound to respect its integrity. The mid-nineteenth-century commentator Rabbi Samson Raphael Hirsch put this rather well in an original interpretation of Genesis 1:26, which reads, "Let Us make the human in Our image after Our own likeness."[79] The verse has always been puzzling, since the hallmark of the Torah is the singularity of God. Who would God consult in the process of creating humans? Hirsch says the "us" refers to the rest of creation. Before creating the human, a being destined to develop the capacity to alter and possibly endanger the natural world, God sought the approval of nature itself. This interpretation implies that we would use nature only in such a way that is faithful to the purposes of its Creator and acknowledges nature's consenting to humanity's existence.

The mandate in Genesis 1 to exercise dominion is, therefore, not technical but moral: humanity would control, within our means, the use of nature toward the service of God. This mandate is limited by the requirement to serve and guard as seen in Genesis 2. The famous story of Genesis 2–3 – the eating of the forbidden fruit, leading to Adam and Eve's exile from Eden – supports this point. God does not permit everything. God provides limits on how we interact with the earth. The Torah has many commandments relating to the earth, from how to sow crops, to how to collect eggs, to how to preserve trees in a time of war, just to name a few.[80]

When we do not protect creation according to God's will, disaster can follow. We see this today as more and more cities sit under a cloud of smog and as mercury poisons large sectors of our fishing waters.[81] Deforestation of the rainforests, largely a result of humanity's growing demand for timber and beef, has brought on irrevocable destruction of plant and animal species.[82] We can no longer ignore the massive negative impact that our global industrial society is having on the ecosystems of the earth. Our unbounded use of fossil fuels to stoke our energy-intensive lifestyles is causing global climate change. An international consensus of scientists predicts more intense and destructive storms, floods, and droughts resulting from human-induced changes in the atmosphere.[83] If we do not take action now, we risk the very survival of civilization as we know it.

The Midrash says that God showed Adam around the Garden of Eden and said, "Look at My works! See how beautiful they are – how excellent! For your sake I created them all. See to it that you do not spoil and destroy My world; for if you do, there will be no one else to repair it."[84] Creation has its own dignity as God's masterpiece, and though we have the mandate to use it, we have none to destroy or despoil it. Rabbi Hirsch says that Shabbat was given to humanity "in order that one should not grow overbearing in his dominion" of God's creation. On the Day of Rest, "he must, as it were, return the borrowed world to its Divine Owner in order to realize that it is but lent to him."[85] Ingrained in the process of creation is a weekly reminder that our dominion of earth must be for the sake of Heaven.

The choice is ours. If we continue to live as though God had only commanded us to subdue the earth, we must be prepared for our children to inherit a seriously degraded planet, with the future of human civilization at risk. If we see in our role as masters of the earth a unique opportunity to truly serve and care for the planet, its creatures and its resources, then we can reclaim our status as stewards of the world, and raise our new and future generations in an environment much closer to that of Eden.

❧ FORBIDDEN FRUIT AND SELF-CONTROL ❧

Genesis 2:17 – But as for the tree of knowledge of good and bad, you must not eat of it; for as soon as you eat of it, you shall die.

The need for human self-control is a central message of God telling Adam and Eve not to eat from the Tree of Knowledge of good and evil. As the story plays out, human lack of restraint clearly leads God to expel people from the Garden of Eden, Rabbi Arthur Waskow teaches. Today, lack of moderation and excessive consumerism are driving the widespread degradation of our planet.[86] We are on the verge of self-induced expulsion.

❧ LEARNING FROM ANIMALS ❧

Genesis 2:19 – And the Lord God formed out of the earth all the wild beasts and all the birds of the sky, and brought them to the man to see what he would call them; and whatever the man called each living creature, that would be its name.

God created animals after people in the second creation story, with the purpose of Adam naming the animals. Adam was engaged in a relationship of recognition and non-violent interaction: I-Thou, not I-It. Today, encountering meat in a supermarket is an I-It relationship, but encountering animals directly – from a bird nesting in a nearby tree, to an eagle soaring high overhead – can be I-Thou.[87] The language the Torah uses for insects, animals, and people is *nefesh chaya*, literally "a soul of life."

According to one midrash, God paraded the various animals before Adam to name them after he studied their respective characteristics.[88] In light of this midrash, the specific names Adam gave to animals reflected his wisdom, each name capturing the outstanding characteristic which made one animal species distinct from the others.

Every letter Adam chose in naming reflected a special meaning. When the Midrash said, "Due to his wisdom, Adam recognized the nature of the lion, *aryeh*," this means he was aware that the lion was the king of the animals due to its fearless posture. The Hebrew letters that make up the word *aryeh – alef, resh, yud, heh* – are letters that also appear in the various names of God. As the prophet Hosiah wrote, using imagery from the natural world, "They will follow the Lord because He roars like a lion."[89]

The lion's name in Hebrew reflects its role in the animal kingdom and its behavior. This is true for the other animals as well. The original human was granted dominion because of his ability to respect and learn about the animal kingdom in this manner. As Midrash Pirkei D'Rabbi Eliezer notes regarding Adam and Eve's burial of their son Abel: "Adam and his partner came and cried [over Abel], and they didn't know what to do… One raven whose companion died said, 'I will teach Adam this is what to do.' The raven set down his friend and dug in the earth before their eyes and buried him. Adam said, 'Like the raven, this is what we will do.'"[90]

Rabbi David Seidenberg writes, "The rabbis that told these stories clearly thought that we could learn God's ways by observing the other animals. The thread that unites these midrashim is that the animals come to us as teachers, providing moral examples for us; they are not just presented as vassals or objects to be taken care of. We can learn from them only by humbly standing in relation to them, i.e., by 'under-standing,' in the truest and deepest sense of the word."[91] As the rabbis said, "Even if the Torah had not been given we would have been able to learn modesty from the cat and an aversion to theft from the ant."[92] Indeed, the Book of Proverbs states, "Lazybones, go to the ant; study its ways and learn."[93]

❧ HOLY EATING ❧

Genesis 3:6 – When the woman saw that the tree was good for eating and a delight to the eyes, and that the tree was desirable as a source of wisdom, she took of its fruit and ate. She also gave some to her husband, and he ate.

The Torah makes it clear that eating is central to human existence: "And God commanded man saying, 'Of every tree of the garden you may freely eat. But of the Tree of Knowledge of good and evil you shall not eat of it, for on the day that you eat thereof, you shall surely die.'"[94]

Adam and Eve broke this commandment with the first sin – eating from the Tree. The Tree of Life represents holy eating, Rabbi Tzadok HaKohen teaches, while the Tree of Knowledge of Good and Evil represents eating suffused with craving for physical pleasure.[95] Based on this teaching, Sarah Yehudit Schneider writes that "humanity's first sin was not Adam and Eve's eating of forbidden fruit, but rather the way they ate it. The Tree of Knowledge…was not a tree or a food or a thing at all. Rather it was a way of eating. Whenever a person grabs self-conscious pleasure from the world, he falls, at that moment, from God consciousness…Whenever we eat without proper *kavanna* [intention] we repeat this original sin. The primary fixing of human civilization is to learn to eat in holiness."[96]

In a somewhat different vein, Or HaChayim (Rabbi Chayim ben Moshe ibn Attar) says Adam did not know he was eating from the forbidden fruit, and his sin was in not trying to find out where Eve got the fruit she gave him.[97] The premodern reality was that most people grew some of the food they ate. How much effort do we make today to find out where our food comes from? Do we know if it was sourced locally or from abroad? Do we know if the farm workers were paid a fair wage? Do we know what potentially harmful toxins were used in its growing? Do we grow any of our food ourselves?

❧ ALL CREATIONS ARE CONNECTED ❧

Genesis 3:11 – Then He [God] asked, "Who told you that you were naked? Did you eat of the tree from which I had forbidden you to eat?"

Why did Adam and Eve not previously realize they were naked? The Midrash explains that initially Adam and Eve were created with translucent suits, like fingernails. This is one reason why many Jews look at their fingernails in the flame light of the candle used at the end of Shabbat each week. This tradition is to remember their God-given state before the sin of the fruit.[98] After Adam and Eve ate the forbidden fruit, the translucent coverings became opaque, and the first man and woman realized they were naked.

Rashi states that before Eve was removed from Adam, the original human was both male and female together.[99] When you look through an infrared (heat imaging) camera at two people standing close together, you see them merge into a single heat unit. Life before the forbidden fruit may have been like that – all of creation merged together without opaque boundaries. There was no "you" and no "me," just "us." When humankind today, or in the future, returns to the understanding that all God's creations are inseparably linked, we will truly have returned to the Garden of Eden.

Indeed, we must learn to view our planet through a lens of inter-connected ecosystems, not just individual species. Modern science has only scraped the surface of understanding how intricately all biological species interrelate – for example how a hummingbird's beak fits so well for collecting nectar from a particular flower species. Therefore, we must preserve the entire web of life around us as much as possible. We can compare our ecosystem to a line of dominoes: If we push down a single species, others will follow. Through our lack or ignoring of deep ecological understanding, we have caused great damage to God's creation. Our challenge is to see life more holistically, just as Adam and Eve saw life before the forbidden fruit.

❧ EATING THE FORBIDDEN FRUIT ❧

Genesis 3:17 – To Adam He [God] said, "Because you did as your wife said and ate of the tree about which I commanded you, 'You shall not eat of it,' cursed be the ground because of you; by toil shall you eat of it all the days of your life."

For the developed world, agricultural technology removes much of the curse of the Biblical expulsion. In material terms, we have all but re-cre-ated the Garden of Eden, with the comfort and assurance of plentiful food. We have re-created the choice that Adam and Eve faced as well – whether or not to eat from the tree. Today, that means whether or not to choose to gratify ourselves without regard to our impact on the sustainability of the planet. If we keep eating from the tree, we will be expelled again from the abundance of the Garden. And this time, it is not clear we will be able to repair the environmental damage we have wrought.

❧ EDIBLE WEEDS ❧

Genesis 3:18 – Thorns and thistles shall it sprout for you. But your food shall be the grasses of the field.

Rashi asks, "What sort of curse is this? Didn't God just bless him with every seed-bearing herb?" Rashi explains, "When you sow the ground with beans or garden vegetables, the ground will cause thorns and thistles and other grasses of the field to grow and you shall have no choice but to eat them."[100]

In the twenty-first century, invasive weed species cost the Chinese more than $14.5 billion per year[101] to remove and pose one of the greatest challenges to local grain farmers. Removal can often involve use of dangerous chemical weed killers. Perhaps, as some researchers suggest, we can transform "some 'neglected' species, sometimes considered as weeds in extensive major crop cultivation, into 'new functional crops.'"[102] In other words, we could recognize "weeds" as natural food resources and spend less effort, cost, and contamination than in trying to eliminate them.[103]

❧ CONNECTED TO THE EARTH ❧

Genesis 3:19 – By the sweat of your brow shall you get bread to eat, until you return to the ground – for from it you were taken. For dust you are, and to dust you shall return.

The Torah reminds us that we are made up, ultimately, of stardust, as is the rest of creation. We share that origin with every substance in the universe. Terrestrial life on our planet absorbs most of its vitality from a six-inch layer of topsoil. Even though we operate daily on the assumption that we are separate from the earth, this verse reminds us in fact we are intricately connected: "For dust you are, and to dust you shall return."

❧ TAKING RESPONSIBILITY FOR OTHERS ❧

Genesis 4:9 – The Lord said to Cain, "Where is your brother Abel?" And he said, "I do not know. Am I my brother's keeper?"

Rabbi Shlomo Riskin teaches that to be a protector means to be responsible. Rabbi Riskin's teacher, Rabbi Joseph Ber Soloveitchik, taught this as a core Jewish value: "I am responsible, therefore I am." Being responsible and taking responsibility is core to being human. This is very clear from Cain's response to God when asked of Abel's whereabouts: "Am I my brother's keeper?" The actual term used is not "keeper" here but "protector" in the same sense of "protection" mentioned in the Garden of Eden. To Cain's question, the Bible surely implies, "Yes!"[104]

Sustainable living involves being attentive to and taking responsibility for the effects of our actions. In a globally and environmentally connected world, today our failure to take responsibility for our actions on a planet of almost eight billion people has major, detrimental consequences. We use the resources of the world – trees, mineral ores, petroleum – without sufficient attention to how these resources are gathered or mined, refined, transported, and disposed of. We often fail to see, or ignore, the consequences to air and water where we live and far beyond, as well as to our own health and other people's health. Studies in the US indicate that minority, especially African-American, communities suffer disproportionately from living near factories that emit high levels of air pollutants.[105] Exposure results in more cases of asthma and other lung diseases, which in turn make people more susceptible to the most severe incidence of diseases like COVID-19.

❧ FROM FARMER TO REFUGEE ❧

Genesis 4:13 – Cain said to the Lord, "My punishment is too great to bear!"

Cain, the farmer, polluted the earth with Abel's blood, and God cursed Cain that the earth would no longer produce for him. There is an ecological warning built into this human story: Cain worked the ground but cared little about others, and asked, "Am I my brother's keeper?" meaning, "Am I a steward?" God consequently made him a wanderer, disconnecting him from the land he knew and, in effect, giving him permanent refugee status – no longer a steward over nature.

Refugees today are often fleeing from hunger caused by climate change and environmental degradation. The World Bank estimated in 2018 that by 2050, Latin America, sub-Saharan Africa, and Southeast Asia will generate 143 million more climate migrants.[106] As a Brookings Institution report notes, "In 2017, 68.5 million people were forcibly displaced, more than at any point in human history. While it is difficult to estimate, approximately one-third of these (22.5 million to 24 million people) were forced to move by 'sudden onset' weather events – flooding, forest fires after droughts, and intensified storms."[107]

Suggested Action Items

1. To get started with your commitment to learn and act on Genesis' ecological messages, calculate your ecological footprint: How many acres of bioproductive space are devoted to supporting your lifestyle? This can be done through an online quiz such as the one at www .carbonfootprint.com.
2. After you complete the quiz, explore the links provided to discover new ways of living sustainably.
3. For one week, walk outside daily and pay close attention to each element of our planet. On the first day, appreciate the warmth of the sun. On the second, feel the ground beneath your feet. On the third, examine rain clouds or bodies of water. On the fourth, count as many stars as you can. On the fifth, feed birds on a park bench. And on the sixth day, try to find as many animals in your neighborhood as possible – a bird or squirrel can be fun to follow. Fostering appreciation and awareness for all of God's creations will bring us closer to spiritual grounding on earth.

Torah portion of Noah

❧ THE ARK AND GREEN BUILDING ❧

Genesis 6:16 – Make an opening [tzohar] for daylight in the Ark and terminate it within a cubit of the top. Put the entrance to the Ark in its side; make it with bottom, second, and third decks.

Rashi offers two possible meanings of *tzohar*, an "opening" or a "stone that emits light."[108] The Ark was a "green building," with a window for natural lighting from the sun, a whole floor dedicated to composting of animal waste, and wood from forests Noah planted, according to the Midrash. Studying the design of the first Divine-commanded building could teach us about Divine green building standards.

The end of this verse states that God commanded Noah to build the Ark with three levels. The Talmud explains why. Humans were to be on the top deck, the animals in the middle deck, and their manure stored at the bottom. Why store the manure? After all, it could have just been thrown into the sea! As farmers in the Midwestern United States learned after the 2019 floods, "Flooding drains nutrients out of the soil that are necessary for plant growth as well as reducing oxygen needed for plant roots to breathe and gather water and nutrients."[109] So perhaps it was not just the vine branches that Noah took out of the Ark after the floodwater receded, but also the wisely-accumulated manure stored on the bottom level of the vessel.[110] This may be the first Biblical reference to organic fertilizer.

Recent years have seen multiple unintended explosions of ammonium nitrate (used as both a chemical, non-organic fertilizer and an explosive). In August 2020, 2,750 metric tons of ammonium nitrate exploded in Beirut, killing 157 people, wounding 5,000, and causing 300,000 to be homeless. Large explosions also occurred in Tianjin, China (2015) and Texas (2013).[111] These disasters reveal another impact of the widespread use of ammonium nitrate.

The Ark was a "green" project in Biblical times. Today, about one-third of US building projects are considered "green," saving an average of 15 percent on water and electricity costs compared to conventional buildings. Natural lighting, solar power, and water recycling (such as diverting sink waste to water external gardens) are just some of the many architectural and design features that ensure buildings will consume less of nature's resources.[112]

❧ POPULATION AND RESTRAINT ❧

Genesis 6:18 – But I will establish My covenant with you, and you shall enter the Ark, with your sons, your wife, and your sons' wives.

Radak explains that God's statement to Noah does not mention husbands and wives together, but intentionally separates them. This signifies to Noah that in a time of limited resources, human energies should go into surviving and not procreating.[113]

The world population has grown from around two billion in 1950 to an expected 9.8 billion in 2050. However, these numbers disguise the fact that almost all of this growth has occurred in developing nations, where resources are most limited, with an anticipated increase of over seven billion people in just 100 years.[114] Population concerns have complex causes, and often controversial solutions, but the needs of our planet's ever-growing population must be addressed in the context not just of development but of environmental preservation. The most immediate impact of so many people is the astonishing 60 percent drop in total wildlife globally.[115]

❧ NOAH AS EARTH STEWARD ☙

by Shimshon Stüart Siegel[116]

Genesis 6:19 – And of all that lives, of all flesh, you shall take two of each into the Ark to keep alive with you; they shall be male and female.

When we take a deeper look, seeing Noah through the eyes of the rabbinic commentaries, we discover a man who spent his life caring for nature and spreading Divine awareness. This fresh look can provide us many lessons as we strive to bring our world back to a state of holy balance. What can we learn from Noah's efforts?

We can learn that caring about the environment requires patience and forethought. The Midrash says that 120 years before the Flood, Noah actually planted the trees from which he would take the wood for the Ark.[117] (No old-growth logging here!) Aware of the massive resources that his project would demand, Noah tried to be as self-sustaining as possible.

The Talmud explains why the Ark had three levels: one for Noah and his family, one for the animals, and one for the waste – tons upon tons of animal droppings.[118] Noah's family spent a lot of their time shoveling manure. Whether they systematically removed it from the Ark, stored it in a designated waste facility, or found a practical use for it, we see that Noah toiled to maintain the cleanliness of the Ark. Noah's lesson teaches us today that the benefits of a clean, healthy living space – clean of both natural and industrially created waste – are worth the effort for humans and animals coexisting on earth.

Another lesson we can learn from Noah is that it helps to see the world as a "closed," integrated system. Noah and his seven-person crew maintained a sort of proto-Biodome inside the Ark, struggling to preserve a functional level of ecological balance in the most challenging of situations. Within such a system, every action has a significant impact and ramifications, and individual elements can be aligned to strengthen and assist one another.

In modern times, this ecological balance is demonstrated by walking, riding bikes, and using public transportation in congested areas. These individual decisions collectively reduce pollution while easing traffic jams. Partly as a result of the coronavirus pandemic, cities are exploring how to permanently block off more areas for walkers and bikers traveling to work or getting outdoors after work and on weekends. Less traffic and cleaner air reduce many kinds of human health risk from both accidents, pollution, and communicable disease. Individually, these very same choices can reduce personal stress and keep us more fit as well.

After the flood, Noah reinvented himself as an agricultural pioneer. The Midrash explains that Noah revolutionized farming techniques to soften the backbreaking toil that had been the way of the land since the sin of Adam and Eve. By easing the burdens on people and the soil, he truly earned the meaning of his name, "rest."[119]

Overall, Noah's relationship with the land was harmonious and pro-ductive, not adversarial or injurious to the planet for his own well-being. Like Noah, modern farmers can promote agricultural techniques, such as organic farming, that keep consumers healthier and keep the land fruitful, both literally and figuratively, for future generations. Also we must not fill our breadbasket at the expense of suffering by farmworkers – such as their exposure in the fields to toxic pesticides.

For Noah, the Ark was an unfortunate but necessary solution to a global crisis. Even when all signs were grim, he maintained his faith, greeting every challenge with further innovation. So, too, must we con-tinue to strive for a better tomorrow, educate others about environmental issues, and ensure that our actions on every level make a difference. When we step outside after a rainstorm and see the rainbow in the sky, we remember God's promise to Noah, and we can believe and know that we are not alone in our efforts.

❧ CARING FOR CREATURES ❧

Genesis 6:21 – For your part, take of everything that is eaten and store it away, to serve as food for you and for them.

Malbim (Rabbi Meir Leibush ben Yechiel Michel) explains that God is telling Noah, "Don't expect that each animal will bring food for itself in the same way that it hides away food during the summer for the winter months, but rather, make sure that you bring all the necessary provisions with you on to the Ark."[120] In other words, due to the disruption of animals' usual behavior in their ecosystems, Noah becomes responsible not just to bring the animals onto the Ark, but to guarantee their survival by supplying appropriate food for all of the animals, birds, and insects. In our times, ecological devastation has a similar impact and puts similar demands on humans. After catastrophic fires in Australia wiped out eucalyptus forests, leaving any surviving koalas without their only food source, human rescuers are relocating koalas to other eucalyptus areas that were not burned.

❧ PLASTIC, FISH, AND PEOPLE ❧

Genesis 7:23 – All existence on earth was blotted out – people, cattle, creeping things, and birds of the sky; they were blotted out from the earth. Only Noah was left, and those with him in the Ark.

Nachmanides asks, "What happened to the fish?!" He suggests that they escaped to the depths of the oceans where they survived, while the floodwaters over the earth were boiling and thus unsuitable even for fish life.[121] Sadly, fish today are not safe even in great ocean depths.

Contemporary researchers investigating nonbiodegradable plastics in our planet's ocean find that they "are ubiquitous even at depths of more than 6,000 meters and 92 percent are single-use products and that these plastics are harmful to sea life and ultimately to us as they are accumulated in our food chain.[122] Single-use plastic has even reached the world's deepest ocean trench at 10,898 meters."[123] By 2050, some analysts believe there will be more plastic (by weight) in the oceans than fish.[124] Much of this plastic breaks down into tinier pieces, which are then eaten by fish and make their way into both the wild and human food chain. So in a sense, we are experiencing a flood of plastics that threatens to blot out sea life, and we must transform our planet into an Ark to preserve God's creation.

❧ SAVING THE RAVEN ❧

Genesis 8:6–7 – At the end of forty days, Noah opened the window of the Ark that he had made and sent out the raven; it went to and fro until the waters had dried up from the earth.

In the Talmud, Reish Lakish (Rabbi Shimon ben Lakish) describes a fascinating conversation between the raven and Noah. The raven (a non-kosher bird) said, "Your Boss [i.e. God] hates me, and YOU hate me. Your Boss hates me because He said that there should be seven pairs of each kosher animal and only one pair of each non-kosher animal. And you hate me because, despite there only being one breeding pair on board, you sent me out to scout the land, risking the extinction of my whole species!"[125] In response, God told Noah to take the raven back into the Ark. Noah then sent the dove, of which seven pairs were in the Ark. Noah is thus seen as preserving the diversity of life on earth.

We would be wise to learn from Noah's example in a century known as the Anthropocene, or great human-caused extinction era.[126] According to recent research on local and regional species loss in China, the estimated proportion of species loss, out of 252 key protected vertebrate species, during the past half-century was 47.7 percent for mammals, 28.8 percent for amphibians and reptiles, and 19.8 percent for birds.[127] Scientists recognize human-induced environmental impacts and climate change as the greatest threats to all species' survival.

❧ RAINBOWS AND RESPONSIBILITY[128]

Genesis 9:13 – I have set My bow in the clouds, and it shall serve as a sign of the covenant between Me and the earth.

Rabbi Samson Raphael Hirsch explains that the symbolism of the rainbow is its multiple colors in one cohesive structure.[129] God's pact of peace with humankind and all of creation is represented by this eternal symbol of diversity. Today we know that our global ecosystem is extremely complex and interlinked, even beyond what humans can currently comprehend. Our actions in diverting a single river or allowing the use of a single refrigerant chemical can have devastating effects on aspects of the planet we don't even know about – including even species not yet identified – that could affect us for generations to come.

Nachmanides teaches that the rainbow signifies an upside-down bow and serves as "a reminder of peace." The feet of the rainbow are bent downward to show that the Heavenly "shooting" (the torrential rains) has ceased.[130] Rabbi Shlomo Riskin explains the meaning of Nachmanides' teaching: "Ancient cultures fought their wars with the bow and arrow, and the side which surrendered, pursuing peace instead of war, would express their will to do so by raising an inverted bow that the enemy could see. Similarly, God places an inverted bow in the heavens as a sign that He is no longer warring against humanity."[131] The rainbow testifies to the Creator's intention for life on our planet to continue to exist. It is a sign that God desires the existence of the world and not its destruction.

Rabbi Riskin continues that the symbolism of the rainbow extends beyond God's commitment – to encompass humans: "The rainbow is a half-picture, lacking a second half to complete the circle of wholeness. God can pledge not to destroy humanity, but since He created humanity with freedom of choice, He cannot guarantee that humanity will not destroy itself."[132] Yet the rabbis make clear that God does not want us to destroy creation either.

At present, humanity is emitting over 36 billion tons of CO_2 per year into the atmosphere. In the past 800,000 years, atmospheric concentrations of CO_2 did not exceed 300 parts per million (ppm).[133] Yet people have dramatically increased the concentration of CO_2 in the atmosphere in the past 200 years, to 417 parts per million and rising every year.[134] A consensus of climate scientists understands that humans are directly causing climate change.[135] Through our consumption, it is as if we are shooting carbon arrows into the atmosphere, inadvertently waging war on God's creation.

In Israel, one first sees rainbows after the Jewish New Year and Day of Atonement, when the winter rains begin to fall in October. According to the Ziv HaZohar commentary, the rainbow as a whole reminds us to turn our hearts to improve our actions.[136] Perhaps the timing of the rainbow's appearance, soon after the period of repentance, can motivate each of us to keep improving ourselves and become better servants of the Creator and collective stewards of creation.

❧ FLOODS AND FAIRTRADE ❧

Genesis 9:20 – Noah, the tiller of the soil, was the first to plant a vineyard.

Rashi was a vintner, and he cites the Midrash:[137] "When he [Noah] entered the Ark, he brought with him vine branches and shoots of fig trees." When he left the Ark, he planted them. Yet the Midrash states that about a foot of soil, "the depth [that the blade of a] plow [digs into], was washed away in the flood."[138] How did Noah succeed in growing a vineyard? Noah may have used the massive stores of dung on the Ark to compost and revitalize the land.

In Kerala, India, during the heavy monsoons of 2018, rainfall was so heavy that more than 450 people died and over two million took shelter in camps – yet the topsoil remained. In the aftermath, the Fairtrade Foundation was able to utilize this topsoil and wisely supported farmers with 200,000 seedlings to replant crops lost in the floods.[139]

❧ LORDING OVER NATURE ❧

Genesis 11:1–3 – Everyone on earth had the same language and the same words. And as they migrated from the east, they came upon a valley in the land of Shinar and settled there. They said to one another, "Come, let us make bricks and burn them hard." Brick served them as stone, and bitumen served them as mortar.

Evan Eisenberg writes that the Tower of Babel, in the Mesopotamian kingdom of Sumeria, represents the arrogance of the world's early farmers who thought their own work cultivated their prosperity. He notes that the Mesopotamians embraced a type of thinking where, "the man-made order is so firmly established that it seems God-made. All is stripped from nature and affixed to the social and technical order." They saw themselves as a source of bounty and power, not as recipients of God's blessing. In spite of all their efforts and mastery, Eisenberg notes,

Sumerian society declined due to unsustainable agricultural practices, which created rising salt content in the soil of the agricultural fields.

By contrast, the Israelites "were neither desert nomads mistrustful of nature nor proud hydraulic despots lording it over nature. They were good farmers living frugally on the margins and using the best stewardship they knew. They were dependent on rain and groundwater, neither of which was overabundant, and on thin and rock-strewn soil, and had to use their wits to conserve both."[140]

❧ THE LIMITS OF TECHNOLOGY ❧

Genesis 11:4 – And they said, "Come, let us build us a city, and a tower with its top in the sky, to make a name for ourselves; else we shall be scattered all over the world."

Dr. Manfred Gerstenfeld states, "Often, the negative effects of uncontrolled technological development are one of the reasons for the deterioration of the environment... The roots of the limitations of technology are stated in the Bible. This is made clear in the story of the Tower of Babel."[141] Ultimately, God does scatter the people who build the Tower of Babel – and whose names are now only remembered in the context of failure, both ecological and social, and disarray.

Dr. Jeremy Benstein writes:

> The Tower was not only a vertical reality, but a virtual one as well, perhaps the first in history. Ancient Mesopotamians built those ziggurats – cultic towers – on the flat floodplain, as a replacement for an actual mountain of God. Even their building materials were artificial substitutes for more natural stones and mortar (see Genesis 11:3). Today's towers, and all that they represent, dwarf those of antiquity. Alienation from the earth, each other, and the divine too often typifies our society. Recent trends of corporate globalization, pointing to a world monoculture – unity through uniformity – threaten that delicate fabric of diversity, of cultures and their habitats. This can serve as a warning to us, like the builders of Babel, not to put our faith in technology for our salvation, especially when it clouds our trust in the Creator.

Real mountains and vast natural phenomena deeply remind us we should feel humble in the face of the cosmos and even in local representations of it, like mountains. Perhaps there is a built-in humility "gene," evolutionarily acquired to engender wonder, to give us a healthy respect for things which we cannot fathom much less control. But when artificial towers like skyscrapers – or technology, or other products of human ingenuity – begin to mimic that effect, to co-opt that feeling, we begin to lose sight of reality, subjugate ourselves to our own tools, and limit our ability to experience wonderment at anything but the work of our own hands.[142]

Technology can be a blessing and a curse. Used well, it can bring peace, progress, and prosperity. Yet it often causes discord and even violence, pollution and environmental degradation.

♣ DIVERSITY SUSTAINS LIFE ♣

Genesis 11:6 – And the Lord said, "If, as one people with one language for all, this is how they have begun to act, then nothing that they may propose to do will be out of their reach."

Shadal (Rabbi Samuel David Luzzatto) explains, "They were one people, with one society and one opinion."[143] In other words, they were a society with no diversity whatsoever. We need diversity for sustainability, both in the animal kingdom and in the human world. While every society must have its own customs and constraints, survival in times of disaster may ultimately depend on learning from outsiders.

Greenland in the Middle Ages was inhabited by two peoples – the Norse from Scandinavia and the native Inuit. According to historical records, the two peoples met on a very occasional basis but never cooperated. In the words of Pulitzer Prize winner and anthropologist Jared Diamond, "If only the Norse, besides eating many of the wild foods used by Native American societies in Greenland (especially caribou, migratory seals, and harbor seals), had also taken advantage of other wild foods that Native Americans used but the Norse did not (especially fish, ringed seals, and whales other than beached whales), the Norse might have survived. That they did not ... was their own decision. The Norse starved in the presence of unutilized food resources."[144]

God sees the people of Babel becoming too uniform and determines to break them up into more diverse groups, each with their own language and ideas. With this, God lays the foundations for sustainable diversity within humanity. Yet human diversity has declined significantly in the past century, including in diet. McDonald's, Subway, Kentucky Fried Chicken, Burger King, and Pizza Hut have 116,000 stores, in a majority of countries around the world.[145] The majority of people in the world eat these chains' food each year, with common ingredients being meat, cheese, wheat, corn, oil, and sugar. The homogeneity in diet worldwide has contributed to a dramatic decline in the biodiversity of food crops, which the UN cites as a threat to global food security. A UN report notes that "the lack of variety and increasing uniformity of crops may render them unsuitable for the changing conditions under which they grow."[146]

With regard to biodiversity, Jared Diamond notes how destroying a lot of little species matters to the same extent that taking out a lot of little screws holding together an airplane matters.[147] The extinction of a single species, the destruction of large tracts of rainforest, ocean pollution, and poisoning of billions of sea animals with plastic – these acts equally diminish the holiness of creation.

Suggested Action Items

1. Try eating one fewer fast-food meal each week – or even none!
2. If you've eaten plenty of meat or fish over the last month, consider changing one meal this coming week to be vegetarian or vegan. Try a new fruit or vegetable, or prepare it in a new way, to "explore the fruits of the land."
3. Noah's hard work paid off for future generations, namely us. Identify an action that you could take in your lifetime that would make a difference for your children or future generations.
4. If you are not ready to commit today to a long-term change, identify a time in the future when you will commit to it, and mark that time on your personal calendar. Also remember that some changes take effort or additional steps. Consider those steps and add them to your calendar as well.

Torah portion of Lech Lecha

❧ PALACE ON FIRE ❧

Genesis 12:1 – The Lord said to Abram, "Go forth from your native land and from your father's house to the land that I will show you."

The Midrash explains how Abram (whose name becomes Abraham) discovered God. It describes Abraham passing by a palace that is on fire. He wonders aloud, "Is it possible that the palace doesn't have an owner? Who is the owner of this palace?" The owner hears him and says, "It is Me!"[148]

In the words of Rabbi Yosef Y. Jacobson: "Abraham's bewilderment is clear. This sensitive human being gazes at a brilliantly structured universe, a splendid piece of art. He is overwhelmed by the grandeur of a sunset and by the miracle of childbirth; he marvels at the roaring ocean waves and at the silent, steady beat of the human heart. The world is indeed a palace. But the palace is in flames. The world is full of…pain."[149]

Rabbi Jonathan Sacks explains that the question, "Is it possible that the palace doesn't have an owner?" speaks to the responsibility of humanity to put out the fire that we have started. The palace is a metaphor for nature.[150] Today with global warming, the world's great rainforests and boreal forests are burning as never before.[151] One could look at the planet and legitimately ask, "Who is in charge of this problem?" And God's response may be to us, just as it was to Abraham, "Go forth," or "Reach into yourself." In other words, we all share responsibility for our common home.

❧ FAMINE IN GENESIS ❧

Genesis 12:10 – There was a famine in the land, and Abram went down to Egypt to sojourn there, for the famine was severe in the land.

The verse emphasizes that Abraham and his family had to migrate due to the famine. In the Land of Israel, the crops that depend on rainfall, like wheat, barley, olives, and grapes, produce little or no grain or fruit during a drought. Fig trees, pomegranate trees, and vegetables that depend on more water produce even less. In a sustained drought, even the springs dry up, which prevents irrigation.

According to Rabbeinu Bachaya (Bachaya ben Asher ibn Halawa), citing the rabbis of the Talmud, there were ten famines from Adam to the end of Genesis.[152] The Midrash states that the Torah explicitly mentions only three famines, one each during the lifetimes of Abraham, Isaac, and Jacob.[153] These three famines occur in a period of about 200 years.[154]

Ten extreme famines occurred in the twentieth century. They killed over 70 million people, predominantly in China, the Soviet Union, and India, and also drove migration of millions more to new regions.[155] This suggests an average of ten years between major world famines. While the immediate and deeper causes of famines are complex, unsustainable agricultural practices contributing to salinity, loss of natural water bodies, or soil erosion can play a role.[156] A 2019 United Nations Climate Change report highlights the increased likelihood of future, major global famine due to climate change, stressing the world's major breadbaskets.[157] Abraham and Sarah had no choice but to become famine refugees. Today, the individual and collective actions of people could reduce the frequency and severity of famines in our times and in the future.

❧ SUSTAINABLE COEXISTENCE ❧
by Rabbi Tuvia Aronson[158]

Genesis 13:6 – So that the land could not support them staying together; for their possessions were so great that they could not remain together.

Abraham and Lot's inability to coexist on one piece of land leaps out at us. In our era, when environmental issues such as population, food, and land distribution divide communities and nations, we can look to this text for guidance. Rabbi Samson Raphael Hirsch and Netziv (Rabbi Naftali Tzvi Yehuda Berlin) explain this verse to show that divisiveness put an extra burden on the land and the people.[159]

It was not because they had too many herds or because there was insufficient pasture for both of them. If they had combined their herds into one, the land would have been sufficient. But if two people cannot agree, separate tents are needed – boxes, crates, everything separate for each of the two parties. Had their personalities been compatible, there would have been no need for separate pastures. Only profits counted in Lot's enterprise, while Abraham's household gave attention to higher interests.

Abraham and Lot's attitudes were incompatible, therefore they could not cooperate. This is why the verse stresses "together" – *yachdav*. Interestingly, the second-century translator Onkelos translates *yachdav* using the wording "as one," connoting the need for a deep interconnection that ultimately enables living in harmony with the Land.[160] The Abrahamic tradition demands that we make our personal and societal decisions based on both environmental and social considerations.

Religious environmental education stresses the importance of togetherness. Community gardens are flourishing, and consumer-assisted farming projects are enhancing life in ways that promote both communal unity and harmony with nature. Hazon's Adamah program in Connecticut is one such example. Intentional ecological communities are gaining momentum. Concern for the environment crosses denominational and philosophical divides. Working as one to take care of our precious resources is incredibly powerful.

❧ THE DEAD SEA IS DYING ❧

Genesis 13:10 – Lot looked about him and saw how well watered was the whole plain of the Jordan, all of it – this was before the Lord had destroyed Sodom and Gomorrah – all the way to Zoar, like the garden of the Lord, like the land of Egypt.

In Biblical times, the Dead Sea region was lush and fertile, like the Garden of Eden. Ralbag (Rabbi Levi ben Gershon) explains that the Dead Sea valley had many fields, suggesting that there was ample water for irrigation at that time.[161] Rashi teaches that it had streams, trees, and crops.[162]

Over the past 60 years, modern irrigation techniques have significantly expanded agriculture in Israel, Jordan, Syria, and Lebanon. In addition, many millions of people now live in the Dead Sea drainage basin. They use water for domestic and industrial uses, including the extraction of Dead Sea minerals. This has threatened the region's ecology, with significant lowering of the Dead Sea's water level and formation of sinkholes around the sea. The diversion of tributary rivers and streams for human use has significantly reduced the annual flow to the Dead Sea, just as climate change has made rainfall in the Dead Sea watershed scarcer.[163] Dead Sea water levels continue to decline at a rate of about 3.4 feet (1.1 meter) per year.[164] Without significant collaborative action, the Dead Sea may suffer a similar fate as two of the world's great lakes – Lake Baikal in Russia, and Lake Mali in Africa, which have shriveled in recent decades. That the Torah describes the Dead Sea valley as comparable to the Garden of Eden should motivate us to stop and reverse the damage we have already done.

❧ HIKING THE LAND ❧

Genesis 13:17 – Get up, walk about the land, through its length and its breadth, for I give it to you.

Abraham connected to God by being alone in nature. Abraham was commanded to walk the width and breadth of Israel. Why is this one of very few commands given to him? Abraham traveled throughout the Middle East by foot and by donkey – from present-day Iraq, crossing through Turkey, Syria, and Egypt, before returning to Israel. His travels and time in nature created a foundation for his spiritual growth and awareness. He also kept himself in good physical shape. At the age of 127, the Bible says, he hiked for three days and climbed Mount Moriah for the binding of Isaac.

Isaac also connected to God through nature when he went out into the fields. So did Jacob when he slept and dreamt of the ladder, alone outdoors. How many city dwellers today have ever slept alone in nature? How can we bridge the ecological gap between our lifestyle and that of our forefathers?

❧ STUCK IN CRUDE OIL ❧

Genesis 14:10 – Now the Valley of Siddim was dotted with bitumen pits; and the kings of Sodom and Gomorrah, in their flight, threw themselves into them, while the rest escaped to the hill country.

The kings of Sodom and Gomorrah fell into pits of "black gold" or bitumen, also known as asphalt (in Hebrew, *chemar*).[165] In ancient times as today, surface seepages of this thick, sticky form of crude oil[166] occurred and still occur in a limited number of places in the world, including Azerbaijan, Iran, Pennsylvania, Alberta, and the Dead Sea.[167] People used and still use the natural tar for its waterproofing qualities[168] and for roads.

Why does the Torah mention this geological detail in relation to the leaders of these ultimately decimated societies? The Torah continues, "The invaders [four Middle Eastern kings] seized all the wealth of Sodom and Gomorrah and all their provisions, and went their way."[169] Once the kings of Sodom and Gomorrah fell into the bitumen pits, they got trapped and lost all of their wickedly gained wealth.

The story of the kings stuck in bitumen relates deeply to our world today. Canada is the planet's fourth-largest oil producer, and 60 percent of its oil comes from the bitumen of oil sands.[170] The Canadian province of Alberta has most of the world's reserves of natural bitumen in the Athabasca oil sands, an area larger than England.[171] Bitumen is considered the dirtiest and most polluting fossil fuel, due to the energy required to separate the crude oil from the sand and the carcinogenic chemicals used to thin it for pipeline transport.[172] In July 2010, the largest oil pipeline spill in US history occurred, spilling over a million gallons of Canadian diluted bitumen (dilbit) into Michigan's Kalamazoo River. As InsideClimate News reported, "The spill triggered the most expensive clean-up in US history – more than ¾ of a billion dollars – and it lingered on for years."[173] Today, we and our leaders are trapped by economic inertia and political resistance. Oil remains our fuel of choice to make gasoline for cars and trucks, jet fuel for airplanes, tar and asphalt for paving the roads, and even plastic which is filling our oceans with trash that never fully breaks down.

The Midrash teaches that Abraham, the prophet of light, pulled the kings out of the bitumen pits.[174] Abraham provides an example of lifting people from being trapped in fossil fuels. Comparatively, scientists published a 2017 study and environmental roadmap on how most countries in the world could transition to 100 percent wind, water, and solar energy by 2050.[175] We do not need to wait until someone rescues us – or until we run out of all fossil fuels – but can now take steps as individuals, communities, and nations to free ourselves from devastating fossil-fuel use.

❧ ABRAHAM AND SELF-SATISFACTION ❧

Genesis 14:22–23 – But Abram said to the king of Sodom, "I swear to the Lord, God Most High, Creator of heaven and earth: I will not take so much as a thread or a sandal strap of what is yours; you shall not say, 'It is I who made Abram rich.'"

Abraham recognizes where wealth and abundance ultimately come from – God. The Maharal of Prague (Rabbi Judah Loew ben Betzalel) taught that Abraham epitomizes "satisfaction with what one has" and being content with what arrives in one's hand based on a normal amount of work.[176] Rashi points out that Abraham made sure to earn his living through honest means, by only grazing his flocks on ownerless land.[177] The trait of being satisfied with what one has flows from an awareness that God provides each person based on their merit. Abraham appreciates the gift of being fully alive through meeting his needs through his own efforts and has no need of gifts from the king of Sodom.

In modern consumer society, we would be wise to learn from Abraham. Being satisfied with what we have, instead of constantly seeking more things, is a root solution for ecological sustainability.

❧ FINDING GOD OUTDOORS ❧

Genesis 15:5 – He took him outside and said, "Look toward heaven and count the stars, if you are able to count them." And He added, "So shall your offspring be."

Why did God take Abraham outside? Ibn Ezra writes poetically of finding God, "Wherever I turn my eyes, around on earth or to the heavens, I see You in the field of stars, I see You in the yield of the land, in every breath and sound, a blade of grass, a simple flower, an echo of Your holy name."[178]

Elie Wiesel relates: When the Holy Seer of Lublin was a little boy, he was known to skip school for hours or even days. Once, his teacher followed the young boy to see what became of these free moments. The Seer walked to the edge of the town, into deep woods, and there, in a small, green circle of trees, he began to pray. The next day the teacher asked the boy what drew him to those woods. The Seer of Lublin replied, "I can find God there." "But," said the teacher, "surely God is the same in the town as in the woods." "That's true," replied the Seer, "but I am not the same!"[179]

❧ THE CURE BEFORE THE SICKNESS ☙

Genesis 15:13–14 – Know well that your offspring shall be strangers in a land not theirs, and they shall be enslaved and oppressed four hundred years; but I will execute judgment on the nation they shall serve, and in the end they shall go free with great wealth.

Rabbi Mordechai Hochman explains that these verses encapsulate the rabbinical dictum that "God gives us the cure before the sickness." In other words, God tells Abraham that his descendants will suffer but emerge much stronger from it.[180]

With regard to sustainability, it is easy to think that the world is doomed to destruction. However, God has given us the cure before the sickness. There have never been so many possible solutions available for reducing carbon emissions (solar panels are cheaper than ever), for conserving water, and for replacing single-use plastics. Our challenge as humankind is in deciding to embrace them.

Suggested Action Items

1. Look for an opportunity to share your resources with others. For example, borrow a book from your local library rather than buying a new one, create an opportunity to share gardening tools with a neighbor, or organize a community swap for books, toys, clothing, or other products. You will then become part of the circular economy.
2. Learn about the environmental challenges faced in your local community. Identify one place where you'd like to focus your attention on the health of the land. Do your part to help preserve it through charity, clean-up or solar projects, or sponsoring a wildlife habitat.
3. Create community opportunities to learn faith-based wisdom on sustainability and creation care, like through a book club, learning circle, or after-school program. See www.interfaithsustain.com for further resources.

Torah portion of Vayeira

❧ RESILIENCE OF TREES ❧

Genesis 18:4 – Let a little water be brought; bathe your feet and recline under the tree.

Rabbeinu Chananel asked why the angels revealed themselves to Abraham under a tree.[181] He answered that in doing so they revealed a message to Abraham: "You, like a tree, will flourish even in your old age," as it says in the book of Job, "For a tree has hope; if it is cut it will again renew itself, and its trunk will never cease,"[182] and in the words of the Psalmist, "He shall be as a tree planted beside streams of water, which brings forth its fruit in its season. Its leaves do not wilt; and whatever it does prospers."[183]

Abraham's resilience and prosperity are compared to a tree. Indeed, trees are one of the most resilient organisms, specifically against drought. This is increasingly important in light of climate change causing unpredictable rainfall, extreme weather events, and stronger pests that threaten forests.[184] Contemporary researchers have discovered that diverse "forests with trees that employ a high diversity of traits related to water use suffer less of an impact from drought."[185] They are also more resilient to forest fires.

❧ VEAL THEN AND NOW ❧

Genesis 18:7 – Then Abraham ran to the herd, took a calf, tender and choice, and gave it to a servant-boy, who hastened to prepare it.

Radak explains that the calf was "fatty."[186] A Biblical fatty calf would have been naturally well fed by its mother and not overworked, so that it could put on weight. Today, however, calves are raised unnaturally for veal, kept in cramped conditions, and fed artificial fluids.

Regarding the permissibility of this modern way of raising calves, Rabbi Moshe Feinstein, one of the greatest twentieth-century authorities on Jewish law, writes, "Regarding the new method of fattening calves in special, narrow stalls where they don't even have enough room to take a few steps, and they are not fed any normal animal feed nor are they allowed to suckle at all but instead are fed with fatty liquids from which they derive no pleasure at all and they are also frequently ill because of this and require all kinds of medication: Those who perform this (the fattening) are surely guilty of the prohibition of causing pain to animals. For even though it (pain) is permitted when there is a purpose, for example to slaughter them for food or to use them for plowing or transport, etc. but not for senseless pain, which is forbidden even if someone makes monetary gain from it ... In any case, it is forbidden to cause pain to an animal, to feed it food which it doesn't enjoy, which causes pain, or which causes it to be ill."[187]

❧ SODOM AND ACID RAIN ❧

Genesis 19:24 – The Lord rained upon Sodom and Gomorrah sulfurous fire from the Lord out of heaven.

According to the Midrash,[188] nothing that descended from heaven was bad, in and of itself. Only when this rain reached the earth's atmosphere did it receive the additive of sulfur and fire.

Acid rain can be seen as a modern-day equivalent. As water evaporates, it combines with the acidic and often sulfurous emissions from cars, factories, and coal-generating plants to form acid rain. In recent years, Taoyuan's Zhongli District in Taiwan measured rain acidity levels equivalent to that of lemon juice (pH of 3.8).[189] Acid rain has been successfully reduced in most Western countries where it was once prevalent. In the US, the EPA emissions trading program "helped deliver annual sulfur dioxide (SO_2) reductions of over 93 percent and annual nitrogen oxides (NO_x) emissions reductions of over 86 percent ... from fossil fuel–fired power plants, extensive environmental and human health benefits, and far lower-than-expected costs."[190]

The success in the US and Europe in dramatically reducing acid rain shows how government environmental policies can rein in high pollution and the ensuing effects on human health and nature. With regard to acid rain, we have a choice about whether or not to experience some of what God rained down on the selfish people of Sodom.

❧ MORALITY AND ECOLOGY ❧

by Rabbi Yuval Cherlow[191]

Genesis 19:24 – The Lord rained upon Sodom and Gomorrah sulfurous fire from the Lord out of heaven.

Two cosmic catastrophes unfold in the book of Genesis. In the flood, God brings waters down from the Heavens to destroy almost all life. In the second, the utter devastation of Sodom and Gomorrah, an area previously known as a fertile and lush "Garden of God,"[192] becomes a desolate land "that cannot be sown, nor sprout, and no grass shall rise up upon it, like the upheaval of Sodom and Gomorrah…which God overturned in His anger, and His wrath."[193]

One of the connections we see between these two events is the word that the Torah employs in both cases – to destroy. When God relates to Noah that He will bring the flood, He says, "I am about to destroy [*mashchitam*] them from the earth."[194] In the case of Sodom we see the same word applied: "When God destroyed [*beshachet*] the cities of the plain…"[195]

The Torah does not elaborate on the sin of Sodom, but the underpinnings are expressed later in the prophecy of Ezekiel: Sodom "…had pride, excess bread, and peaceful serenity, but did not strengthen the hand of the poor and the needy."[196] The prophet's description, combined with what the Torah reveals to us, gives us the following picture: The people of Sodom insisted on preserving their high quality of living to such an extent that they established a principle not to let the poor and homeless reside in their city.

Consequently, when a destitute person would come seeking help, they would revoke their right to any welfare, public or private! In this rule, the Sodomites figured they would preserve an elite upper class community that could monopolize the profits that the bountiful land offered, without having to distribute any revenues to a "lower class" of people.

An opinion in the Mishnah further strengthens this picture of moral depravity when it defines the Sodomite as one who says, "What's mine is mine and what's yours is yours."[197] The Mishnah decries a man who wishes to remove himself from the social responsibility of welfare by closing himself and his wealth from others, even if he makes the claim that he is not taking away from anyone else.

But the Torah also uses the verb "to destroy" in relation to the environment, regarding the prohibition of wanton destruction during a military siege: "Do not destroy [tashchit] the trees."[198]

What could be the connection between the corruption of the generation of the flood, the people of Sodom, and environmental sins? Humanity itself is part and parcel of its environment and is not separate from it. Having been created in the image of God, we may think that we are detached from creation.

The central point in the connection between moral behavior and environmental behavior comes from the understanding that both behaviors go hand in hand. One without the other corrupts the Divine vision for human action. That is, a society may be passionate about preserving its natural environment while maintaining a complete disregard for the welfare of its citizens. Sodom is a perfect example of this, where they cared so much for their "garden of God" that they refused to aid anyone in need.

In effect, the people of Sodom's perverted ways were extremely unsustainable – causing God to turn one of the most fertile and lush ecosystems on earth into what today is infamous for its barrenness and desolation. From the mistakes of the people of Sodom, we can learn the essential character traits that allow one to live in balance with the Creator and creation.

The moral human being is devoted to the holiness and purity of life, refrains from harming others, and sacrifices some personal pleasure for an ethical and upright path. When we are capable of fulfilling this ideal, we will naturally be triumphant in attaining the great spiritual task of infusing our religious/moral lifestyle with one that is also environmentally sustainable.

❧ ABRAHAM AND THE BURNING KILN ❧

Genesis 19:25 – He annihilated those cities and the entire Plain, and all the inhabitants of the cities and the vegetation of the ground.

Rashi comments on the verse, "He [Abraham] saw the smoke of the land rising like the smoke of a kiln,"[199] saying this was like the smoke rising from a kiln burning limestone to create lime used for bricks.[200] Today, burning of tropical rainforests not only devastates the region where the burning occurs, but puts pollution in the air that is carried far beyond a nation's borders. Burning of the environment is an international ecological threat.

Chizkuni (Rabbi Chizkiyahu ben Rabbi Mano'ach) explains why vegetation is also mentioned in this verse: It teaches that anyone who takes a handful of earth from Sodom, even to this day, and transfers it to a garden, will make the garden infertile.[201]

Today, scientists teach us, "When acid rain [from pollution] falls, it can affect forests as well as lakes and rivers. To grow, trees need healthy soil in which to develop. Acid rain is absorbed into the soil, making it more difficult for trees to survive. As a result, trees are more susceptible to viruses, fungi and insect pests."[202]

The acid rain effect is reversible with the addition of large quantities of alkaline lime to the soil. In Sweden, the cost of such treatment is over $50 million per year.[203] This is an example of an "externality," a cost of operating our cars and factories that is paid by taxpayers instead of by polluters. If such treatment costs were included in the costs of fossil fuels, according to some analysts, fuel prices would rise by up to 50 percent.[204]

❧ SUSTAINABLE PEACE ❧

Genesis 21:33 – [Abraham] planted a tamarisk [eshel] at Beersheba, and invoked there the name of the Lord, the Everlasting God.

Malbim explains that the *eshel* was an orchard.[205] The peace pact made with Abimelech, king of Gerar (today's Gaza), is concluded with the planting of fruit trees, representing the importance of sustaining long-term and environmental prosperity for all, and demonstrating that true peace is based upon a joint hope for a better future. This is comparable to modern Israel and Jordan basing a 1994 peace pact on sharing water resources.[206] The Israeli-Palestinian-Jordanian NGO Eco Peace has proposed a shared, cross-border nature park as a way to promote peace.

Suggested Action Items

1. Look for an opportunity to be generous to another human being this week. For example: give money to the poor, schedule a time to volunteer at a local shelter, or find time to join a local team which is fulfilling a community need.

2. Learn about the challenges of environmental justice and environmental racism. These topics will show you how our environmental choices can disproportionately impact others.

3. Focus your attention on living "in balance" with the Creator and creation. One way to do this is by focusing on buying and preparing only as much food as you will eat. Clean out your refrigerator and note which food items have gone to waste so that you will buy less next time.

Torah portion of Chayei Sarah

❧ SARAH AND SUSTAINABLE BURIAL ❧

Genesis 23:4 – I am a resident alien among you; sell me a burial site among you, that I may remove my dead for burial.

Abraham seeks to buy land to bury Sarah. While he purchases both a field and cave in Hebron, Sarah was buried in a cave. Rabbeinu Bachaya explains that there was a custom for every family to have their own burial area.[207] Contemporary scholar Eldad Keynan explains the Biblical method of burial: "The body was not laid and covered with dust for eternity, like the trench graves practices. Instead, it was laid in a shallow pit or on a shelf for the first year, during which the flesh decayed, while the soul underwent the purifying process. A year after the burial, the relatives returned to the tomb, collected the bones, and put them in stone boxes: ossuaries... Now they moved the bones to the ossuary, and put the ossuary in a niche, carved into the tomb wall."[208]

Contemporary researchers have identified two major ecological risks posed by modern cemeteries: contamination of local water sources and of the soil.[209] Traditional Jewish burial practices in Israel overcame these two issues through burial in a rock cave to minimize water contamination, and through burial in simple cloth, without a coffin or other non-decomposable objects.

Modern Jerusalem, a society that lives mostly in urban space and spends most of its time in buildings, now buries many of its dead in multistory structures that resemble parking lots. The main cemetery is next to an urban area and expanded highway, which is common in many cities. A different recent burial design in West Jerusalem's main Har HaMenuchot cemetery is based on the Biblical method of burying in a cave, but creates crypts that are up to 160 feet underground in order to leave space above ground for the living.[210] This may be needed since Israel faces a shortage of 1.5 million burial plots in the coming decades, according to a report from the State Comptroller.[211]

❧ RELATIONSHIP WITH EARTH ❧

Genesis 23:13 – And [Abraham] spoke to Ephron in the hearing of the people of the land, saying, "If only you would hear me out! Let me pay the price of the land; accept it from me, that I may bury my dead there."

Rabbi Matis Weinberg explains:

> God tells humankind in the Creation story that we "will return to the earth for you were taken from it. For you are dust, and to dust you will return."[212] God does not inform people of mortality per se, but of burial: to dust you will return. It is the underlying relationship with the earth that needs to be restored. That relationship, as with a spouse, is not like the use of an object, but rather through the deep connection we make with the other party.
>
> It is because we were "taken from the earth" in the first place, that we are able to "return to it" and ultimately to find peace. The Midrash teaches that "God collected the dust for man's creation from the four corners of the earth, so that wherever he would die he would find his place for burial."[213] The earth, *adama*, is the name

of our species humankind *adam*, just as "human" is drawn from the Latin "humus" meaning "earth." If we lose sight of that connection we lose all connection to ourselves and to life. Burial is a restoration of that connection.[214]

To invoke the philosopher Martin Buber, our connection to the earth should not be an I–It relationship, but rather an I–Thou relationship, much like an ideal marriage.[215]

❧ SARAH AND TREES ❧

Genesis 23:17–18 – The field with its cave and all the trees anywhere within the confines of that field – passed to Abraham as his possession in the presence of the Hittites, of all who entered the gate of his town.

The Torah tells us about the eternal transfer of the cave of the Patriarchs to the seed of Abraham. But why does the Torah need to tell us that the trees were also sold? In ancient societies, trees next to burial sites were protected from being cut down.[216] Near Jerusalem today, at Sataf, one of the only old-growth oak groves in the Judaean hills is adjacent to a Muslim sheik's burial site. In downtown Jerusalem, a Sufi sheik's tomb is surrounded by mature trees.

The Talmud tells the story of Choni HaMe'agel: "One day he was journeying on the road and saw a man planting a carob tree. He asked, 'How long will it take [for this tree] to bear fruit?' The man replied, 'Seventy years.' He then asked the man, 'Are you so certain that you will live another seventy years?' The man replied, 'I found carob trees in the world that my ancestors planted for me, so I am planting these trees for my children.'"[217]

Trees represent continuity and sustainability, producing fruit for many decades. The Torah makes the connection between the death of Sarah and the purchase of the trees to stress that just as the trees will benefit future generations who will eat their fruit and breathe their oxygen, so, too, will Sarah's life continue to have meaning for future generations.

In the time of Choni HaMe'agel, the old man advocated sustainable agriculture, planting a tree for his grandchildren to enjoy. Today, we see youth increasingly engaging with environmental causes and even influencing policy at the UN.[218] Nowadays, children are more likely to be convincing their parents of the importance of sustainability than the other way around.[219] The most visible face of the global climate movement has been a Swedish teenager, Greta Thunberg. In August 2018, at age 15, she began a strike for climate action outside of the Swedish Parliament, following the heat waves and wildfires during Sweden's hottest summer in at least 262 years.[220]

❧ REBECCA'S KINDNESS TO CAMELS ❧

Genesis 24:14 – Let the maiden to whom I say, "Please, lower your jar that I may drink," and who replies, "Drink, and I will also water your camels" – let her be the one whom You have decreed for Your servant Isaac. Thereby shall I know that You have dealt graciously with my master.

Kli Yakar (Rabbi Shlomo Luntschitz) suggests that just as the Talmud explains why the heron is called *chasidah* in Hebrew – because it does *chesed* (kindness) with others of its species – so too the camel is called *gamal* because it does acts (*gemilut*) of kindness with other camels.[221] The Bible encourages us to learn from animals and birds, as the Book of Job states, "God teaches us by the animals of the earth, and makes us wiser by the birds of the sky."[222]

It is significant that the one test for the appropriate wife for Isaac was whether the woman would not only show kindness to people, but also to animals. Rebecca is selected to be one of the four matriarchs because of her compassion, giving water to animals.

Rebbetzin Chana Bracha Siegelbaum explains that Rebecca's kindness is revealed by the challenging work she is prepared to perform for Eliezer and his camels: "How much water would that take? There are different opinions of how long a camel can go without drinking, but at the very least for six to eight days under desert conditions. Thereafter, a camel must drink to replenish its body water, and when water is available, it may drink more than a third of its body weight.[223] When a camel has become dehydrated and then suddenly has access to water, it is capable of drinking up to 35 gallons (135 liters) of water in thirteen minutes.[224] Keep in mind, we have to multiply this number by ten for all of the camels that Rebecca watered in her incredible act of kindness!"[225]

❧ PRAYING IN THE FIELDS ❧

by Drew Kaplan[226]

Genesis 24:63 – And Isaac went out walking in the field toward evening and, looking up, he saw camels approaching.

There may have been an agricultural element to Isaac's outing in the field. Rashbam (Rabbi Shmuel ben Meir) suggests that Isaac was planting trees as well as checking his agricultural efforts.[227]

This verse is understood in the Talmud to refer to Isaac praying outdoors, in the field.[228] In line with this, Rabbi Yochanan in the Talmud said that one may not pray in a house without windows.[229] Rashi explained that this is because looking outside causes one to focus toward heaven and one's heart will be humbled.[230] In contrast, when praying in a house without windows, one is surrounded by human handiwork, with far less power to inspire awe and appreciation for God.

Rebbe Nachman of Breslov instructed his followers to engage in meditation, or to speak with God in nature for an hour every day.[231] In explaining Rebbe Nachman's teachings, Rabbi Natan Greenberg states that real prayer involves conversation with the surrounding natural world. Indeed, the strength of prayer comes from the Divine, spiritual energy flowing from nature. He explains that we need the spiritual energy of the earth to give strength to our prayers. Isaac first manifests this type of prayer through his connection to nature. He comes to it because he finds it difficult to relate to the world around him. He wants to be in a simple world, God's world, so he walks and prays in the field.[232]

For Isaac, praying to God in nature was a central part of his Divine service, and it can be for us as well. Our ability to connect to our Creator in the world He created is an indicator of our ability to live in balance with that natural world. However, a primarily urban, post-industrial generation that is alienated from God's Oneness as manifested in the natural world will certainly misuse that which God has given us.

The litany of ecological problems we face – from air and water pollution to species extinction and urban sprawl – testify to our disconnect from the natural environment which God gave us. Reconnecting to the inspired outdoor prayers of our forefathers can help us regain a sense of the grandeur of God's world and of our responsibility to live in balance with it.

Suggested Action Items

1. Pray or meditate outside. This allows you to surround yourself in God's handiwork.
2. Plant a garden, or even just a few herbs in pots. As you care for these plants, pray that your produce will grow and help sustain you!

Torah portion of Toldot

❧ SUSTAINABLE LUXURIES ❧

Genesis 25:23 – And the Lord answered her, "Two nations are in your womb, two separate peoples shall issue from your body; one people shall be mightier than the other, and the older shall serve the younger."

Rashi comments: "These [two nations] are Antoninus and Rabbi, for neither radish nor lettuce ceased [to be found] on their tables neither during the sunny season nor during the rainy season."[233] The Talmud states: "They [Antoninus and Rabbi] were 'proud ones' in that they were so wealthy that they could afford to have seasonal products all year round."[234] Antoninus was the Roman emperor, and Rabbi (Judah the Prince) was a key Jewish leader in Roman Judaea.

This Talmudic teaching reveals how food availability has changed dramatically in the transition from pre-modern, pre-industrial society to modern industrial society. Today most Westerners take for granted the availability of seasonal produce all year. Ironically, Israel exports significant amounts of "summer produce" grown in greenhouses in the winter to Europe, including Rome. This does not just include radish and lettuce but an array of tropical fruits, including mango, which was unheard of in the time of Rabbi and Antoninus. While the amounts of vegetables exported have declined somewhat in the last decade, exports of avocados and dates have increased.[235]

This can help us gain perspective on how we define need versus luxury. What were considered luxuries for our parents and grandparents are now essential items to our generation. Yet choosing to live with fewer material products and favoring local produce is a critical part of sustainable living. It becomes much easier when religious communities encourage and exemplify sustainability. In this regard, the emergence of "green teams" at houses of worship is an encouraging development. These green places of worship champion sustainability, often by using solar power, composting, and maximizing the use of locally grown fruit and vegetables in their events.

❧ THE CONFLICT OF JACOB AND ESAU ☙

by Rabbi Shaul David Judelman[236]

Genesis 25:27 – When the boys grew up, Esau became a skillful hunter, a man of the outdoors; but Jacob was a mild man who stayed in camp.

The verse describes the growth of the two children. We can interpret this as saying Esau lives his life in the field, a place of open uncertainty, while Jacob is of the tent and the home, a place of stability and conviction. Esau and Jacob are destined for conflict, as prophetically related to Rebecca when she inquired of the unrest she felt in her womb. The dichotomy here is between the driving force of Esau's unbridled desire and Jacob's *tikkun*, or repair, of this urge. Resulting tension pervades their interactions.

Kabbalistic interpretations teach that Esau's soul came from the world of *tohu* (chaotic and wild).[237] This phrase refers to the story of creation and the status of the world before light and the beginning of order.[238] *Tohu* is a spiritual state with recognizable manifestations in this world. In environmental terms, this state would be deemed unsustainable, though it is far more than this. Often, *tohu* is dominated by urge over thought, the moment over the future. In this aspect, Esau's actions represent much of what we see in the world today.

Esau returns from a day of hunting while Jacob has been cooking soup. Incidentally, these verses seem to tell us that Esau is also called Edom (red) because of his desire to pour the "red, red soup" down his throat upon his coming home tired. Esau offers a phenomenal reason for selling his birthright to Jacob for the soup: "I am at the point of death, so of what use is my birthright to me?"[239]

The Torah's description of Esau's decision offers deep insights for any society that so readily swallows the values of Esau. The culture that wants things now has given us fast food, fast cars, and quickly melting polar ice caps. This culture is out of balance. What does balance mean? Balance means that my own physical needs are balanced against a nexus of relationships. These might include other people's needs, my future needs, or the availability of resources. There is a strong critique within environmental discourse against the nature of the society that developed modern technology. However, this is not a diatribe against technology or modernity, but rather a strong statement about the manner in which we pour things down our throat. This analysis occurs both on the personal level of our private consumption habits and on the societal level of manufacturing and pursuing lifestyles that have not yet proven their balance.

Esau and the energies of *tohu* have a tendency toward destruction. The Kabbalah refers to the doomed Kings of Esau as the unsustainable elements of the creation process.[240] They are the destroyed worlds. The lights broke the vessels. Their desires and abilities shattered the physical world's capacity to contain them.

The Kings of Esau are still alive (though maybe not for long!) in our day. Consider the following statistic: If the whole world lived with the same consumption pattern as the average American, it would take 5.3 earths to support everyone.[241] The Esau of today is living as if he's going to die tomorrow. That is not without a kernel of truth. He will.

The crucial question is will we leave a livable earth for our children to inherit? Will there be fresh drinking water, fish in the seas, and birds in the trees? Will our children be able to run freely and breathe fresh air?

❧ LOVE OF MEAT ❧

Genesis 25:28 – And Isaac loved Esau, because venison was in his mouth.

The Torah emphasizes that Isaac preferred Esau because of Isaac's love of meat and Esau's ability to bring him roasted meat. The Torah uses the word "love" three times in relation to Isaac and food and in particular a meat dish: "Then prepare a dish for me such as I love, and bring it to me to eat, so that I may give you my innermost blessing before I die." ... Rebecca said to her son Jacob, "Go to the flock and fetch me two choice kids, and I will make of them a dish for your father, such as he loves ... He got them and brought them to his mother, and his mother prepared a dish such as his father loved."[242]

Of all the things that the Torah could describe Isaac "loving," it refers to meat. According to Rabbi Raphael Zarum, Isaac's love of meat caused him to pass over his relationship with Jacob.[243] A desire for meat can cause a person to overlook negative practices by those who produce the meat; in this Biblical case it is Esau. These days, people's love of meat causes them to overlook and tolerate inhumane treatment of most of the 80 billion factory-farmed animals. Too many people ignore that meat production processes and facilities are a leading driver of the climate crisis, and a contributor to the spread of diseases, including those caused by pathogens in the animals and meat, and among the meat plant workers.

❧ HOLY EATING

by Rabbi Yonatan Neril[244]

Genesis 25:30 – And Esau said to Jacob, "Pour into [me] some of this red, red [pottage], for I am faint"; he was therefore named Edom.

Esau's consumption represents a classic case in the Torah of a human being eating in an unrefined, base way. The Midrash links Esau to a camel through the word *hal'iteini* – a word used to describe pouring food down a camel's throat into its stomach, so it will walk on a long journey without needing to stop to eat.[245] Based on this, Rabbi Samson Raphael Hirsch explains *hal'iteini* as "greedily to gulp down."[246] Esau's mindless animalistic eating therefore serves as an example of an inappropriate and unholy way to eat.

Eating food can be a significant part of spiritual living, and rabbinic teachings and practices provide guidance for how to eat in a holy manner. These include being selective and mindful of which foods we eat and how we eat them. In Rabbi Tzadok HaKohen's "A Treatise on Eating," he cites the mystical book of the Zohar, which calls the moment of eating "the time of combat."[247] This is because in eating, a person must engage in the spiritual fight to ensure the act is a holy one. If Esau teaches how *not* to eat, what wisdom does the Torah offer for how we *should* consume in holiness?

Why am I eating? Rebbe Nachman of Breslov identifies the desire for food and drink as the central desire of the human being, and the one from which other desires emanate.[248] Rabbi Shlomo Wolbe teaches that a person needs to distinguish between eating because of a healthy desire of the body (eating in order to be healthy) versus eating out of base physical desire.[249] Of course we also know that many people today also eat out of emotional desire. It is therefore important to clarify, before eating, that it is for the right reason. To eat in a spiritual way, we should eat when we are hungry, to fulfill our body's needs, rather than out of physical or emotional cravings.

How fast do I eat my food? While it is possible to eat a meal quickly in a few minutes, the rabbis caution against doing so. Rabbi Nathan of Breslov states: "Be careful not to swallow your food in a hurry. Eat at a moderate pace, calmly and with the same table manners that you would show if an important guest were present. You should always eat in this manner, even when you are alone."[250] Along with the physicality of his cravings, Esau's fast eating is also considered unholy. A spiritual way of eating includes eating food slowly and consciously.

Where do I eat? In the Talmud, Rabbi Yochanan and Reish Lakish teach that a person's table atones for a person like the Temple did in ancient times. One understanding of their statement is that when a person eats in holiness at their own table, they have made proper use of their table in a way parallel to the altar of the Temple.[251] This underscores the significance in Jewish thought of eating at a table, rather than while standing or walking. Today some of our eating takes place at a desk or even in a car! We will eat more healthfully if we take wholesome meals at a table.

With whom do I eat? Rabbi Shimon teaches: "Three who eat at one table and do not speak words of Torah, it is as if they have eaten sacrifices of the dead . . . But three who eat at one table and speak words of Torah, it is as if they have eaten at God's table . . ."[252] The act of eating with others and sharing not only food, but also Torah wisdom, bestows upon the meal an aura of sanctity, and elevates eating to a holy act. A shared opportunity for blessing before and after one eats also serves to connect the act of eating to a higher purpose.[253]

Bringing greater spiritual awareness to our eating will likely have an effect on how much food we eat. The link between *how much* we eat and the environmental "footprint" has been made clear by several studies. Adults in the United States today eat on average 500 calories more per day (about one large hamburger) than they did in the 1970s.[254] Between 1983 and 2000, US food availability (food consumption including waste) increased by 18 percent, requiring an additional 3.1 percent of total US energy consumption as well as more land and water to produce the food.[255] Agriculture, forestry, and other land use contribute about 24 percent of global greenhouse gas emissions globally, making them major factors in addressing climate change.[256] Modern food production and consumption also contribute to rainforest deforestation (to clear land for cattle and crops) and water pollution (from pesticide and fertilizer use).

Expanding agriculture to meet growing demand based on overeating only exacerbates these impacts. Practices that elevate our eating to become an act of holiness and devotion can also make our food consumption more ecologically sustainable.

❧ FAST AND SLOW FOOD ❧

Genesis 25:34 – Jacob then gave Esau bread and lentil stew; he ate and drank, and he rose and went away. Thus did Esau spurn the birthright.

In explaining that Esau "ate and drank and rose," the HaKetav VeHaKabbalah commentary[257] suggests that he did not sit to eat like his father, Isaac (to whom Jacob beckons, "Please sit up and eat of my game"), and his grandfather Abraham (when he served the angels, "he waited on them under the tree as they ate").[258] Esau is uncouth, eating on the run, which shows his lack of self-control and ultimately his lack of qualification to hold the birthright. Esau is the root of wasteful consumption. The first use in the Torah of the word for wasting in relation to a person occurs with regard to Esau. He just thinks about the present without regard for the future, which causes him to waste the future. This is one of the spiritual roots of today's ecological crisis.

With a healthy-looking snail as its logo, the Slow Food Movement (SFM), conceived in 1986 in Bra, Italy by Carlo Petrini,[259] has grown and inspired the broader "Slow Movement."[260] Slow cities, slow tourism, slow money, slow journalism, slow travel, and slow fashion are a few examples. From its humble origins in a protest against the first McDonald's in Italy (at the Piazza di Spagna in Rome), SFM now has more than 1,500 "convivia" or local chapters, with more than 100,000 members in 160 countries.[261] Its members advocate a return to simple local food and leisure, benefiting local communities and reducing our carbon footprint. Esau is the antithesis of this ideology, and Jacob is its advocate – described by the Torah as "a mild man who stayed in camp."[262]

❧ ISAAC AND WATER MAPPING ❧

Genesis 26:12,15 – Isaac sowed in that land and reaped a hundredfold the same year. The Lord blessed him . . . The Philistines stopped up all the wells which his father's servants had dug in the days of his father Abraham, filling them with earth.

The Midrash explains that Isaac's bountiful harvest came during a year of famine in the region.[263] God blessed him with a successful crop when the rest of the country was suffering a famine. The Philistines apparently stopped up the wells of Abraham only after Isaac's bountiful harvest. Isaac therefore likely knew the locations of these wells, perhaps with maps, and drew water from them before they were stopped up.

Today, computerized maps known as Geographic Information Systems (GIS) are critical in the identification and management of underground water sources and inland fisheries.[264] Yet underground water sources are threatened by a relatively new form of fossil fuel extraction – hydraulic fracturing.[265] Fracking uses water to break up rock in order to force out natural gas. Most of the water used remains in the rock.

As Rabbi David Seidenberg writes:

Fracking is unique, because the many billions of gallons of water involved are being used up, taken out of the cycle that would have seen them flow through the earth's streams and seas and atmosphere as part of the life-blood of this planet, for potentially millions of years.

What does it mean to lose that water, essentially forever? According to Kabbalah, it could be considered a sin against the water itself.

The way the natural world is imagined in Kabbalah, its elements are yearning, longing to be raised higher and higher into consciousness, into the process of life and love. This can happen whenever a more sentient life form like a human being takes in a more basic substance (like when we drink water or eat plants), and it happens through the process of evolution itself, where life comes from the elements and develops greater and greater capacities for connection and awareness. In Kabbalah, the very symbol of blessing and life – of *chesed* (or "loving-kindness") – is water. If we take these ideas seriously, then the water that stays in that fracked rock is deprived of fulfilling its deepest purpose.[266]

❧ WATER WARS ☙

by Rabbi Yuval Cherlow[267]

Genesis 26:20 – The herdsmen of Gerar quarreled with Isaac's herdsmen, saying, "The water is ours." He named that well Esek *[contention], because they contended with him.*

Isaac's conflict with the Philistines and the people of Gerar is rooted in the age-old struggle for scarce water. The shepherds of Gerar claim, "The water is ours," and effectively expel Isaac from the area of the well in contention, forcing him to find a new source of water. The Philistines go further, filling the wells Isaac used with dirt rather than sharing them with him. So fierce is their enmity that they destroyed some of their own vital water sources to expel him and attain their political end.

Access to fresh water is arguably the primary environmental issue in the history of humankind. Our need for clean water is the concern that requires us to directly face the undeniable and harsh consequences of depleting a critically limited natural resource.

The narrative of Isaac and the wells offers us insight into how to deal with the contemporary water crisis. The first teaching is the necessity to protect natural resources from destruction in times of conflict and war. The deliberate destruction of the wells by the Philistines, to expel Isaac from their midst, illustrates the danger of war fought without regard for the environment. The Torah places limits on how harshly we respond during war. It forbids us from wantonly destroying fruit-bearing trees as a military tactic.[268] Even in the midst of struggle, we must consider the "day after" and understand the profound need for sustainability for both sides of the conflict.

The narrative continues with Isaac developing additional water sources after being forced to abandon the wells of his father, as well as some of his own. He continuously searches for new sources of water.[269] We too are bound by the unremitting task of expanding and protecting our water resources, rather than relying solely on our current "wells." There are many ways to increase access to potable water. One is to capture rainwater, instead of letting it run off into the sea. Another highly successful method is recycling and purifying waste water, as is commonly done in Israel's agricultural sector and increasingly in other countries. In addition, the Israeli invention of drip irrigation in 1965 revolutionized agriculture. Implemented in over 110 countries, over 150 billion dripper mechanisms have been sold.[270]

The ethics for wise and appropriate water consumption practices are included in the general prohibition of wanton destruction (ba'al tashchit). Due to the direct connection between water and life, the conservation of water also becomes a Jewish legal obligation.

In the semi-arid and arid Middle East, the lack of fresh water often adds fuel to the existing political conflagrations. Climate change is making the Middle East drier and water scarcer. Some scientists understand the 2006–7 drought – the worst in 900 years – to be a key driver of the Syrian civil and regional war.[271] May we look to a future where peace between nations is fostered by our shared water resources.

❧ HUNTERS AND FARMERS ❧

Genesis 27:6–9 – Rebecca said to her son Jacob, "I overheard your father speaking to your brother Esau, saying, 'Bring me some game and prepare a dish for me to eat, that I may bless you, with the Lord's approval, before I die.' Now, my son, listen carefully as I instruct you. Go to the flock and fetch me two choice kids, and I will make of them a dish for your father, such as he likes."

Esau was a hunter and Jacob a farmer. In investigating why ancient communities transitioned from hunting to more sustainable farming, researchers found three drivers: populations structured into small groups, farming-friendly property rights, and a conservative mindset.[272] We learn that Isaac set up a small settlement in Beersheba, away from the Philistines.[273] Additionally, property rights had just been established through a pact with the king of the Philistines, Abimelech.[274] The final ingredient, a conservative mindset, was more an aspect of Jacob's personality ("a mild man who stayed in camp")[275] in contrast to Esau's ("a man of the field").[276] This may be why Jacob became the farmer.

Today, society is structured into large groups, property rights are well established in most countries, and the greatest challenge to greater sustainability is creating a conservationist mindset that thinks long term about preventing future environmental risks. How does humankind become more long-term oriented? This is an important role for religious educators who are accustomed to seeing life patterns over thousands of years, more so than for politicians who typically are focused on the next two or four years.

❧ DOING ALL WE CAN ❧

Genesis 27:28 – "And may God give you of the dew of heaven and the fat of the earth, abundance of new grain and wine."

Kli Yakar explains that the blessing is introduced with the word "and" because God's blessing is given only after a person has done all they can do. Then, and only then, "nature will complete the miracle."[277]

How can one do all that is possible? The work of achieving sustainability in our lives and on our planet seems infinite, and potentially discouraging to any one person. Group, community, and even interfaith collaboration greatly expands our capacity. Since 2010, The Interfaith Center for Sustainable Development has been revealing the connection between religion and ecology and has been mobilizing people to act. It has co-organized twelve conferences in Israel and the United States, bringing together current and emerging clergy from many faiths for engagement on religion and ecology.[278]

Suggested Action Items

1. To save water, make a commitment to turn off the faucet while brushing your teeth, between washing hands, and while lathering dishes. This small action will raise your consciousness about all your water use.
2. Learn about water challenges in your local community.
3. Feast upon lentil soup – a delicious, vegan, and protein-filled soup that tempted even Esau the hunter.

Torah portion of Vayeitzei

❧ SLEEPING ALONE IN NATURE ❧

Genesis 28:11 – He came upon a certain place and stopped there for the night, for the sun had set. Taking one of the stones of that place, he [Jacob] put it under his head and lay down in that place.

Ibn Ezra explains that the stone was the Foundation Stone, the location of the Holy of Holies on the Temple Mount in Jerusalem.[279] Rabbi Daniel Kohn explains the significance of this location, saying, "Jacob is connected to the holism of reality and existence. The Midrash states that the rocks united under him and the land of Israel folded underneath him.[280] It reflects this aspect of Jacob, of a deep connectedness to the planet and the One that is. Jacob, by virtue of being a *tam*, a whole-hearted individual, encounters a magical moment when he sleeps at the core of creation, sleeping on the Foundation Stone itself. Lying on the earth creates such a deep engagement with the planet that he becomes conscious of all that this planet has to offer."[281]

Jacob connects to God while alone in nature; this time alone produces ripe moments for spiritually transcendent experiences. King Solomon teaches: "When you lie down, you should not fear."[282] Sleeping alone in nature can help a person trust in God due to the vulnerability of sleeping without visible protection from animals, people, and the elements. Jacob's spiritual dream of the ladder with angels occurs precisely when he is sleeping alone in nature. Perhaps Jacob learned about being alone in nature from his father and grandfather. Abraham was commanded by God to walk "the width and breadth" of the land, and he built altars outside. Isaac is mentioned as one who "went out to pray in the field."

❧ CONNECTING WITH THE EARTH ❧

Genesis 28:13 – And God was standing beside him and He said, "I am the Divine, the God of your father Abraham and the God of Isaac: the ground on which you are lying I will assign to you and to your offspring."

God emphasizes to Jacob that he is lying on the land. Jacob established a connection with the land by lying on it. According to scientist Gaétan Chevalier and others:

> Emerging scientific research has revealed a surprisingly positive and overlooked environmental factor on health: direct physical contact with the vast supply of electrons on the surface of the earth. Modern lifestyle separates humans from such contact. The research suggests that this disconnect may be a major contributor to physiological dysfunction and unwellness. Reconnection with the earth's electrons has been found to promote intriguing physiological changes and subjective reports of well-being. Earthing (or grounding) refers to the discovery of benefits – including better sleep and reduced pain – from walking barefoot outside or sitting, working, or sleeping indoors connected to conductive systems that transfer the earth's electrons from the ground into the body.[283]

Richard Louv's book *Last Child in the Woods: Saving Our Children from Nature-Deficit Disorder*[284] has raised public attention about the importance of devoting time to being in nature. In 2019, 24 scientists published a groundbreaking study on the link between nature and mental health, including "the impacts of nature experience on cognitive functioning, emotional well-being, and other dimensions of mental health." They then indicate "how ecosystem service assessments can be expanded to include mental health."[285] That is, humans receive tremendous value from nature in balancing and maintaining our mental health, and environmental economists try to put a price on such value.

❧ JACOB'S SIMPLICITY ❧

Genesis 28:20 – If God remains with me, if He protects me on this journey that I am making and gives me bread to eat and clothing to wear.

We see the simplicity of Jacob's request compared to what someone today might ask. Maimonides (Rabbi Moses ben Maimon) writes, "When a person has enough food for two meals, it is forbidden for him to take from the charity pot designated for daily donations to the poor. When he has enough food for fourteen meals, he should not take from the charity pot designated for weekly donations to the poor."[286] In our modern society, we have far greater expectations than in times past. In fact, if everyone in the world today were to adopt the average diet of the United States, we would need to convert all of our habitable land to agriculture, and we'd still be 38 percent short. For a New Zealand diet (even more meat), we'd need almost twice as much land as we have on the planet.[287]

❧ JACOB AS SPIRITUAL ACTIVIST ❧
Rabbi Avi Neuman[288]

Genesis 28:21 – And I return in peace to my father's house, then God will be a God to me.

It was necessary for Jacob to leave the comforts of home and society in order to gestate, transform, and become. It then became necessary for him to reenter society and bring that which is holy into all that is profane. That is a labor that can only be accomplished through bringing awareness to action. Jacob is perhaps the first spiritual social activist.

Jacob teaches us that environmental or any other social action is rooted in the recognition that our lives can manifest the world as it should be, rather than accepting what it is or appears to be. A truly "religious" ecology must recognize spiritual orientation, or reorientation, as the starting point for meaningful, practical action. Following his encounter, Jacob doesn't withdraw into meditative prayer and ecstatic communion with the Divine. Alive with a new purpose, he "lifted his feet" and stepped forward to struggle with the realities of sustenance, family, social living and justice.[289] Sforno tells us that when a person travels to a place with purpose, it drives him to lift his feet.[290]

✦ JACOB'S SPIRITUAL AND MATERIAL DREAMS ✦

Genesis 31:10–13 – "Once, at the mating time of the flocks, I had a dream in which I saw that the he-goats mating with the flock were streaked, speckled, and mottled. And in the dream an angel of God said to me, 'Jacob!' 'Here,' I answered. And he said, 'Note well that all the he-goats which are mating with the flock are streaked, speckled, and mottled; for I have noted all that Laban has been doing to you. I am the God of Beth-el, where you anointed a pillar and where you made a vow to Me. Now, arise and leave this land and return to your native land.'"

Jacob dreams about angels while in Israel and about sheep when outside of Israel. He lived in southeastern Turkey, likely near the fertile Euphrates river. According to Rabbi Michael Melchior, when Jacob starts dreaming about sheep (his material possessions and his work) and not about angels or God, God sends an angel to tell him to leave the land of Aram and go back to Israel, because dreams of amassing wealth are indicative of an unhealthy connection to the material, especially strong outside the Biblical Land of Israel.

Social pressure can make people increasingly focused on acquiring wealth and material possessions. In many respects, global ecological degradation is an international outgrowth of that focus. And the goals of one nation's citizens can adversely impact another nation. One key aspiration of billions of people is larger home size. In China, per capita living space increased significantly in both urban and rural areas between 2002 and 2017.[291] China banned logging in its own state forests in 1998, so about half of its timber is imported, primarily from southeast Asia, Russia, and Africa.[292] Hundreds of millions of people achieving more spacious living spaces has contributed to deforestation and species loss in the world's forests.

❧ LARGE HERDS OF LIVESTOCK ❧

Genesis 31:18 – Jacob drove off all his livestock and all the wealth that he had amassed, the livestock in his possession that he had acquired in Paddan-aram, to go to his father Isaac in the land of Canaan.

Malbim states that someone who is fleeing would probably convert their assets to cash in order to avoid being slowed down by their flocks.[293] This suggests that Jacob wanted Laban to know he was leaving. Livestock is one of the main capital assets in developing countries today. On a small scale, they preserve wealth, produce food, enhance crop production, and provide additional economic goods and services as well as a cash income. Nonetheless, large-scale animal farming in industrialized countries is increasingly considered damaging to the environment, creating excessive pollution and emission of greenhouse gases as well as being unnecessarily cruel to the animals. Even in developing countries, increased herd size is associated with the degradation of rangelands and soil erosion. Additionally, large-scale livestock development generally favors the richer segments of society, both producers and consumers, rather than the most vulnerable, and competes directly with humans for land and water resources in the production of grain.[294]

Suggested Action Items

1. Set aside 20 minutes, at least once a week, to engage in alone-time. Choose a space without distractions, preferably outside. Shut off your cell phone and computer. Reflect inward and make decisions concerning who you are, how you want to grow, and the impact you have on the social, spiritual, and physical environments you inhabit.

2. Make conscious decisions about your patterns of consumption and begin taking specific actions to shift the balance. For example, before you buy something, ask: "Is this something I want or something I need?" Explore the differences between these two impulses. For one week, buy only things that you "need." See what that feels like.

3. Teach your children healthy patterns of giving and try to infuse them with behaviors based on sharing. Include children in family

decisions about donating to nonprofits that help people in need or the environment.

Torah portion of Vayishlach

❧ SMALL VESSELS ❧

Rabbi Yonatan Neril[295]

Genesis 32:24 – After taking them across the stream, he sent across all his possessions.

Before Jacob's epic encounter with Esau – reuniting with his brother after decades of estrangement – Jacob brings his family and possessions across a stream. He then returns at night to the other side of the stream, and the Torah narrates that "Jacob remained alone." The rabbis see the word "alone" (*levado*) as superfluous and understand it as related to the similar sounding *lekado*, "for his vessel," yielding "Jacob remained for his vessel." That is, say the rabbis, he recrossed the stream at night to recover a few small vessels he forgot to bring across.[296] Why does Jacob, facing an imminent confrontation with Esau and his 400-man militia, leave his family alone and vulnerable at night to recover a few forgotten flasks? Why were they so important to him?

The seeming absurdity of Jacob's action becomes understandable when one examines his worldview: he believes that everything in his possession comes from God, has a specific purpose, and must be used to its full potential. As one rabbinic commentary explains, each material item that a righteous person uses is a means toward spiritual repair in the world.[297] Jacob went back for the vessels to ensure he would use them optimally and realize their full potential.

The righteous strive to recognize the value of their God-given possessions and to be careful with them, no matter how small or seemingly insignificant they are. While not overly attached to material things, they do not dispose of objects prematurely or use them inappropriately.

Jacob's recrossing of the stream exposes a striking contrast between two worldviews on material possessions. One sees the things we own as essential and indispensable. The other views them as expendable and disposable. Jacob's example presents a particular challenge for those of us who live in a world of abundance and built-in obsolescence where it is so easy to throw things away and often difficult to get older things repaired.

In 1955, the retailing analyst Victor Lebow highlighted a trend in consumer society, one moving away from greater mindfulness regarding possessions and toward a more short-term view. He wrote, "Our enormously productive economy demands that we make consumption our way of life, that we convert the buying and use of goods into rituals, that we seek our spiritual satisfactions, our ego satisfactions, in consumption ... We need things consumed, burned up, worn out, replaced, and discarded at an ever increasing pace."[298] Harvard economist John Kenneth Galbraith wrote on how advertising tends to confuse the public and direct them away from their core values.[299]

Today, we throw away usable items because they are a few years old and may be outdated by new products. Instead of repairing clothing and appliances, we often just buy new ones. Our relationship with the resources we consume has significant consequences for the planet. Yet how is it possible that human beings could cause such widespread imbalance? Most of the big things that happen in the world result from an accumulation of many small things – like the mining of aluminum needed for each can, the fuel needed to truck each glass bottle to a faraway dump – combined with countless small acts, and multiplied by 250 years of industrial society and billions of people.

Today's global environmental crises can be pinned on no one group of people or nation. This holds for plastic in the ocean, vast garbage dumps, and climate change. Solving these challenges will require the participation of billions of individuals. It is on this crucial level of the individual that Jacob's actions can speak so profoundly.

Rebbe Nachman of Breslov offers a teaching based on kabbalistic sources that can also help us understand the likely reason for Jacob's actions. He wrote, "Everything in the world has in it sparks of holiness ... According to this understanding, an object comes to a person for the purpose of spiritual elevation, and reuse of a physical object enables a further spiritual elevation of the sparks of holiness within the object."[300] By raising the sparks to Heaven, we also refrain from littering the earth. These examples show the relationship our sages had with material objects, and the effort they invested in elevating the holy sparks in the objects.

❧ BEING CONTENT WITH WHAT WE HAVE ❧

Genesis 33:9–11 – Esau said, "I have enough, my brother; let what you have remain yours." But Jacob said, "No, I pray you; if you would do me this favor, accept from me this gift; for to see your face is like seeing the face of God, and you have received me favorably. Please accept my present which has been brought to you, for God has favored me and I have plenty." And when he urged him, he accepted.

Esau said, "I have enough," which rabbinical commentators explain to mean "I have a lot" of material items, "much more than I need."[301] Jacob responded, "I have plenty," which Rashi interprets as "I have all my necessities"[302] – meaning Jacob is satisfied and does not seek more. A Jewish morning blessing states, "God provides me all that I need."

Rabbi Matis Weinberg writes with regard to Esau, "The man who thinks in terms of having 'much, much more than I need' will never have enough. His possessions are external and his connection to them remains superficial... To Jacob, happiness is a consequence of fulfillment; to Esau, happiness is a goal to be pursued. Esau indulges... in the terrifying and compulsive *pursuit* of happiness, endlessly chasing after something that is only to be found within... To Jacob, the connection and relationship are what count, not the actual possession."[303]

King Solomon teaches: "One who loves money will never be satisfied by money."[304] J. Paul Getty, one of the world's first billionaires, was asked how much wealth would be enough for him. He replied, "Just a little more."[305] People who relate to the world as a place of acquisition and control can have a lot but never all they "need." They will remain unhappy and frustrated because their need has no end.

Rabbi Daniel Kohn teaches that only a simple man or woman can say "I have it all," because they are beyond the stage of "I want a lot," and are content with what they have. Spiritual acquisition, through spiritual discipline leading to growth, is far more rewarding and in line with the Divine Will than physical acquisitions.[306] Spiritual acquisition should not harm the environment, while material acquisition contributes to decimation of nature in so many ways.

A recent study of the South Korean population census supports this idea, revealing that people who prioritize religion or spirituality are the most likely to report that they are happy, followed by those who prioritize social relationships including family, friends, and neighbors. Those who prioritize extrinsic achievements (money, power, educational attainment, work, and leisure) are least likely to report happiness.[307]

The more people find spiritual satisfaction, the less they will be driven to overconsumption, which is one of the main drivers of overproduction and ecological degradation.

❧ HOW FAST WE MOVE ❧

Genesis 33:12–14 – And [Esau] said, "Let us start on our journey, and I will proceed at your pace." But he [Jacob] said to him, "My Lord knows that the children are frail and that the flocks and herds, which are nursing, are a care to me; if they are driven hard a single day, all the flocks will die. Let my Lord go on ahead of his servant, while I travel slowly, at the pace of the cattle before me and at the pace of the children, until I come to my Lord in Seir."

Rabbi Shaul David Judelman teaches: "Thus the paths of Esau and Jacob split. We must learn the lesson that Jacob tries to give Esau: that the considerations for our children and animals must also determine the pace of our travel. We must find sustainable vessels for our tremendous creative abilities. When we consider how to act in the moment at hand, our attention must focus on our shared futures on this earth, and we must remember to make responsible decisions in accordance with this reality."[308]

Here, we see the brothers' different views: Esau with his rapid pace, and Jacob with patience to accommodate the needs of his children and nursing flocks and cattle. According to the Midrash, Esau's offspring become Rome,[309] and more broadly, Western civilization. In recent centuries, the West has promoted a pace of life much faster than in pre-modern societies.

We can relate this verse to how the rate of technological change today is occurring faster than our conscious ability to consider its implications.

One example is the BP oil spill. Federal investigators found that the companies BP, Halliburton, and Transocean acted in haste in trying to complete the cementing of the oil well, which was weeks behind schedule.[310] Due to the great depth of the drilling, it took engineers 87 days to stop the oil spill, although it continued to leak for years. BP's Deepwater Horizon rig drilled and spilled at a depth of 18,360 feet, in 5,100 feet of water, which shows what happens when humans lose control. A 2020 study found that the extent of the spill was much greater than commonly thought.[311] Ten years after the spill, oil drilling has moved further offshore and deeper underwater. The bipartisan National Commission on the BP Deepwater Horizon Oil Spill and Offshore Drilling "accused Congress of a near-complete failure to adopt their recommendations on drilling safety."[312] New oil wells at even greater depths are now operating near the site of the BP Macondo well that spilled.[313]

A second, more recent, example is the Boeing 737 Max 8 airplane. Boeing produced and sold thousands of 737 Max 8 airplanes before it was revealed, through two crashes that took 346 lives, that there was a defect. The development of the aircraft was rushed through in order to compete with a new plane from Boeing's rival, Airbus. As reported by *The New York Times*, "The pace of the work on the 737 Max was frenetic, according to current and former employees. They weren't going to stand by and let Airbus steal market share," said Mike Renzelmann, an engineer who retired in 2016 from Boeing's flight control team on the 737 Max.[314]

In deep water or high in the air, in particular, the process of moving too fast can be catastrophic. At a global level, a humanity that is moving too fast is generating a global ecological crisis.

❦ BUILDING INFRASTRUCTURE ❦

Genesis 33:18 – Jacob arrived safe in the city of Shechem which is in the land of Canaan – having come thus from Paddan-aram – and he encamped before the city.

The Talmud expounds on the word "encamped," which has the same Hebrew root as the word "benefited," and gives three possible ways that Jacob might have benefited the city through developing its infrastructure:

by introducing a new currency; by setting up bathhouses; or by establishing a marketplace.

The Talmud seems to suggest that infrastructure development is a "benefit." However, it also describes an argument between three leading sages about the moral value of Roman infrastructure development in Israel in the second century. Rabbi Yehuda said, "How great are the deeds of the Romans – they built marketplaces, bathhouses, and bridges." Rabbi Shimon said, "Everything they built was only for their vanity – marketplaces for prostitution, bathhouses to beautify themselves, and bridges to charge tolls!" The third sage, Rabbi Yosei, remained silent.[315]

In support of Rabbi Yehuda, who praises the value of Roman infrastructure, one of the biggest obstacles to progress in developing countries today is lack of infrastructure. Food grown in one region spoils before it can be sold to those who need it in a neighboring region. The World Food Program is using innovative technology to enable millions of refugees to pay for food through their mobile phones in regions without financial infrastructure. Additionally, these transactions can be made online in a virtual marketplace.[316] These infrastructure initiatives serve to increase the amount of food available for locals.

However, in support of Rabbi Shimon, much of the infrastructure currently being built in the developing world is not for the benefit of the local population, but for export to populations thousands of miles away. Infrastructure development in some of these locations is being used to deprive locals of their sustenance in order to support foreign states.

In 2018, China imported almost $100 billion of raw materials from Africa[317] and built railways and roads in Africa to bring these products to port. To fund this new infrastructure, China issued billions of dollars of debt to some of the world's poorest countries, such as Ethiopia, which is struggling to repay it.[318] Infrastructure development that deprives populations of their local resources is seen by some as a form of neo-colonialism and drives poorer nations to neglect their natural environment in favor of industry and exports.

Suggested Action Items

1. Buy food in bulk if possible. Bring your own cloth bags or reusable containers to the store to reduce plastic waste.
2. Giving a gift? Wrap presents in wrapping paper that you saved from a gift you received. Or get creative and use the gift as its own wrapping; for example, tie an item in a scarf or fill a reusable mug with fair-trade coffee beans or candy.

Torah portion of Vayeishev

❧ SHEPHERD CONSCIOUSNESS

by Rabbi Fivel Yedidya Glasser[319]

Genesis 37:2 – This, then, is the line of Jacob: At seventeen years of age, Joseph tended the flocks with his brothers, as a helper to the sons of his father's wives Bilhah and Zilpah. And Joseph brought bad reports of them to their father.

The patriarchs and matriarchs were shepherds. The Torah tells us that Abraham, Isaac, Jacob, Rachel, Joseph and his brothers, and later Moses, his wife Zippora, and young King David, all herded goats and sheep.[320] The greatest of the early Biblical leaders chose this profession, a livelihood scorned by surrounding cultures. Years after Joseph's exile to Egypt and rise to viceroy to the king of Egypt, when his brothers came to him in exile, Joseph presented them to Pharaoh, the king of Egypt. The question that most interested the king was: "What is your occupation?" "We are shepherds," they replied to Pharaoh, "like our fathers before us."[321] Shepherding was not a respected occupation in Egypt, and Pharaoh relegated Joseph's family to the far-off land of Goshen.

Why did so many Israelite original leaders become shepherds? Rabbi Abraham Isaac Kook explains that the advantage of shepherding may be found in the shepherd's secluded lifestyle.[322] While engaged with flocks, ambling through hills and valleys, the shepherd is removed from the noisy distractions of society, providing him or her with ample time for inner reflection. Unlike farming, shepherding does not require great exertion. Shepherds engage constantly with the real world, seeking water, shade, and good fodder for the animals.

What is the value of the solitude and simplicity of the shepherd? And how can it translate into our own lives? How do we balance reclusive behavior with the greater ideals of refining humanity and elevating the universe?

Rabbi Kook explains, "The greater the soul, the more it must struggle in order to find itself; the more the depths of the human soul are hidden from the conscious mind. One must have extended solitude and self-reflective prayer, examining ideas, deepening thoughts, and expanding the mind, until finally the soul will truly reveal itself, unveiling some of the splendor of its brilliant inner light."[323]

In order to cultivate one's greatness, it is first necessary to develop a deep soul-awareness, including through silence and isolation. When one truly engages in such a practice, one will experience a positive impact on both their personal life, as well as on their surroundings. Ultimately, the intent of this withdrawal is to benefit the larger world, and not only to gain personal spiritual fulfillment. The intent of the personal spiritual path of growth is to positively impact the larger world, both in the immediate orbit of the individual, but also on a deeper and more spiritual level for the world as a whole.

The "silence" of the shepherd is not just the absence of speech. It is a sublime language of silence, flowing from an outpouring of the soul, a vehicle of Divine inspiration. The depths of the soul demand silence. Silence is full of life, revealing treasures from the beauty of wisdom. Yet today's high-tech, Internet-connected world does not leave space for an individual to hear silence. Does wireless access enable us to access the inner recesses of our own being?

Rebbe Nachman of Breslov teaches that one should spend an hour of every day in self-reflective prayer.[324] This significant investment of time, to simply be with God – without formal prayers, and without study or engaging in religious commandments, provides a platform to simply "be." This time could include mundane conversation with God or soul-wrenching self-analysis. Regardless of the content, in this sacred time, we can come to taste the Divine encounter that our forefathers exemplified as shepherds. This one hour of being with God, of simply being, will come to inform who we are and what we do in the world.

When we are too caught up in experiencing the world without "shepherd consciousness," we tend to make decisions from our own narrow, "get-ahead" reality. When we focus too much on "doing," without making time for "being" – that is to say, communing with the Divine – we are more likely to make decisions that transform the earth in negative ways. This is the source of many environmental problems today. A society driven by consumption and industrial development can overlook deforesting the rainforests or irrevocably harming the climate. It is precisely the accessing of our inner selves that enables us to encounter the larger picture of our own reality.

If everyone, from the average consumer to the corporate CEO, dedicates time each day to rekindle their own inner potential as vehicles for God in the world, their use of the natural world will be informed by their relationship with the Creator of the natural world. Mindfulness of the bigger picture is an essential tool for any individual who cares about the world in which we live.

We do not need to become shepherds in the field to learn "shepherd consciousness." A simple commitment to withdraw from the world for brief periods and engage with more spiritual realms will provide us with a broader perspective on our own lives and the decisions we make. We need to focus on human being, not human doing. If we stand any chance of returning to ecological balance, we must find inner spiritual balance and clarity of vision that our ancestors may have found more easily in simpler times.

❧ NATURE AND VIOLENCE ❧

Genesis 37:12 – Now his brothers had gone to pasture their father's flock at Shechem.

The incident of how Joseph's brothers maltreated him near Shechem exemplifies how acts of violence against others inevitably turn to acts of violence amongst one's own family and community. This may explain why the Torah mentions Shechem, the brothers' location before throwing Joseph into the pit, three times. The repetition seems unnecessary, but points to the earlier incident where Simeon and Levi massacred the men of Shechem in response to the rape of their sister, Dinah.[325] The Torah appears to be teaching that one act of violence leads to another, ultimately with more victims.

Jared Diamond, in his book *Collapse*, provides many maps: one illustrates the world's war zones, another shows the world's areas of greatest environmental degradation. The two maps are essentially identical, underscoring a correlation between war and environmental impact.[326] Does war cause environmental degradation, the other way around, or both? When humankind wages war on itself, nature and the environment are often the greatest victims. At the same time, pollution of critical natural resources, like rivers, can foment competition for survival so intense, it can turn to war.

❧ NATURE AND OUR WORK ❧

Genesis 37:14 – And he said to him, "Go and see how your brothers are and how the flocks are faring and bring me back word." So he sent him from the valley of Hebron.

The Midrash asks, "We can understand why Jacob asks about the welfare of his sons, but why the flock? From this we can see that a person has to inquire about the welfare of anything that benefits him."[327] Jacob's concern for his animals, second only to caring for his sons, could be seen as concern for his financial assets. As the Midrash explains, "A righteous person is concerned about all his or her possessions after working hard for every penny."[328] Or, it could be seen as worry for the animals themselves, as we know this took place during the dry season: "The pit was empty; there was no water in it."[329]

In contrast to a shepherd's concern about his flock, Jacob's son Joseph appears more focused on agriculture. Joseph shares a dream with his brothers: "Behold, we were binding sheaves in the midst of the field, and behold, my sheaf arose and also stood upright, and behold, your sheaves encircled [it] and prostrated themselves to my sheaf."[330] Rabbi Shlomo Riskin teaches that Joseph's dream was particularly frightening to the brothers because they were shepherds, but his dream was agricultur-al.[331] This meant Joseph longed for the ways of Egypt, the preeminent agricultural civilization, over his own family's shepherding path. (Much later, Joseph allays his brothers' fear, providing them with pasture land for their flocks in Egypt.)[332]

Today, many of the remaining shepherd cultures of the world are being squeezed into ever smaller areas, or being supplanted by mass agriculture, industry, or cities. But thousands of years of shepherding can give us insights into spiritual and ecological living today. Shepherds gen-erally walk on the land and manage their flocks grazing on wild-growing shrubs and grasses. Traditionally, shepherds have used little technology, and have had more time for contemplation, spiritual connection, and a close relationship with the animals that they raise. Most of their day is spent outdoors in nature.

Farmers have more domination of the land and animals, but still much of their day is spent outdoors on the land they farm. Industrial, technology, and service workers base their livelihoods on technologies. Most people now work indoors, using machines or screens for nearly every work function. They live, for the most part, in cities and suburbs and may have to travel some distance to connect with nature. Their experience in the outdoors and with animals is much more limited.

Paradoxically, with our increasing embrace of, and dependence on, "life enhancing" technologies, we are becoming less in touch with the natural sources of our survival, with the earth that gives us nourishment and the weather patterns that determine our fate, and with the most profound Source of our existence. The Torah reminds us to stay aware of our "flocks" and not to take the earth and its creatures for granted.

❧ FROM SILK ROUTE TO AIR FREIGHT ❧

Genesis 37:25 – Then they sat down to a meal. Looking up, they saw a caravan of Ishmaelites coming from Gilead, their camels bearing gum, balm, and lotus to be taken to Egypt.

While some consider globalization a recent phenomenon, the trade of luxury goods between peoples goes back thousands of years, as this verse attests to. About 1,500 years after this caravan of camels descended to Egypt, the silk route developed, with the main routes passing to the north and south of Israel. Yet in recent decades, the amount of global trade has increased to the highest rates in history. Since 1980, global trade increased tenfold to about $20 trillion per year,[333] even though the world population increased by only about 50 percent.

The ecological footprint of this caravan of people and camels bearing gum, balm, and lotus (and Joseph) to Egypt was minimal. Yet the footprint of trade today is tremendous. As the International Transport Forum (ITF) notes:

> Supply chains have become longer and more complex, as logistics networks link more and more economic centers across oceans and continents. Changing consumer preferences and new manufacturing requirements also affect international trade and thus shape freight patterns. This has led to more frequent and smaller freight shipments and, as a result, to less-full containers, more empty runs, and increased demand for rapid, energy-intensive transport such as air freight. Freight transport – whether by air, land, or sea – relies heavily on fossil fuel for propulsion and is still a long way from being able to switch to cleaner energy sources. The ITF estimates that international trade-related freight transport currently accounts for around 30 percent of all transport-related CO_2 emissions from fuel combustion, and more than 7 percent of global emissions. Projections based on the ITF's International Freight Model foresee an increase of trade-related freight transport emissions by a factor of 3.9 to 2050.[334]

The ITF notes the incompatibility of skyrocketing global trade emissions with national commitments to decrease global carbon emissions.

✣ CONSIDERING OTHERS ✣

Genesis 40:7 – He asked Pharaoh's courtiers, who were with him in custody in his master's house, saying, "Why do you appear downcast today?"

The story of Joseph begins with him relating an apparently egocentric dream, one that arouses the hatred and jealousy of his brothers. In this passage, he is sitting in a prison in Egypt, far away from his entire family.

An opening to his redemption comes when he stops thinking only about himself and begins listening to the dreams and problems of others, according to Rabbi Michael Melchior. When Joseph asks Pharaoh's servants why they are downcast, we see the first time that Joseph is thinking about someone else.[335] By being open to listening to other people's concerns, Joseph rose out of a low place to a more redemptive space. His question is the beginning of his personal redemption from prison, and of Egypt's salvation from famine. In addition, Joseph is showing concern for people from a different culture and different religion, and so the Torah is teaching us the importance of asking about the welfare of all whom we encounter.

Joseph's sphere of concern expands further in Pharaoh's presence when Joseph suggests a plan for averting catastrophe during an impending famine. Joseph's transition from selfishness to concern for others offers an ecological teaching. Rabbi Abraham Isaac Kook taught about a person singing four songs, representing four levels of concern. The first level is as an individual. On a higher level, a person is concerned for their nation or people. On an even higher level, a person cares for all of humanity. The highest level is to connect to and care for all of creation.[336]

❧ WINE AND BREAD ❧

Genesis 40:11, 17 – Pharaoh's cup was in my hand, and I took the grapes, pressed them into Pharaoh's cup, and placed the cup in Pharaoh's hand . . . In the uppermost basket were all kinds of food for Pharaoh that a baker prepares; and the birds were eating it out of the basket above my head.

Professor of Biblical Studies Jonathan Grossman points out that one of the main differences between the dream of the cupbearer and that of the baker is that the grapes are picked and pressed freshly into Pharaoh's cup, whereas the bread in the baker's dream is pecked away by birds.[337] Based on the differences between the dreams, Joseph correctly understands that the cupbearer is to be returned to his job and the baker is to be hanged. The sign is that his bread has gone to waste, from the perspective of human consumption.

Wine making is an ancient method for preserving grape juice. Fermentation allows the wine to stay drinkable for many years. Even in ancient times, people regularly stored wine for twelve months, until the following harvest.

In contrast, bread is a relatively wasteful product. Contemporary research states that "34–44 percent of all bread produced in the UK is wasted and that only half of that occurs in our homes … [Grains] are lost in the field due to crop damage, cancelled orders or other unforeseen circumstances, and in the factories of food processors during the production of bakery products. Bread is wasted by sandwich makers who discard the heel end of loaves … At the end of the supply chain, retailers dispose of loaves that are damaged or past their sell-by-date, even though they are usually perfectly edible."[338] Today, even with modern preservatives and packaging, a loaf of bread will become hard and then moldy in days or weeks. In our times and likely in ancient times, far less wine would have been wasted than bread or grain.

Modern technology has given us many ways of extending the shelf-life and expanding the transportability of food products. Yet, according to the UN, about one-third of all food in the world is lost or goes to waste.[339] This includes good food discarded by satiated diners or edible leftovers thrown away from the refrigerator. With predictions of massively increasing hunger worldwide, we need much more awareness to make our own lifestyles sustainable, and action to sustain billons of people worldwide.

Suggested Action Items

1. Before purchasing a new bottle of wine, research the different types of planet-healthy wines. The main differences lie in the agricultural process: organic is purity of product, biodynamic is holistic agriculture, and sustainable is mitigating and reducing wastefulness in the process.[340]
2. Consider saying this prayer, formulated by Rebbe Nachman of Breslov: "Grant me the ability to be alone; may it be my custom to go outdoors each day among the trees and grass – among all growing things and there may I be alone, and enter into prayer, to talk with the One to whom I belong. May I express there everything in my

heart, and may all the foliage of the field – all grasses, trees, and plants – awake at my coming, to send the powers of their life into the words of my prayer so that my prayer and speech are made whole through the life and spirit of all growing things, which are made as one by their transcendent Source."[341]

3. Awareness can often be gained through small details and changes. Set aside one day a week in which you will engage the world with more ecological awareness. Try a different activity each week: walk or cycle instead of driving to work, don't throw anything out, only buy recycled products or products in recyclable packaging, pick up street litter, don't use any disposables, cut your shower down by five minutes, bring a travel mug with you to your favorite cafe, or carpool.

Torah portion of Mikeitz

❧ ON THE NILE RIVER ❧

Genesis 41:1 – After two years' time, Pharaoh dreamed that he was standing by the Nile.

Bekhor Shor (Rabbi Joseph ben Isaac Bekhor Shor) explains that the dream took place by the Nile, as the Nile is the source of all irrigation and abundance in Egypt.[342]

In 1970, Egypt completed construction of the Aswan High Dam on the Nile. On the world's longest river, it is also the world's largest embankment dam. The dam was intended to improve flood control, increase water storage for irrigation, and generate hydroelectricity. In the 50 years since it began operation, it has caused a number of unintended ecological consequences, including increased coastline erosion around the Nile Delta, and increased soil salinity, which affected crop yields.[343]

Today, the Egyptians are in conflict with the Ethiopians (up river) who are building a dam across the Nile for hydroelectric power. The dam threatens the water supply to the Nile delta, and hence the livelihoods and sustenance of the majority of the Egyptian people. According to a recent *New York Times* article, "The dam has become the focus of Egypt's water anxieties. The main sticking point with Ethiopia is how quickly it should be filled. Ethiopia says as few as four years, but Egypt, fearing a drought during the filling period, has argued for 12 or longer."[344] Pharaoh dreams about standing next to the abundant Nile, but modern-day Egyptians fear that it will cease to flow. As the world becomes more connected, we are increasingly aware of our ecological dependence on other humans and their choices.

❧ THE SONG OF THE LAND ❧
Rabbi Shaul David Judelman[345]

Genesis 41:4 – And the ugly gaunt cows ate up the seven handsome sturdy cows. And Pharaoh awoke.

The environmental movement that has sprung forth from the West bears many imprints of the thought paradigms that have led to the environmental crisis itself. There is a tendency to rush toward results and overlook the process required to organically arrive at those results. Part of our work in healing is to redress these internalized ways of thinking to arrive at a truly sustainable way of living. Through the Torah, we are learning this lesson of process.

In Pharaoh's prophetic dream seven robust cows are devoured by seven frail ones.[346] The signs seem clear for all to see: seven good and seven so bad that they devour the good that was. It is a vision that may foretell of our human endeavors with technology: a golden age of Enlightenment and invention, industrialization, and higher qualities of life, now quivering under the unknown threat of today's environmental crisis.

Why weren't the Egyptians able to understand the dream? Upon hearing Joseph's interpretation, it seems fairly clear. Was it myopia? Was it denial? How do we, aware of the "dreams" (predictions) of our scientists, share the interpretation? For the last 30 years, environmentalists have been struggling with this challenge of "giving over the bad news." With news that nobody wants to hear, how do they spread the message?

And as their goal is not to share bad news, but rather to inspire, motivate, and guide necessary changes that society and individuals need to make, how do they achieve this?

The environmental movement faces this challenge to catalyze change in two distinct realms: action and spirit. In the realm of action, consumer patterns, industrial pollution, and carbon footprints are the terms of discourse and site of change. But from a broader perspective, those actions are the result of a deeper problem: an imbalance of spirit or exile. If our lifestyle is out of balance with the ecosystems we inhabit, is it fair to assume that our inner dimensions are also out of balance? And while we are seeing great advances and potential in addressing the action side of our crisis, are we paying enough attention to the inner dimensions of disconnect?

As green technologies increase in public awareness and economic reality, the actions seem easier to fix, while our personal and intimate awareness of our surroundings remains as disconnected as ever. How do we address this experiential exile from our Place?[347] How do we share that a connection to our larger self is the true importance of a personal connection to one's habitat, the seasons, the fruits and the land, and the living experience of connection to a place?

An answer is given later in the story of Joseph's family coming down to Egypt. Joseph, the favorite son – who, years before, was left for dead by his jealous brothers – has come to power in Egypt and is in charge of dispensing the only food stores in the region. Jacob, his father, sends a "care package" down with his brothers to the ruler, gifting him with fruits of the Land of Israel.

Jacob does not point out the bad points of Egypt; rather he sends Joseph the fruits of the land. Rebbe Nachman writes that Jacob was sending this mysterious ruler of Egypt a taste of what the Land of Israel is.[348] This is perhaps the true core of environmental work: to pass on the awareness of ourselves within our surroundings.

The taste and song of green living are our greatest allies in affecting substantial organic change in our patterns. For if we end up with an environmentally sustainable lifestyle, but don't grow more aware of our surroundings and our personal connection to that which is outside of us, we may be missing one of the ultimate lessons that the environmental crisis can teach us.

❧ FORESEEING FUTURE CHALLENGES ❧

Genesis 41:8 – Next morning, his spirit was agitated, and he sent for all the magicians of Egypt, and all its wise men; and Pharaoh told them his dreams, but none could interpret them for Pharaoh.

Rabbi Michael Melchior teaches that the Egyptians could not interpret Pharaoh's dream because they knew only abundance from the Nile. They could not imagine the Nile not flooding each year to provide water for their crops. Joseph, who experienced scarcity in Israel, was able to envision a famine in Egypt.[349] Certainty and stability in the past can mislead us as we try to prepare for an uncertain future. For many people who have enjoyed material stability and abundance in the past half-century, it is difficult to imagine that the next half-century will be much different. One role of spiritual leadership is to see more deeply into where our current lifestyle is leading us, and to help us to change accordingly.

❧ COWS AND CROPS ❧

Genesis 41:20, 24 – And the seven lean and ugly cows ate up the first seven cows, the sturdy ones . . . And the thin ears swallowed the seven healthy ears. I have told my magicians, but none has an explanation for me.

Why did Pharaoh have two such similar dreams, and why did the dream about the cows precede the one about the crops? Rabbi Matis Weinberg explains: "The proximate failure of the earliest links in the food chain (ears of grain) would lead to the rapid destruction of their only stockpile (the cows) and the collapse of society."[350]

In 1891, a severe famine in Russia affected 13 million people. Along with the severe drop in crop yields, analysts assert, "the most serious effect of the famine was . . . the widespread destruction of livestock in the famine area . . . only a third of the horses remained alive and one-eighth of the cattle."[351]

Pharaoh has a nightmare about the economic impact of a famine on his empire. Since cattle consume valuable crops that can sustain humans, they cannot be fed during the famine. We see evidence of this later in the story when the Egyptians willingly exchange their cattle for grain.

Today, about one billion cattle are raised for beef and milk.[352] This requires grain and water that could sustain tens of billions of people. A cow weighing 1,300 pounds (590 kg), making 100 pounds (45.5 kg) of milk per day, or producing 490 pounds of beef (222 kg) requires 40,000 kcal/day of feed.[353] This is approximately 16 times a human's daily food consumption. In addition, such a cow would drink 20 gallons of water, compared to an average of half a gallon by a person – a multiple of 40 times. In a world with a rapidly growing human population, and with increasing food and water scarcity, should we be rearing a billion grain and water guzzling cows?

In Pharaoh's dream, the cows and grain are separate. In modern times, the cattle (as well as hogs and chickens) consume much of the agricultural crops grown by people. Indeed, "Livestock takes up nearly 80 percent of global agricultural land yet produces less than 20 percent of the world's supply of calories."[354]

❧ FEEDING ALL THE PEOPLE ❦

Genesis 41:41 – Pharaoh further said to Joseph, "See, I put you in charge of all the land of Egypt."

Pharaoh trusted Joseph to maximize food production for the Egyptian people, and to store grain during the good years in advance of the coming famine. Joseph's success certainly required immediate attention to the natural world – sun, rain, wind, and insects – and long-term attention to the coming drought and famine. The rabbis proclaim, "Who is wise? One who sees the long-term effect of their actions."[355] Joseph was one such wise man, ensuring that everyone received food during the famine.

In contrast, many of today's large corporations buy agricultural land from indigenous people, then leave the local population without sufficient means to feed themselves. Globally between 2001 and 2013, 227 million hectares of land – an area the size of Western Europe – were sold or leased around the world, mainly to international investors. (This trend actually intensified after the 2008 food crisis.) Much of this land is now left unused, despite being greatly needed by local populations for food production.[356] If we want to be ecologically wise like Joseph, shouldn't we be concerned that while our world produces enough food for every person on earth, some 820 million people go hungry and two billion remain malnourished?[357]

❧ LOCAL FOOD ❧

Genesis 41:48 – And he gathered all the grain of the seven years that the land of Egypt was enjoying, and stored the grain in the cities; he put in each city the grain of the fields around it.

Malbim explains that there was no central storage for the Egyptian state, but rather, local storage for each city.[358] Rashi explains that this prevented the food from rotting.[359]

Sourcing food from local suppliers cuts down on waste and transport costs. In a globalized world, the more we can source local food and products, the better it is for the environment and for our budgets. Since 2005, the Transition Movement has promoted more local, resilient communities. It has spread to over 50 countries, in thousands of communities. One of their guiding principles relates to sustainability: "The urgent need to reduce carbon dioxide emissions, greatly reduce our reliance on fossil fuels and make wise use of precious resources is at the forefront of everything we do."[360]

❧ JOSEPH AND FAMILY PLANNING ❧

Genesis 41:50 – Before the years of famine came, Joseph became the father of two sons, whom Asenath daughter of Poti-phera, priest of On, bore to him.

The Torah mentions the births of Joseph's two children immediately before mentioning the beginning of the famine. Joseph intentionally abstained from having more children during the famine, according to the Levush Ha'Orah commentary. And Joseph may have decided, even before the famine, to limit the number of children he had – knowing that extreme resource limitations were imminent.[361] Rashi comments based on the Talmud: "From here [we see] that it is forbidden for a person to have marital relations during years of famine."[362] The Jerusalem Talmud puts it bluntly (to men): "When you see great deprivation entering the world, keep your wife childless."[363] This constraint in the face of ecological disaster is codified in Jewish law.[364] Generally, according to Jewish law, the Biblical injunction to "be fruitful and multiply"[365] is fulfilled in having one son and one daughter.[366] The rabbinic understanding of Joseph's pre-famine restraint suggests that a society that cannot sustain an increasing population should engage in permissible methods of birth control. While Isaac and Rebecca had only two children, their son Jacob and his four wives had at least 13 children and large herds of livestock. When famine came to the land, they were not able to feed their family, and were forced to send their children to Egypt to buy grain. Jacob's brother Esau, with five sons and large flocks, left the Land of Israel for what is now Jordan.

Dr. David Goldblatt writes, "Joseph's decision was, in part, pragmatic, based on a broad, socially aware perspective that, in times of famine, the collective is not served by having more mouths to feed, as Rabbi Natan Greenberg teaches.[367] In addition, as a high Egyptian official, Joseph made a principled decision to involve himself personally in the suffering of his community. The Ba'al HaTurim and Maharim[368] commentaries note that Joseph's restraint here caused him to merit the abundance which Moses states in relation to the tribe of Joseph – 'Blessed of God be his land, with the bounty of dew from heaven.'[369] In today's developed countries, birthrates are already relatively low, so reducing environmentally significant consumption becomes especially import-ant."[370] Perhaps more troubling than the prospect of ten billion people on earth in the coming 50 years is 150 billion factory-farmed animals, three billion personal automobiles, eight billion air conditioners, and 30 billion smartphones, laptops, and tablets.

Population growth becomes most significant when it is multiplied by the energy consumption of the machines that billions more people will use. To ignore population growth and consumption in relation to sustainability is to miss how these factors multiply impact.

❦ SONG OF THE TREES ❦

Genesis 43:11 – Then their father Israel said to them, "If it must be so, do this: take some of the choice products [zimra] of the land in your baggage, and carry them down as a gift for the man – some balm and some honey, gum, lotus, pistachio nuts, and almonds."

Jacob used the word *zimra* in describing to his children what to take. This word means both choice products and song. According to Rebbe Nachman of Breslov, Jacob taught the melody of the Land of Israel to his sons before they went to Egypt, since every land has its own melody.[371] According to Rebbe Nachman, this song is based on the melody of the trees – note that all the products are from trees – the honey being from dates. Jacob requested that his sons bring this song to Joseph. The trees helped the brothers to reconcile. For us, going into a forest can help to restore balance within ourselves.

Suggested Action Items

1. Hire a guide to explain your local geology, plants, and wildlife, providing you with a glimpse of how your neighborhood or town was formed and continues to develop. Transform walking to your corner store into a historical and environmental hike!
2. Connect to the Transition Movement in your town or city.
3. Buy foods from local farms, which can reduce the carbon miles of your food and can also bring you and your family into meaningful contact with the people, plants, and soil that grow your food.
4. Experiment with local, organic, and/or heirloom corn recipes. Whether you bake cornbread or boil soup, you'll have the perfect food to feast upon while learning about Pharaoh's dreams.
5. Teach your children songs with environmental themes. Music can be a great teacher.

Torah portion of Vayigash

❧ TO PLOW OR NOT TO PLOW ❧

Genesis 45:6 – It is now two years that there has been famine in the land, and there are still five years to come in which there shall be no plowing or gathering.

Riva (Rabbi Yitzchak ben Asher HaLevi) asks why the Torah needs to say "no plowing or gathering." Surely if there is no plowing, then there is no gathering, so why not just write "no plowing?" Rabbeinu Yaakov ben Meir (Rabbeinu Tam) answers that the verse wishes to include those fields that do not require plowing.[372]

Today the question of plowing or not plowing is a significant one in many places, including Africa. Climate change is forcing people to rethink their traditional farming methods, and the practice of conservation tillage has proven widely beneficial. Conservation tillage involves leaving the previous year's residue of corn stalks or wheat stubble on the fields, before and after planting the next crop, to reduce runoff and soil erosion by up to 60 percent.[373] It saves labor and adds healthy organic matter to the soil. It decreases fuel and planting expenditures because fewer tractor trips across the field are needed. Finally, it reduces tractor-related soil compaction, which can interfere with plant growth.

Research has shown that conservation tillage accompanied by crop rotation and the use of cover crops (planted after the cash crop, to manage pests and retain water out of season) increases harvest yields and improves the soil. In a case study performed by the UN's Food and Agriculture Organization (FAO) in Tanzania, crop yields increased 130 percent over a six-year period of conservation tillage.[374]

These gains in crop yields are significant since hunger remains a pervasive problem for hundreds of millions of Africans. As World Vision notes, "…237 million sub-Saharan Africans are chronically undernourished, more than in any other region. In the whole of Africa, 257 million people are experiencing hunger, which is 20 percent of the population. Successive crop failures and poor harvests in Zambia, Zimbabwe, Mozambique, and Angola are taking a toll on agriculture production, and food prices are soaring. In the past three growing seasons, parts of Southern Africa experienced their lowest rainfall since 1981. Other areas suffered widespread destruction from Cyclones Idai and Kenneth in March and April 2019, near the time for harvesting."[375]

❧ JACOB, PHARAOH, AND REUSE ❧

Genesis 45:20 – And never mind your belongings, for the best of all the land of Egypt shall be yours.

Pharaoh bids Jacob and his family not to bring much with them to Egypt as Pharaoh can provide them with new vessels once they arrive.

Jacob, apparently, does not listen to Pharaoh's advice, as we learn later: "Israel set out with all that was his."[376] (Years earlier, Jacob had returned at night to retrieve small vessels when he encountered the angel with whom he wrestled – see the commentary to Genesis 32:24. The Da'at Zekeinim commentary explains that Pharaoh somehow heard about Jacob's commitment to keeping even the smallest vessels.[377])

Pharaoh represents extreme wealth and disposable income – one that does not hold sentimentality for possessions and does not hesitate to replace things that could still be usable. Jacob represents sustainable living, living the value of reuse.

❧ SHEPHERDS AND FARMERS ❧

Genesis 46:32–34, 47:1 – The men are shepherds; they have always been breeders of livestock, and they have brought with them their flocks and herds and all that is theirs. So when Pharaoh summons you and asks, "What is your occupation?" you shall answer, "Your servants have been breeders of livestock from the start until now, both we and our fathers" – so that you may stay in the region of Goshen. For all shepherds are abhorrent to Egyptians ... Then Joseph came and reported to Pharaoh, saying, "My father and my brothers, with their flocks and herds and all that is theirs, have come from the land of Canaan and are now in the region of Goshen."

Rabbeinu Bachaya explains that Abraham, Isaac, Jacob, Moses, and David were all shepherds because shepherding is work that took them out of the city, away from gossip, theft, and other temptations.[378] Here, Joseph is instructing his family, now in Egypt, to continue to live away from the main city, in the pastoral region of Goshen. Doing so would keep them away from the threats of urban life, and maintain their spirituality and time spent in peace and contemplation.[379]

The interactions between Pharaoh and Joseph, the brothers and Jacob, capture an encounter between a people with shepherding in their blood and the head of the great Nile agricultural society.

In the Book of Exodus, Moses requests that Pharaoh let the Israelites go into the desert to worship God. Pharaoh is willing to let the Israelites leave, but he refuses to allow them to take their cows, goats, and sheep with them.[380] This is a red line for Pharaoh in the negotiations. The leader of the world's greatest farming nation downright refuses to allow a shepherding people to go with their flocks to worship God. These verses touch on a central tension and competition within ancient societies, between shepherds and farmers, for control of land and for power.

Ibn Ezra gives a different explanation for the Egyptians' abhorrence of shepherds – that Egyptians at the time were vegetarians who did not eat meat or drink milk.[381] This understanding by Ibn Ezra is confirmed by contemporary researchers from Lyons University, based on analysis of carbon isotopes in ancient Egyptian teeth and bone samples.[382]

❧ REPLACING ANIMALS WITH PLANTS ❧

Genesis 47:17 – So they brought their livestock to Joseph, and Joseph gave them bread in exchange for the horses, for the stocks of sheep and cattle, and the donkeys; thus he provided them with bread that year in exchange for all their livestock.

Netziv, in his commentary Ha'amek Davar, asks why the animals are listed in this way, and he answers that they are listed in order of importance to the state and economy. First come the horses required for Pharaoh's army and national defense; next the sheep that provide wool, milk, and meat; then the cows that provide milk and meat; and finally, the donkeys suitable only for transportation.[383]

In a time of crisis, Egyptians gave up their animals for a plant-derived food – bread – demonstrating that a plant-based diet consumes far fewer resources of land, nutrients, and water. Eating less meat has also been associated with better health. In the words of the *Harvard Women's Health Watch*, "a Mediterranean eating pattern – known to be associated with longer life and reduced risk of several chronic illnesses – features an emphasis on plant foods with a sparing use of meat."[384]

In our modern society we are far less reliant on animals for things like agriculture, clothing, and transportation than in Biblical times. In warfare, tanks and airplanes have replaced horses. We have largely replaced sheep's wool with other fibers. We use trucks instead of donkeys to transport goods. And many people replace animal protein with soy or other food sources of plant-based protein. We have the potential to consume far fewer resources in our lives than previous generations could, yet we consume far more. Our choice to consume more and more meat and dairy products, despite the environmental cost, is one of our generation's key challenges.

✤ JOSEPH'S FORESIGHT AND RESTRAINT ✤

by David Goldblatt[385]

Genesis 47:18 – And when that year was ended, they came to him the next year and said to him, "We cannot hide from my Lord that, with all the money and animal stocks consigned to my Lord, nothing is left at my Lord's disposal save our persons and our farmland."

Joseph embodies foresight, self-discipline, and concern for the larger community. He used his prophetic insight to instruct Egypt to make provisions, during seven years of plenty, for seven years of famine that would follow. Anticipating an impending human-ecological disaster, he had Egyptians gather grain in the time of plenty as insurance against hard times to come. Egypt benefited because Joseph forced the Egyptians to show restraint ahead of a crisis – to consume less in the short term, in return for some non-material gain, and survival in leaner times to come.

Pharaoh (whose name implies *paru'ah*, undisciplined) is the quintessential self-indulger. By contrast, Joseph exemplifies self-discipline. (Jacob likens him to an ox, *shor*, which also means to see.[386]) Self-restraint, discipline, and making pleasure secondary to the pursuit of goodness create a path to the World to Come. In this case, Joseph shows how societal restraint and discipline are also the means to secure one's future survival in this world.

In the words of Rabbi Avraham Greenbaum, "Joseph used the Seven Years of Plenty to teach the Egyptians to put limits on immediate consumption and gratification in order to save for the future."[387] This is a discipline modern societies sorely need to learn. If we do not plan for the future, we will be unprepared when it arrives.

During the second year of the famine, all the Egyptians' grain rotted and after selling their livestock for food, they sold their land to the state.[388] Rabbi Daniel Kohn says that Joseph ultimately brought the Egyptians into a caring relationship with the earth ("and the land will not become desolate"[389]). Even though the land no longer belonged to them, they followed Joseph's insistence that they symbolically commit themselves to a path of self-restraint.

Today we lack two distinct advantages Joseph had in implementing his plan to safeguard Egypt. His knowledge of the future was perfect for

God revealed to Joseph what would transpire, in the form of Pharaoh's dreams. And Joseph's control was absolute over managing the Egyptian agrarian system and achieving his plan, as Pharaoh's appointed leader.

We do not have perfect knowledge of our impact on the environment, nor does any single leader have absolute power to change that impact. Some level of uncertainty is inherent in most current environmental problems.

Our challenge is to deal with this uncertainty responsibly, incorporating the Precautionary Principle, which demands "a willingness to take action in advance of [complete] scientific proof of evidence of the need for the proposed action on the grounds that further delay may prove ultimately most costly to society and nature, and, in the longer term, selfish and unfair to future generations."[390] We may not have the luxury of Joseph's God-given absolute knowledge and power, but we do have the past to learn from, and dreams for our future to drive us to action.

❧ LET US NOT PERISH ❧

Genesis 47:19 – Let us not perish before your eyes, both we and our land. Take us and our land in exchange for bread, and we with our land will be serfs to Pharaoh; provide the seed, that we may live and not die, and that the land may not become desolate.

The verse shows the desperation people experience when environmental problems reach a crisis stage. Nature, through the famine, overwhelms the Egyptians.

In today's world, environmental problems are reaching crisis stage for millions of people. In September 2019, Hurricane Dorian decimated the Bahamas. A *New York Times* article quotes Cindy Russell, a resident of Marsh Harbour in the Bahamas, whose home was destroyed: "It's like we just need to be rescued and put on another island to start over again," she said. "Complete devastation."[391] The ravages of such a storm – and the increasing frequency and intensity of storm activity – are the canary in the coal mine, a sign of imminent danger if we don't curb climate change. This was reinforced in August 2020, when Hurricane Isaias struck the Bahamas, and impacted people living in tents or unrepaired houses damaged by Dorian the previous year.

Suggested Action Items

1. Support an effective energy policy in your city, state, or country – one that strongly reduces fossil energy use, such as investing in city-owned electric vehicles, and strongly supports development of carbon-free energy sources such as solar panels on the roofs of homes and municipal buildings.
2. Plan a family trip to a local, organic, free-range, cage-free, and/ or certified humane farm! To celebrate Joseph reuniting with his family, unite with your own family over nature and animals in an environment where both are respected.
3. Volunteer with your family or friends at a local food bank or wildlife rescue center.

Torah portion of Vayechi

❧ THE MIRACLE OF WATER ❧

Genesis 49:4 – Unstable as water, you [Reuben] shall excel no longer; for when you mounted your father's bed, you brought disgrace – my couch he mounted!

The HaKetav VeHaKabbalah commentary explains that just as spilt water evaporates rapidly without leaving a trace (unlike more viscous oil drops that form a puddle, or wine that leaves a smell), so did Jacob's son Reuben's merits evaporate.

The dispersion of water molecules turns out to be essential for life on our planet, and the unique chemical properties of water are some of God's revealed miracles.[392] Our bodies are partly made of water. Water is an excellent solvent, dissolving nutrients in the soil and transferring them to plants. Frozen water is less dense than liquid water, and under a floating layer of ice, fish can survive a frigid winter. Water in the form of clouds becomes life-giving rain. Water has a high specific heat capacity (it takes a lot of applied heat to warm up water), which buffers how rapidly the sun warms the oceans, enabling heat-sensitive sea life to thrive.

❧ LIONS AS SUSTAINABLE PREDATORS ❧

Genesis 49:9 – Judah is a lion's cub. On prey, my son, have you grown. He crouches, lies down like a lion, like the king of beasts – who dare rouse him?

Malbim explains that Jacob likens Judah to a lion cub for enthusiasm and to an adult lion for strength.[393] Yet isn't a lion mostly destructive? And since King David was to come from the tribe of Judah, is calling Judah a lion a compliment or condemnation?

Lions in Africa are the "apex" predator, meaning no other animals prey on healthy adult lions. Lions account for the killing of 30 percent of zebras in the Serengeti region. This sounds like a destructive force, but from the perspective of the whole ecosystem, lions limit the zebra population and therefore allow less competitive plant-eating animal species to survive in the region. By hunting and killing lions – which lets zebra populations increase too much – humans disturb the region's ecological balance. The result is the death, by starvation, of giraffes, buffalo, and other herbivores that can't effectively compete with zebra herds for food.[394]

So referring to the ruling line of King David as the Lion of Judah carries complex ecological meaning – connecting him with another of God's creations that protects the weaker by containing the strong.

❧ HOLY FOOD ❧

by Rabbi Yedidya Sinclair[395]

Genesis 49:11 – He tethers his donkey to a vine, his donkey's foal to a choice vine; he washes his garment in wine, his robe in blood of grapes.

Do we know who grows our food or prepares it? Do we need to know? Is the idea of having a relationship that is in any way personal with one's food, or the people who grow and prepare it, quaint or ridiculous? Rashi suggests otherwise.

When Jacob on his deathbed blesses his many sons, he highlights characteristics unique to each son and to the tribes of his sons' descendants. According to Rashi, five of Jacob's blessings focus on the agricultural (today we would also add aquacultural) specificity of each tribe's territory in the Land of Israel. On Judah's blessing – "Binding his foal to the vine…he washes his garments in wine"[396] – Rashi comments on the Midrash: "It was prophesied about the Land of Judah that it will gush forth wine like a fountain."[397] Likewise Talmudic commentary abounds in sensuous descriptions of the grapes and wine grown in the lands of Judah: "Any palate that tastes it says, 'Give me! Give me!'"[398]

On the promise that "Zebulun shall dwell at the edge of the sea. His will be a shore for ships,"[399] Rashi observes, "He will always be found on the shores by the ports to which ships bring merchandise."[400] The Talmud further tells how the beaches of Zebulun were home to the mollusks from which blue dye could be extracted.[401] His territory was agriculturally poor but a lucrative resource for snail farming. The ports would also be sources of fish harvested from the ocean.

Interpreting Jacob's blessing to Issachar – "He saw a resting place, that it was good, and the land that it was pleasant"[402] – Rashi writes, "He saw that his part of the land was blessed and would produce good fruit."[403] Issachar's tribe's destiny was traditionally understood as immersion in Torah learning. He rejoiced in a region where food gathering was less labor intensive, allowing time for greater devotion to study.

Two ecological themes stand out from Rashi's comments. First, Biblical food production is regional. Each part of the Biblical Land of Israel is known for the particular kinds of crop, produce, and natural product native to the area. Second, Biblical food production is personal. We know that the earliest members of Judah's tribe grow grapes, those in Asher's make olive oil, those in Issachar's harvest fruit, etc. In Biblical times, people could easily trace the short and transparent journey of each item from the ground or water, via the grower or gatherer, to their plates and lives.

Contemporary city and suburban dwellers don't readily find relevance in these notions. In the United States, for example, people often have no idea of the source of industrially produced and packaged food they buy in identical supermarkets coast to coast. Most contemporary Western eaters have lost connection with the people who grow their food and the places where it is grown. (Typical food on an American dinner plate has traveled 1,500 miles.)[404]

Does this matter? Michael Pollan, in his influential book *The Omni-*

vore's Dilemma, argues that it matters greatly. Pollan claims the industrial food chain deliberately casts a thick veil of ignorance between us and its production processes, partly through our complacency. From meat raised in CAFO's (Concentrated Animal Feeding Operations) to methane-belching corn-fed cattle, to the raising of monoculture fruits, vegetables and grains, to the use of chemical fertilizers and pesticides on our produce, many of us do not want to know too much about how what we eat arrives on supermarket shelves. The COVID-19 pandemic has dramatically revealed the risk of disease spread among workers in cramped meat-processing plants, and even further among their families and communities.

If we were fully aware of the cruelty frequently involved in raising our food, the environmental degradation caused by growing it, the health risks to workers and consumers in processing and preserving it, and the immense expenditure of fossil fuels in transporting it, we would be extremely troubled, if not repulsed. Pollan's achievement is to rip away the veil of ignorance and open our eyes to the raw and disturbing facts about so much of our food.

How should we exercise the ethical responsibility that comes with knowledge about modern food production? Pollan writes about Polyface Farm, a pesticide- and fertilizer-free farm where the animals are free-range. The farm's owner, Joel Salatin, says, "The only meaningful guarantee of integrity is when buyers and sellers can look one another in the eye." Knowing the people who grow our food, we can take a measure of responsibility for how it reaches us.

How can people living far from the nearest farm possibly do this? One step is through Community Supported Agriculture (CSA) projects. City dwellers subscribe at the beginning of the growing season and pay a few hundred dollars to receive a box of local produce each week. CSA projects enable farms to connect with customers right in their regions.

Rashi's description of a localized personal agriculture may serve as a model for how to find our way back from the tortured, depersonalized complexity of the industrial food chain toward a healthier, more informed, and empowered relationship with what we eat.

❧ SNAKES AND SEEDS ❧

Genesis 49:17 – Dan shall be a serpent by the road, a viper by the path, that bites the horse's heels so that his rider is thrown backward.

Radak explains that the serpent is a solitary animal that can kill many other animals, like Samson (from the tribe of Dan) was a solitary fighter who killed many Philistines.[405] Jacob's words about his son Dan do not seem all that favorable. But what admirable features of a snake in the ecosystem can lend Dan a more positive image by comparison?

Not only are snakes essential in pest control, consuming small rodents that would otherwise become rampant and potentially spread disease, they are also critical in seed dispersal. One snake eats around 20 rodents per year and travels over 1.2 miles (2 kilometers), further than the rodents would have traveled while alive. Each devoured rodent has previously eaten a variety of seeds. So these seeds make their way through the snake's gastrointestinal tract, and are excreted as the snake travels – making the snake an effective seed distributor.[406]

"Even those creatures deemed by you superfluous in the world – like serpents and scorpions – still have their definite place in the scheme of creation," says Rabbi Acha ben Chanina in the Midrash. "For God said to the prophets, 'Do you think that if you refuse to fulfill My message, I have none else to send? No! My message will be fulfilled even by a serpent, scorpion, or frog.'"[407]

The Torah values wildlife, since every creature has a role in creation, even animals wrongly perceived as just pests.

❧ TRIBES AND LOCAL TRADE ❧

Genesis 49:20 – Asher's bread shall be rich, and he shall yield royal dainties.

Jacob's blessings to his sons speak of the different foods that they will grow within the different tribal lands of Israel. The tribe of Judah will settle a mountainous region ideal for growing grapes. The tribe of Zebulun will engage in fishing by the sea, and the tribe of Asher will grow wheat on its flat land.

Clearly Jacob is blessing the tribes with an optimized food and agricultural policy. With efficient trading, each tribe could produce the crops or gather the food animals most suited to its territory. Then the tribes would barter or sell them to one another, to ensure a balanced diet at the lowest overall cost. The close proximity of the tribes reduced the carbon footprint of their food. What would Jacob think about modern Israel, where rice is imported from the United States, meat from Argentina, and coffee from Peru?

❧ GOD THE SHEPHERD ❧

Genesis 49:24–25 – Yet his bow stayed taut, and his arms were made firm by the hands of the Mighty One of Jacob – there, the Shepherd, the Rock of Israel – the God of your father who helps you and Shaddai who blesses you with blessings of heaven above, blessings of the deep that couches below, blessings of the breast and womb.

A shepherd bears responsibility for the safety and welfare of the flock. The shepherd herds the flock to graze in areas of good forage, and protects the animals from eating poisonous plants or being attacked by predators.[408] God is likened to a shepherd who leads His flock to pastures and cares for every animal. The allusions to nature suggest an ideal harmony between humanity and the environment, with God in charge.

In the Book of Job, God invokes His mastery of nature when He asks Job, "Who provides food for the raven when its young cry out to God and wander about in search of food? Do you know the season when the mountain goats give birth? Can you mark the time when the hinds calve?... Who sets the wild ass free?...Do you give the horse his strength? Do you clothe his neck with a mane?... Does the eagle soar at your command, building its nest high, dwelling in the rock...?" Job responds, "See, I am of small worth; what can I answer you?"[409]

We would be wise to learn from Job about humility as regards our place on God's earth.

❧ THE BLESSING OF WOLVES ❧

Genesis 49:27 – Benjamin is a ravenous wolf; in the morning he consumes the foe, and in the evening he divides the spoil.

Or HaChayim explains that a real wolf guzzles down its prey rapidly, and that Jacob's blessing of his youngest son Benjamin alludes to King Saul, who was impulsive and from the tribe of Benjamin.[410] Wolves still roam the wild in the Negev desert region of Israel, as well as the Egyptian Sinai and the Arabian peninsula, and many parts of the world.[411]

In Yellowstone National Park, in the US, scientists are carefully documenting how gray wolves affect the ecosystem, and note that the wolves have brought many changes for the better since they were reintroduced into the park.[412] Americans once treated gray wolves as pests and poisoned them until the 1950s, before scientists better understood the importance of ecosystem balance between predators and prey. Absent for 70 years, the wolves of Yellowstone are now increasing in number.

The growing wolf population is triggering direct and indirect effects, including that more diverse species are thriving throughout the Yellowstone ecosystem.[413] Wolves have reduced the numbers of elk grazing in the area,[414] and scavenging species such as eagles, bears, and magpies are thriving on remains of elk prey that wolves leave behind.[415] Wolves, like other key predators, are critical to the health of ecosystems. Perhaps this ecological understanding can help us better appreciate Jacob's words of blessing invoking the power of a wild predator.

Suggested Action Items

1. Learn about the local farms and food producers near you and buy from them directly. You might find that not too far from you is a delicious jam producer or an organic peach and berry farm where you can pick your own fruit!

2. Attempt to buy food that is grown or produced locally, with as little packaging and transportation as possible involved in the process. One way to do so is by joining a Community Supported Agriculture project near where you live.

3. Write a short review for *Eco Bible* on Amazon: https://www.amazon.com/review/create-review/.

Part Two

Commentary on the
Book of Exodus

Torah portion of Shemot

❧ SOARING POPULATION ❧

Exodus 1:7–9 – And the Israelites were fruitful and prolific; they multiplied and increased very greatly, so that the land was filled with them. A new king arose over Egypt who did not know Joseph. Look, the Israelite people are much too numerous for us.

Seven words in this verse – *fruitful, prolific, multiplied, increased, very, greatly,* and *filled* – emphasize the rapid growth of the Israelite population. Rabbi Yaakov Tzvi Mecklenburg explains that the Egyptians worried that the Israelites would increase at a greater rate than native Egyptians and would overthrow the government.[416]

The Bible uses similar language in this first chapter of Exodus as in the first chapter of Genesis ("be fruitful and multiply and fill the earth"). Yet in Exodus it says that the land was filled with the people. According to scholars, ancient Egypt at that time had two to three million people in total,[417] and the Israelites were only part of the population – perhaps one million. So the Bible itself calls the land of Egypt "full" with even one million Israelites, while today Egypt has 100 million people. *The New York Times* states in regard to Egypt in 2020, "the most pressing threat facing the Nile stems from population growth and climate change. Egypt's population increases by one million people every six months – a soaring rate."[418]

Today, the world population is growing exponentially, and 97 percent of growth in the next decade is expected from the developing world.[419] The pressure of high population growth rates and strain on natural resources in Africa and Asia have led to many civil wars.[420] Over the past 70 years, the top ten wars by death toll have all been in Asia and Africa.[421]

In the first four months, the COVID-19 pandemic spread the most in megacities of about 20 million people, including Wuhan (19,000,000), New York City metropolitan area (23,000,000), and Tehran metropolitan area (23,000,000). The coronavirus stays alive by multiplying and spreading from person to person where people are in close proximity to each other, so the dense, fast-paced life of a megacity is the optimal place for the coronavirus to spread. In Israel, recent research confirmed that the more crowded a city was, the greater the risk of being infected by the COVID-19 virus, a phenomenon consistent with dozens of similar studies conducted worldwide during other epidemics.[422]

According to the authoritative Shulchan Arukh code of Torah law, "Once a man has had a son and a daughter, he has fulfilled the obligation to be fruitful and multiply."[423] The intention of the Creator is that our being fruitful should lead to life, blessing, and prosperity, and not the opposite. In light of how population growth multiplies ecological impact, what does the Bible's injunction to "be fruitful and multiply" mean in our time?

❧ ECOLOGICAL LIBERATION ❧

Exodus 1:11 – So they [the Egyptians] set taskmasters over them [the Israelites] to oppress them with forced labor; and they built garrison cities for Pharaoh: Pithom and Raamses.

Rabbi Benjamin Weiner writes:

> The Book of Exodus draws a sharp distinction between oppressor and oppressed – the Egyptian overlord and the Israelite slave. While our world is plagued by such stark imbalances of power, I find myself preoccupied with the way that our society locks us, its beneficiaries, into oppressive roles. My daily routine is sustained by the ceaseless extraction and burning of fossil fuels. When I take stock of this, I want to cry out to God, not as an enslaved Israelite, but as an Egyptian, sickened by the destructive power entangled in my hands. Going back to the land – learning to grow a large portion of my family's food with regenerative techniques, drawing sustenance from the parcel of earth where we make our home while also doing my best

to restore it as habitat to birds and bees, bears and butterflies – has felt, in this regard, like liberation.[424]

❧ BITUMEN: BIBLICAL AND MODERN ❧

Exodus 2:3 – When she [Miriam] could hide him [Moses] no longer, she got a wicker basket for him and caulked it with bitumen and pitch. She put the child into it and placed it among the reeds by the bank of the Nile.

Pitch is obtained by distilling tar or petroleum and is used for water-proofing. Pitch and bitumen, an extract of crude oil, are mentioned four times in the books of Genesis and Exodus – twice for good in lining Noah's Ark and Moses' basket and twice for evil (in Genesis, in the building of the Tower of Babel, and involving the kings of Sodom and Gomorrah).[425] We see from these verses that bitumen and pitch were used in limited quantities for thousands of years. Yet in the past several decades, petroleum use has grown exponentially both for fuel and for making plastics. Today, we manufacture plastics from extracts of crude oil and use the plastics in products that range from frivolous to vital – for example, from single-use plastics to durable medical devices. Microplastics are now showing up in the rain. As John Schwartz reports in *The New York Times*, "More than 1,000 tons of tiny fragments rain down each year on national parks and wilderness areas in the American West alone, equivalent to between 123 million and 300 million plastic bottles worth."[426] We are only now beginning to realize the implications of a lifestyle in which almost everything we eat reaches us in plastic. Bitumen, like most resources, can be used for good or for bad. The choice is ours.

❧ PRECIOUS GROUNDWATER ❧

Exodus 2:16 – Now the priest of Midian had seven daughters. They came to draw water and filled the troughs to water their father's flock.

Rashi explains, "The troughs were channels of running water [that were] made in the ground."[427] This description indicates a sustainable rainwater collection system built in the desert. (Deserts are not all sand.) Many ancient civilizations had advanced methods of rainwater capture in the desert providing a key source of water. By digging wells above an underground aquifer, people could draw water up with buckets. By digging channels, desert dwellers could direct local streams into the well system, to top up the groundwater when it ran low.[428] Rashi seems to be alluding to these practices in this commentary.

Today, depletion of groundwater is a global concern. Many regions are experiencing recurrent water stress, including the Sahara, South Africa, Australia, India, Pakistan, and Northeast China. It is estimated that over two billion people, or 35 percent of the world population, suffer from severe water stress.

In these regions and others, people often use groundwater as an additional water source. As one study notes, "If groundwater extraction exceeds groundwater replenishment for an extended time, the resulting lowering of groundwater levels can have devastating effects on … ecosystems and lead to land collapse and saltwater intrusion. Current levels of groundwater depletion are more than 100 percent higher than 1960 and are contributing 0.8 mm per year toward sea-level rise."[429]

Humanity is extracting water unsustainably, and at some point, many regions will exhaust underground water supplies that have been a key source for millennia.

❧ SHEPHERDS BECOME NATIONAL LEADERS ❧

Exodus 3:1 – Now Moses, tending the flock of his father-in-law Jethro, the priest of Midian, drove the flock into the wilderness, and came to Horeb, the mountain of God.

The Midrash explains that Moses was looking for a lost lamb when he stumbled upon the burning bush.[430] This demonstrates Moses' care for each member of his flock – a strong recommendation for leadership. Just as for Abraham, Isaac, Jacob, and David, Moses' occupation as a shepherd was great training for national leadership. Apparently, compassion for animals was a key qualification for leadership in ancient times.

Kli Yakar suggests that being in the wilderness enabled Moses to achieve a state of prophecy, like many of the prophets who prophesied in the wilderness.[431] As it says in Psalms, "When I behold Your heavens, the work of Your fingers … how majestic is Your name throughout the earth!"[432] This suggests that a strong love and appreciation for nature can lead us to a greater understanding of God.

Rebbe Nachman of Breslov emphasizes the significance of the shepherd-flock relationship: "Know that every shepherd has a special song according to the grasses and according to the place where he shepherds, because every animal has its appropriate grass that it needs for feeding and the shepherd does not tend his flock continuously in the same place. And according to the grasses and the place...so is the tune. Because every single grass has a song that it sings...and from the song of the grasses, the tune of the shepherd is made...and through the shepherd's knowledge of the tune, he gives power to the grasses, and the flock is able to graze."[433]

The grazing of flocks, especially goats and sheep, has significant ecological benefits. Environmental scientist Alon Tal notes that grazing in woodlands helps promote biodiversity and decrease the frequency and intensity of fires. He writes, "Not only do grazing animals provide a wonderful mechanism for spreading seed and enriching soils with nutrients; long-term grazing can improve the competitive ability of other plant species less palatable to animals." About shepherding in modern Israel, Tal notes: "Modern regulations and paperwork make pastoral occupations increasingly bureaucratic and less profitable... The profession of 'shepherd' is not a lucrative one, and nomadic grazers have difficulty competing with feedlots." He calls for government incentives "to revitalize grazing as a societally valuable occupation."[434]

❧ RENEWABLE DIVINE FIRE ❧

Exodus 3:2 – An angel of the Lord appeared to him in a blazing fire out of a bush. He gazed, and there was a bush all aflame, yet the bush was not consumed.

God appears to Moses as a form of sustainable energy – fire that emanates from a source that is not consumed. In this way, God is demonstrating His ability to endure forever.

Our planet's supply of unsustainable energy is running out. According to scholars from Stanford University, the world's oil reserves will last until 2052, gas until 2060, and coal until 2090.[435] At that point, humankind will have burned through fuel resources formed over the past hundreds of millions of years, and will have done so in a 200-year period.

In today's world, we are dangerously dependent on fire that consumes, in our cars, airplanes, power plants that supply our electronic gadgets, home appliances, and much more. Yet there are different forms of "fire" that we can relate to. Billions of creatures on earth such as "fireflies" (nocturnal beetles) make their own "fire" which is actually bioluminescence. Chinese medicine contains a diagnosis of "'internal fire," where the body suffers as a result of excess heat.[436] The burning bush is an example of God appearing to a person as spiritual fire. In what ways might we find our spiritual fire and use it to protect our planet?

❧ HOLY LAND ❧

Exodus 3:5 – And He [God] said, "Do not come closer. Remove your sandals from your feet, for the place on which you stand is holy ground."

God is speaking to Moses at the burning bush. Rabbi Bradley Artson explains, "The Torah directly proclaims the sanctity of a site outside of the Land of Israel… This passage tells us that *land* is holy, not just *a* land. In Genesis, God is the Creator of the heavens and the earth; therefore, all lands are touched by God. Perhaps this appreciation that all the earth is God's place contributes to the age-old Israelite tradition that extols the wilderness as a place of holiness and purity."[437]

❧ WATER, STAFF, SNAKE, AND LEPROSY ❧

Exodus 4:3–9 – He said, "Cast it on the ground." He cast it on the ground and it became a snake; and Moses recoiled from it. Then the Lord said to Moses, "Put out your hand and grasp it by the tail" – he put out his hand and seized it, and it became a rod in his hand – "that they may believe that the Lord, the God of their fathers, the God of Abraham, the God of Isaac, and the God of Jacob, did appear to you." The Lord said to him further, "Put your hand into your bosom." He put his hand into his bosom; and when he took it out, his hand was encrusted with snowy scales! And He said, "Put your hand back into your bosom." – He put his hand back into his bosom; and when he took it out of his bosom, there it was again like the rest of his body. – "And if they do not believe you or pay heed to the first sign, they will believe the second. And if they are not convinced by both these signs and still do not heed you, take some water from the Nile and pour it on the dry ground, and it – the water that you take from the Nile – will turn to blood on the dry ground."

The signs that God gives Moses before going to Egypt cover the whole of creation. The staff comes from a tree; the snake is an animal; the leprosy that occurs on Moses' hand is a human blight; and water is inanimate. The signs begin with plant and animal life – perhaps the easiest for humans to control. If this is not enough to convince Pharaoh that God is behind these wonders, then next comes the leprous hand – humans are more difficult than animals to control. Yet the most compelling sign, the water turning to blood, is frightening because humankind has the least control over the inanimate aspects of nature.

In a sense, this order follows the track of human development. First, we learned how to raise livestock and grow crops. Then we learned how to cure human disease and create democracies. The final challenge for humankind is to live sustainably with nature.

Suggested Action Items

1. Learn the names of the sanitation employees, maintenance workers, and gardeners who service your neighborhood, apartment building, school, or workplace. Consider ways in which you could ennoble their work and include them in your community.
2. Learn the names of the trees and plants that grow in your neighborhood. To do so, you can join a foraging class or a guided nature walk, or use an app.
3. Find out which major retailers and manufacturers utilize dehumanizing sweatshop labor. Make a commitment to reduce your use of products from these companies. Many websites feature lists of such companies: The American Federation of Labor and Congress of Industrial Organizations (AFL-CIO) and Green America are good places to start.

Torah portion of Va'eira

❧ HARD LABOR AND WORK'S YOKE ❧

Exodus 6:6 – Say, therefore, to the Israelite people: I am the Lord. I will free you from the labors of the Egyptians and deliver you from their bondage. I will redeem you with an outstretched arm and through extraordinary chastisements.

Rashi understands the "labors of the Egyptians" to be "the yoke of the burden of Egypt." According to Yosef Hallel, this means "the feeling that they are duty bound to do the bidding of the Egyptians, even at times when they are not actually engaged in hard labor."[438] In modern society, it is common to feel the pressures of work well after the work day is officially over. Upon leaving their office, many feel obligated to continue work from home and answer texts and emails at night, over the weekend, and even during vacation. Many modern white-collar workers have internalized the taskmaster. Technologies like smartphones and email play a role in enabling a person to always be "on call."

In the US, 85.8 percent of men and 66.5 percent of women work more than 40 hours per week.[439] In the "gig" economy, many cannot get full-time jobs with benefits. They must work multiple jobs to make ends meet, including service jobs that involve a lot of driving and fossil-fuel use.[440] One root of the ecological crisis is a human population whose work policies and attitudes place an increasing burden on lower-income workers.

Those who have more options are choosing a reduction in income and taking part-time work as a way of establishing a healthier balance between paid work, family, and personal nourishment[441] (and spiritual practice).

❧ THE PLAGUES AND NATURE ❧

Exodus 7:5 – And the Egyptians shall know that I am the Lord, when I stretch out My hand over Egypt and bring out the Israelites from their midst.

Ibn Ezra explains that when God intervenes in the world, God is often concealed in natural phenomena.[442] God acting through nature in no way diminishes the Hand of God in these miracles, since God created and can intervene in nature.

For decades, archaeologists and other researchers have put forth theories about connections between events in nature and the plagues that occurred in Egypt. Based on this large body of research, pathologist Dr. Stephen Mortlock explains the plagues in light of natural systems.[443] For the (first) plague of blood, certain algae flourish in warm, sluggish water. Their algal blooms can color the water red. An algal bloom may have killed the fish that eat amphibian eggs, potentially increasing frog numbers. When the water of the Nile goes out of balance, the frogs go out of balance soon thereafter (second plague). They flee the water, move onto land, and become a pest to the Egyptian society. Frogs normally keep flies and other insects in check by eating their eggs, larvae, and flying adults (third plague). With the frogs and other amphibians dead, populations of midges, stable flies, and other insects would have greatly increased (fourth plague). Scientists have theorized that African horse sickness (spread by midges) may have killed the Egyptians' horses (fifth plague). Stable flies can infect animals and humans with *Staphylococcus aureus*, a bacterium that can cause boils (sixth plague).

The plagues may have occurred around the time of the volcanic eruption that destroyed the island of Santorini.[444] Massive eruptions can affect the atmosphere, weather, and resulting climate. The particulates in smoke from the Santorini volcano may have affected the weather and caused dramatic hailstorms (the seventh plague). After periods of significant precipitation, the numbers of locusts naturally increase. The hailstorms may have created the conditions that caused the desert locust to change from its solitary form to its swarming form (the eighth plague). The volcanic plume could have blocked out the sunlight for days (the ninth plague).

❧ GRATITUDE TO NATURE ❧

Exodus 7:17 – Thus says the Lord, "By this you shall know that I am the Lord." See, I [Moses] shall strike the water in the Nile with the rod that is in my hand, and it will be turned into blood.

Rabbi Yitzchak Breitowitz writes, "In addition to our gratitude to God, there is also a concept that we owe appreciation to the animals and inanimate natural resources. For example, the first plague was not carried out by Moses, but by Aaron. Why? Rashi says that since the Nile had taken care of Moses as a baby, he owed the Nile a debt of gratitude. As a result, it would be inappropriate for him to turn the Nile into blood. We have this concept of gratitude to that which takes care of us, even natural resources like rivers and rain."[445]

❧ WAKING UP IN TIME ❧

Exodus 7:18 – And the fish in the Nile will die. The Nile will stink so that the Egyptians will find it impossible to drink the water of the Nile.

Malbim explains that fish can live in cold water, but not in blood which is hot and foul.[446]

Today, the oceans have a number of "dead zones" where no sea life can live. These can occur naturally, but scientists are concerned about the zones created or worsened by human activity. There are many physical, chemical, and biological factors that combine to create dead zones, but nutrient pollution is the primary cause of zones created by humans. Excess nutrients – such as nitrogen from fertilizer – that get washed off the land, and wastewater piped into rivers and coastal water, can stimulate an overgrowth of algae, which then sinks and decomposes in the water. The decomposition process consumes oxygen from the water and depletes the supply available to healthy marine life.[447]

After the 1970s, dead zones became more widespread, almost doubling each decade since the 1960s. The largest dead zone in the world lies in the Arabian Sea, covering almost the entire 63,700-square-mile (102,500-square-kilometer) Gulf of Oman, which is the size of Florida. This dead zone's vastness was only measured in 2018.[448] The second largest sits in the Gulf of Mexico south of the United States, averaging almost 6,000 square miles (9,650 square kilometers) in size, about the size of New Jersey.[449] Climate change exacerbates dead zones by raising water temperatures; higher temperatures interfere with the water holding enough oxygen.

With the first plague, the water became a red zone and dead zone. With the tenth plague, Egyptian society became a dead zone. The plagues of the water, frogs, lice, and wild animals were nuisances, but they went away. If the Egyptians had listened to Moses and learned from God's signs, they wouldn't have had to suffer the rest of the plagues. The remaining plagues did not only become more severe in terms of magnitude, but they encroached more and more on Egyptian society and their lifestyle. Each subsequent plague brought more damage and devastation upon the human population of Egypt. The longer Pharaoh refused to humble himself to God's will, the more intense the impact became.[450]

Today's ecological crisis has striking parallels. Decades ago, scientists warned of the ecological impacts that people are currently experiencing. With each subsequent decade of inaction, the impacts increase.

❧ FROGS – EARTH'S EARLY WARNING SYSTEM ❧

Exodus 7:27 – If you refuse to let them go, then I will plague your whole country with frogs.

Of all the 15 million species on earth, why are frogs the first animals mentioned in the plagues?

Frogs are a key bioindicator species of ecosystem health.[451] In the case of some natural disasters, it is as if they "know" what's coming. One study found that frog behavior changes dramatically in the five days leading up to a major earthquake or tsunami.[452] In Hebrew, the word for frog – *tzfarde'a* – can also be read *tzipor-de'ah*, an insightful bird, according to Rebbe Nachman of Breslov.[453]

When it comes to ecosystem destruction, however, frogs do not seem able to respond fast enough to save their own species. In this light, the plague of frogs is particularly relevant today. Scientists estimate that more than 40 percent of the world's amphibian species are in decline – a decline significantly more severe than that of birds or mammal species.[454] Research also shows that amphibians are particularly sensitive to pollutants because of their highly permeable skins and the many stages of their life cycle. This maximizes their exposure to toxic pollutants both on land and in water, and from feeding on both plants and animals.[455]

Our silent extermination of entire amphibian species has implications both spiritual – degrading God's creation – and practical. Medical researchers are particularly interested in amphibians as sources of new medications. Australia's White's tree frog, for example, produces skin secretions with antibiotic and antiviral characteristics.[456]

The plague of water turning to blood symbolizes extreme pollution, as the water becomes undrinkable. Here, frogs play the role of the indicator species, warning humankind of worse things to come. After the plague of frogs, the natural world really goes out of balance – lice, locusts, lions, and other wild animals run rampant.

The plagues then culminate in the death of humans, demonstrating that human beings ultimately suffer when the natural world collapses. This occurs when human society continues to live stubbornly in an unjust, selfish, and short-sighted way. Frogs can provide lifesaving cures for human disease or be an indicator of oncoming doom.[457] It is up to us.

❧ FROGS, PESTS, AND SONG ❦

Exodus 8:2 – Aaron held out his arm over the waters of Egypt, and the frogs [literally "frog"] came up and covered the land of Egypt.

The rabbis ask why the frogs are referenced in the singular here while the plural "frogs" appears throughout the rest of the story. One answer the rabbis give is that initially one frog came out of the Nile and multiplied quickly when people started hitting it.[458]

This can instruct us on how we relate to "pests." Some pesticides have been shown to kill natural predators, like birds, and inadvertently create an outbreak of a different insect pest.[459] Other pesticides create resistant insect species, with more dangerous potential. Among mammal "pest" species, coyote population numbers often rise in response to humans hunting them – exactly the opposite of what is intended. One study found that with reduced adult coyote numbers, and thus more prey, the number of newborns per coyote mother could double.[460]

Perhaps we can learn from the rabbis' teaching about how to approach natural problems in a naturally effective way – not violently or coercively but with contemplation about the true source of the problem.

Another traditional explanation for the initial reference to a singular frog is that the first frog whistled, calling its friends to pester the Egyptian slave-masters.[461] All animals communicate, and frogs, in particular, can produce a lot of noise to communicate with each other over other sounds (like waterfalls). When King David finished his monumental work of Psalms, he was feeling confident. But the Midrash tells us that along came a frog and said, "Don't be full of yourself; for every sound I make, there are 3,000 deep parables that I am saying."[462] The rabbis teach that frog sounds mean, "Blessed is the name of God's glorious Kingdom forever and ever!"[463]

There is a hasidic story that after the Maggid of Mezeritch passed away, his students gathered to discuss their great teacher and his customs. They wanted to understand why the rebbe went to the pond early in the morning before prayers. One of the students recalled the Maggid explaining this practice as a way to learn the song of the frogs because it is so deep and complex.[464] When we extinguish even a single species, we lose the wisdom of 3,000 deep parables.

❧ SPECIES ON THE MOVE ❧

Exodus 8:7 – The frogs shall retreat from you and your courtiers and your people; they shall remain only in the Nile.

The issue was not only the frogs' numbers, but their migration to land after their natural habitat, the river, became polluted. Climate change today is leading to species moving into new habitats. This can lead to many infectious diseases that jump from an animal to a human, possibly including coronavirus.[465]

❧ PRAYING OUTDOORS ❧

Exodus 8:23 – We must go a distance of three days into the wilderness and sacrifice to the Lord our God as He may command us.

Moses insists to Pharaoh that the Israelites worship God deep in nature, and not in built-up Egypt. There is something special about praying in a natural environment, even if it's not a wilderness three days away but a park a few blocks away. In the words of Rebbe Nachman of Breslov, "How wonderful it would be if we were worthy of hearing the song of the grass; every blade of grass sings a pure song to God, expecting nothing in return. It is wonderful to hear its song and to worship God in its midst."[466]

❧ SOOT, SKY, AND SKIN ❧

Exodus 9:8 – Then the Lord said to Moses and Aaron, "Each of you take hand-fuls of soot from the kiln, and let Moses throw it toward the sky in the sight of Pharaoh."

Rabbi Samson Raphael Hirsch describes the kiln as "an oven in which substances such as limestone are completely mastered, calcined, and reduced."[467] And Rashi comments that the plague-borne "boils" were hot, perhaps burning. Moses and Aaron threw handfuls of furnace ash into the air, and hot boils erupted on the skin of Egyptians. The waste products from Egyptian industry catalyzed the plague on their skin.

In our times, pollutants such as lead in household water – as happened in Flint, Michigan – can cause skin afflictions among other very serious health problems. Also, the proliferation of unregulated chemicals used in cosmetics, paints, cleaning products, and more has caused workers and consumers to experience increasing levels of acute and lasting skin diseases. The US Centers for Disease Control and Prevention (CDC) estimate that more than 13 million US workers, spanning a variety of occupational industries and sectors, are potentially exposed to high doses of chemicals that can be absorbed through the skin.

❧ THE EARTH IS THE LORD'S ❧

by David Goldblatt, PhD[468]

Exodus 9:14 – For this time I will send all My plagues upon your person, and your courtiers, and your people, in order that you may know that there is none like Me in all the world.

Divine chastisement, brought in the form of affliction and suffering, can be an effective, if painful, instrument for individual and social learning. The ten plagues that God visits on the Egyptians and Pharaoh publicly demonstrate God's power to both Egypt and Israel.

In the warnings and reproofs accompanying the plagues, God and Moses use ten variations of the phrase "to know the Lord." After Pharaoh beseeches Moses to end the seventh plague of hail, Moses tells him it will stop once he (Moses) leaves the city and spreads out his hands to God.

Moses admonishes Pharaoh: "That you may know that the earth belongs to the Lord."[469] This phrase, expressing the dominion of God and the limits to human power and control over the earth, has relevance for and resonance with modern humans' place in the world and humanity's role in the current environmental predicament.

The plague of hail was much harsher than the ones preceding it, and God's forewarning was correspondingly the longest and most severe until then. This warning, however, expressed a strong measure of Divine compassion for the Egyptians. God urges them to bring in their servants and animals from the field to spare them from destruction. The God-fearing among the Egyptians heed and live, while the heedless perish.

It was this Divine compassion that moved Pharaoh to repent, albeit temporarily, for the first time following a plague, according to Chizkuni.[470] Pharaoh summons Moses and declares, "This time I have sinned; the Lord is the Righteous One; and I and my people are the villains."[471] Here Moses describes how he will leave the city and spread out his hands to heaven, upon which God will stop the hail "that you may know that the earth belongs to the Lord." The instant cessation of the unprecedented, torrential hail and thunder displays the supernatural, miraculous quality of God's control over meteorological phenomena.[472]

The Da'at Mikra commentary explains: "'That you may know': Your request will be granted, and the plague removed, not because you can be trusted to fulfill your promise to let the people go, but rather so that it will be proved to you and you will know that the earth is under God's control, and He can do what He wants with it – at His word it hails, and at His word it ceases."[473]

The plagues were expressions of God's power over the earth. They were intended as a reproof to the arrogant Pharaoh and a demonstration to the Egyptians of the limits to his power and the fallacy of their trust in him. Modern humans have set themselves as the absolute master of the biophysical world. In pursuit of technological mastery and material prosperity, many in modern society have lost the sense of a greater transcendent power and of a meaning and purpose beyond the world they know. This has had drastic moral and environmental ramifications. To paraphrase author Ze'ev Jabotinsky, if people make a slave of the natural world, they will degenerate, first morally, and in the end, materially.[474]

Now, modern-day "unnatural plagues" are occurring with greatly increasing frequency around the world: land degradation, including deforestation and soil erosion; water stress, leading to pollution and depletion of freshwater and decimation of ocean fish stocks; stress on animal and plant life, resulting in extinctions and the spread of invasive species; and atmospheric pollution, including local and regional air pollution, ozone layer depletion, and greenhouse gases.[475]

God's display of power and mercy during the plague of hail was enough to bring about a temporary change of heart in Pharaoh. But his sins and stubbornness had already set him and his nation on the road to ruin. Together, let us work and pray to heed the mounting environmental warning signs and change course in time to avoid consigning ourselves to the same fate.

♣ ARROGANCE AND HUMILITY ♣

Exodus 9:17 – Yet you continue to tread upon My people, and do not let them go!

Rashi translates "tread" as "trample underfoot."[476] Pharaoh was trampling on the Israelites and was the archetype of arrogance. He contrasts with Moses, whom the Torah describes as "a very humble man, more so than any other man on earth."[477] According to the Midrash, Pharaoh is a descendant of Nimrod, who, according to rabbinic tradition, threw Abraham into a furnace.[478] Pharaoh epitomizes the universal dominance of the egotistical conqueror, Rabbi Daniel Kohn explains.[479]

In our times, industry has had unparalleled success in extracting resources from the earth, and refuses to let go of its controlling position. The first oil well in history drilled 32 feet underground, in 1859.[480] As oil close to the surface has been mostly extracted in the past 150 years, companies now drill 1,000 times deeper. BP's Deepwater Horizon drilling rig went down 5,100 feet (1,550 meters) of water, and then drilled an additional 18,360 feet (5,600 meters) in land under the water, which shows what happens when humans lose control of technology. The BP oil spill released about five million barrels of oil, and caused widespread damage to wildlife, people, and coastal ecosystems.[481] The world's deepest oil well, in Russia, reaches 40,000 feet (12,200 meters) underground.[482] In our hubris, we are trampling the earth underfoot, as evidenced by oil spills that take months to control and years to fully stop. A more humble approach would limit the depths of offshore oil drilling, and leave most of offshore oil in the ground.

❧ ADMITTING GUILT BEFORE IT'S TOO LATE ❧

Exodus 9:27 – Thereupon Pharaoh sent for Moses and Aaron and said to them, "I stand guilty this time. The Lord is in the right, and I and my people are in the wrong."

God had warned the Egyptian people: "Order your livestock and everything you have in the open brought under shelter; every man and beast that is found outside, not having been brought indoors, shall perish when the hail comes down upon them!"[483] Malbim explains that the deaths of Egyptians and their animals in the plague of hail were avoidable. God was right, and Pharaoh and his people were wrong, leading to avoidable casualties.[484]

This is about the closest that Pharaoh gets to admitting fault during the plagues. He realizes, belatedly, that he could have prevented some of the damage. Humankind seems capable of admitting fault in hindsight, but often it's too late. By the time Pharaoh comes to fear God, his land and empire are destroyed.

The contemporary moral philosopher Lawrence Torcello, discussing the world's current lack of action on climate change, writes: "The principled condemnation of large-scale atrocity is, too often, a luxury of hindsight…There can be no greater crime against humanity than the foreseeable, and methodical, destruction of conditions that make human life possible. Hindsight isn't necessary."[485]

❧ NATURE AND CIVILIZATION ❧

Exodus 9:29 – Moses said to him, "As I go out of the city, I shall spread out my hands to the Lord; the thunder will cease and the hail will fall no more, so that you may know that the earth is the Lord's."

Why did Moses need to leave the city in order to pray to God? According to Rebbe Nachman of Breslov, prayer flows best in nature and not in a city. In his story "The Master of Prayer," Rebbe Nachman describes how "the Master of Prayer . . . lived away from civilization."[486] As Rabbi Natan Greenberg describes, for Rebbe Nachman, "away from civilization or human settlement" means in the forest, outside the parameters of society. The description of the Master of Prayer "living" implies a degree of stability, while being "outside of civilization" implies living in a state of nature – unstable, wild. Many Westerners think of the city as civilized and nature as wild and savage. Rebbe Nachman teaches through this story how that characterization is upside down. From a spiritual perspective, the city is more barren and nature is the place where one can pray and find God. The Hebrew word, *yishuv*, settlement, implies rigidness. The level of civilization in a human society is a function of its closeness to God, not determined by wealth or technological achievement.

❧ CROP DIVERSITY ❧

Exodus 9:31–32 – Now the flax and barley were ruined, for the barley was in the ear and the flax was in bud; but the plain wheat and the hulled wheat were not hurt, for they ripen late.

The diversity of crops in Egypt insulated the impact of the plague of hail. Diversifying crops increases resilience. Ecologist Brenda Lin writes, "Crop diversification can improve resilience in a variety of ways: by engendering a greater ability to suppress pest outbreaks and dampen pathogen (disease) transmission, which may worsen under future climate scenarios, as well as by buffering crop production from the effects of greater climate variability and extreme events." Today, crop diversity is on the decline globally. According to a 2019 University of Toronto study led by ecologist Adam Martin, "We're seeing large monocultures of crops that are commercially valuable being grown in greater numbers around the world." Soybeans, wheat, rice, and corn make up about 50 percent of crops grown on the world's entire agricultural lands.[487]

Suggested Action Items

1. Reduce the use of toxic household chemicals by replacing them with ecological alternatives.
2. Communal: Encourage your government representatives to support stronger national environmental legislation and international treaties, including trade agreements that prioritize environmental considerations.
3. Investment: Invest in funds that screen for corporate environmental performance or sensitivity; invest in and encourage government investments in developing renewable energy technologies.
4. Communal: Help your community organize a beach, stream, or forest clean-up. While there, learn about the plagues of the Nile and then picnic on vegetarian dishes.

Torah portion of Bo

❧ POVERTY AND POLLUTION ❧

Exodus 10:3 – So Moses and Aaron went to Pharaoh and said to him, "Thus says the Lord, the God of the Hebrews, 'How long will you refuse to humble yourself before Me? Let My people go that they may worship Me.'"

Rashi explains: "The word *le'anot*, to humble, is derived from the word *'ani*, poor. You have refused to be humble and meek [poor] before Me."[488] The implication of this statement is that if Pharaoh were humble, he would properly feel the effects of the plagues, and act differently.

Currently, poor people are more impacted by environmental degradation. According to a study published in the *American Journal of Public Health*, those living in poverty had a 35 percent higher air pollution exposure than the overall population.[489] Related diseases such as asthma have higher prevalence in poorer areas, especially where people live near factories spewing fumes.

❧ LOCUST SWARMS THEN AND NOW ❧

Exodus 10:4–5 – For if you refuse to let My people go, tomorrow I will bring locusts on your territory. They shall cover the surface of the land, so that no one will be able to see the land. They shall devour the surviving remnant that was left to you after the hail; and they shall eat away all your trees that grow in the field.

The desert locust is usually a solitary creature. However, it can switch to social swarming behavior when its numbers increase, and it then depletes local food resources. This often starts with a heavy rain or hailstorm, which produces a new flush of vegetation in the desert. With new food, the locust population booms. The booming locusts consume the vegetation and crowd together on what little food remains. Under such crowded conditions, chemical signals in their feces trigger a serotonin release in their brains, prompting gregariousness and swarming.[490]

In 2020, the largest locust swarms in more than 50 years spread from Kenya to Iran and impacted tens of millions of subsistence farmers. An article in *Nature* noted how one swarm in Kenya had tens of billions of locusts and was three times the size of New York City.[491] Journalist Bob Berwyn explains the role of climate change: "Warm weather and heavy rains at the end of 2019 set up a perfect storm of breeding conditions for the destructive bugs . . . Changes in plant growth caused by higher carbon dioxide levels, as well as heatwaves and tropical cyclones with intense rains, can lead to more prolific and unpredictable locust swarming."[492]

❧ TAKING GOOD ADVICE ❧

Exodus 10:7 – Pharaoh's courtiers said to him, "How long shall this one be a snare to us? Let the men go to worship the Lord their God! Are you not yet aware that Egypt is lost?"

The plagues occurred because of Pharaoh's selfish refusal to give up a population of cheap Israelite labor. For Pharaoh to agree with his advisers and release the Israelites from bondage would require restructuring the economy. Striking parallels exist to our situation today with regard to climate change, with Pharaoh's courtiers replaced by today's scientific advisers. Rabbi Arthur Waskow and Rabbi Phyllis Berman teach that "in 2002, the United States submitted a report to the United

Nations on the expected impact of global warming. The report was written by the president's own advisers. It stated that the United States will be substantially changed in the next few decades – with the likely disruption of snow-fed water supplies, more stifling heat waves, and the permanent disappearance of high mountain meadows and coastal marshes.[493] The report concluded that 'some of the goods and services lost through the disappearance of natural ecosystems would be costly or impossible to replace.'"[494]

The American government ignored the report and made no commitments to change, in part because of the outsized political influence of the fossil-fuel industry. Rabbis Berman and Waskow note how "this kind of response has not been limited to one country, nor has it been ended by one election. The dangers of top-down, unaccountable, irresponsible power transcend the borders and the centuries."[495] While ecological science is well established, governments in many of the world's major countries – including the US, Australia, and Brazil – implement policies that accelerate ecological degradation. What can bridge the disconnect between ecological science and government policy?

❧ TAKING NOTICE IN OUR TIME ❧

by Rabbi Shaul David Judelman[496]

Exodus 12:2 – This month shall mark for you the beginning of the months; it shall be the first of the months of the year for you.

The Kabbalah (mystic tradition) describes reality using three prime components: place, time, and soul. These are the basic dimensions in which we exist and interact with our world. Environmental ideas are most often communicated through the dimension of place, as the physical world has inherent ecological import. In the middle of the Exodus story, however, our attention turns to time: "This month will be to you the head of the months." An exploration of this unique commandment can reveal profound insights into the Torah's concept of time and unlock the secret of how the realm of time is also of deep environmental significance.

The commandment to mark the Hebrew month of Nisan is the very first commandment given to the Israelites as a people. While still in Egypt, the people are commanded to note the month so that they may prepare to observe the first Passover in springtime, the season of the Exodus. What is so crucial about the awareness of the new month that it holds the significance of being the Torah's first national commandment?

Far from being purely linear, the Torah calendar reflects the cyclical nature of the year with a precise system of holidays and observances connected to each moment and season. The beginning of the year, the month of Nisan, is the linchpin of that connection. The Torah calls Passover, "the spring holiday," and that is the reason that an extra month is added in a Jewish leap year, in order to ensure that Passover always occurs in the spring.

This is a dramatic statement of environmental consequence. The sages could have declared a purely astronomical, lunar-based calendar. But based on the Torah's prescription, they took steps to ensure that the calendar also reflects the cycles of nature. This demonstrates the Torah's deep awareness of the Divine character of nature's cycle.

The confluence of redemption and springtime is no coincidence. Everyone is aware of the tremendous energy of renewal that occurs in the springtime. The rebirth of flowers and greenery, the new life in the fields – these are symbols of our redemption.

The Hebrew word we receive with the commandment of time is *chodesh*, meaning month, or more literally, newness. It is extremely instructive that the Hebrew word for this basic time unit implies renewal and revelation, as opposed to a continuation of the status quo. Even the word for year, *shana*, is connected to the word for change, *shinui*.

The times that the Sabbath enters and leaves are published online and in print, yet it is not uncommon today for people to look up at the sky to count the three stars that mark the end of Shabbat, rather than to consult their watch. The Torah's attention to the natural cycles still brings people outdoors to deepen their connection with God.

❧ APPRECIATING NATURE'S BEAUTY ❧

Exodus 12:2 – This month shall mark for you the beginning of the months; it shall be the first of the months of the year for you.

The month begins with the appearance of a new moon, according to Jewish tradition. The moon's monthly cycle gives us the ability to mark holidays, which are fixed based on the moon's cycle.

Numerous verses in Psalms mention the moon and other parts of nature praising God. For example: "Praise Him, sun and moon, praise Him, all bright stars. Praise Him, the most exalted of the heavens and the waters that are above the heavens. Let them praise the name of God, for He commanded and they were created . . . Praise God from the earth, sea giants and all watery depths. Fire and hail, snow and vapor, stormy wind fulfilling His word. Mountains and hills, fruitful trees and cedars. Beasts and cattle, crawling things and winged fowl."[497]

Psalms recall the beauty and consistency of nature and how much we rely upon it and its Creator. Because the rhythms of nature are so constant, we may forget how special it is that the sun rises each day, that the moon rotates monthly around the globe, that waters continue to flow in the streams, and that intricate ecosystems thrive with numerous creatures in our forests and preserves. We are part of nature and our survival depends on the water we drink, the sun to warm the earth, the rain for our crops, the animals to pollinate flowers and fruits, and so much more that we often forget.

❧ CHANGE FOR A WEEK ❧

Exodus 12:15 – Seven days you shall eat unleavened bread; on the very first day you shall remove leaven from your houses, for whoever eats leavened bread from the first day to the seventh day, that person shall be cut off from Israel.

Rabbi Alexandri in the Talmud recites the following prayer on clearing out his leavened produce for Passover: "God of all worlds, it is known and revealed before You that we wish to do Your will. But what prevents us? The yeast in dough!"[498] The commentators understand this to mean that just as yeast puffs up dough to make bread, so human "puffery" or arrogance drives us away from doing the will of God.

What prevents us from living a healthy, sustainable lifestyle? The facts are generally well known – certain foods are healthier than others, some means of transport and other activities are more sustainable than others. But we humans are arrogant. How often do we choose to live "our own way," convincing ourselves that we know better than the accumulated knowledge of thousands of years of sages and the current research of thousands of scientists?

The Torah commands that before Passover, one's home is cleaned of leavened products, with the message that to be truly "religious" one has to adopt a level of modesty, to admit "that I don't know it all." So why just a week? Why not keep a leaven-free home all year round? Rabbi Yishmael teaches, "Everything that is learned by an exception to the rule comes to teach us about the rule itself."[499] This is an important insight into human nature. In order to best absorb a moral message, a short burst of change of behavior (maybe for just a week) can have the strongest impact. Just as a week of eating unleavened breads can make us refocus our over-inflated egos, a week of eating vegetarian food could help us to think more about the pain of caged animals during the year, and a week of walking or cycling to work could help us to think more about global overheating (while making us fitter).

❧ THE ISSUE OF OUR GENERATION ❧

Exodus 12:37 – The Israelites journeyed from Raamses to Succoth, about six hundred thousand men on foot, aside from children.

The Sefat Emet commentary explains that every generation has a "coming out of Egypt" regarding a key issue for that generation.[500] The "issue" of our generation is best understood when we realize that the average person in North America, Western Europe, Japan, and Australia consumes 32 times the amount of resources (such as fossil fuels) and creates 32 times more waste than the average person in some developing countries, as of 2008.[501] So even if the world population were to peak at 12 billion, the aspiration of humanity to achieve "first world" status in consumption levels would increase world consumption by a factor of 32, which would require multiple planets to support this.

There are those who believe that the world could sustain twice its current level of consumption, but no one claims that it could sustain a level of 32 times. And so our generation's "issue" or challenge is how to wean ourselves off a consumption-heavy lifestyle that is destroying our planet – just as ancient Egypt had to wean itself off the exploitation of its slaves.

Suggested Action Items

1. Pray with the sunrise. The sunrise is a constant source of inspiration to the day it brings. The tradition of praying at sunrise is a tried and tested way of increasing our awareness and connection to each day.

2. Set a regular time to be outdoors. This could be a weekend afternoon walk or hike, a family picnic, or an after-work/school stroll that will help you notice the changing seasons.

3. Spend a week eating only vegetarian food, or only cycling or walking to work.

4. Eat seasonally. Buy local produce to become aware of what foods are available in each season. Many point to health benefits of eating foods that become naturally available in each season, possibly supplying even more nutrients for our bodies at that time.

5. Visit a natural history museum to learn about insects and other fascinating wildlife!

Torah portion of Beshalach

❧ SPLITTING THE SEA AND STORM SURGE ❧

Exodus 14:21 – Then Moses held out his arm over the sea and the Lord drove back the sea with a strong east wind all that night and turned the sea into dry ground. The waters were split.

Nachmanides explains that God made the sea parting appear less like a miracle and more like a "natural occurrence" by using the wind, all to entice the Egyptians into entering the sea.

A recent computer-modeling study by researchers at the US National Center for Atmospheric Research and the University of Colorado at Boulder shows how the movement of wind as described in the book of Exodus could have parted the waters. The computer simulations show that a strong east wind, blowing overnight, could have pushed water back at a bend where an ancient river is believed to have merged with a coastal lagoon along the Mediterranean Sea. With the water pushed back into both waterways, a land bridge would have opened at the bend, enabling people to walk across exposed mud flats to safety. As soon as the wind died down, the waters would have rushed back in. They found that a wind of 63 miles an hour (101 kilometers an hour), lasting for 12 hours, would have pushed back waters estimated to be six feet (1.8 meters) deep. The water would be pushed back into both the lake and the channel of the river, creating barriers of water on both sides of newly exposed mudflats.[502]

The researchers were investigating the extent to which Pacific Ocean typhoons can drive storm surges, the sudden increase in water levels that cause severe destruction on land. Increasingly strong typhoons are partly the result of human-caused climate change, and the largest loss of life associated with tropical cyclones is caused by storm surge.[503]

❧ WONDERS OF CREATION ❧

Exodus 14:31 – And when Israel saw the wondrous power which the Lord had wielded against the Egyptians, the people feared the Lord; they had faith in the Lord and His servant Moses.

The Children of Israel found faith in witnessing the great miracle of the splitting of the sea. Today many rabbis state that we no longer need miracles to find faith, we just need to learn to see God in the wonders of nature.

Rabbi Shlomo Wolbe writes, in a letter to his grandson, "You ask in which book to find faith? Actually every tree you see is a book on faith! Do trees sprout of their own accord? Isn't every tree a creation! And so too each flower, not to mention each star, the sun and the moon! And the Chafetz Chayim writes that it is a commandment to meditate on creation. As the prophet Isaiah says, 'Lift high your eyes and see: Who created these?'[504] Since it is a daily commandment, one should fulfill it before eating in the morning – just stand for some minutes and admire creation! How much faith can one achieve just from that!"[505]

❧ APPRECIATING WATER ❧

by Rabbi Yonatan Neril and Evonne Marzouk[506]

Exodus 15:22 – Then Moses caused Israel to set out from the Sea of Reeds. They went on into the wilderness of Shur; they traveled three days in the wilderness and found no water.

Even before the Israelites entered the Land of Israel, water was central to their collective experience. In the desert, uncertainty about water resources inspired numerous complaints and lessons for the wandering Jews. The Talmud teaches that in the spiritual merit of Miriam's song, a well appeared in the desert and accompanied the Israelites wherever they went. God gave this essential resource, without which one cannot live for more than a few days, in the water-scarce desert. But the long-term security of the resource was never certain. The Biblical experiences with water in the desert can be understood as a spiritual training to cultivate appreciation for God's goodness. Through the process of taking water for granted, losing it, and then receiving it directly from God, the desert wanderers certainly appreciated water and the One who provided it. Thus, at the end of the Israelites' desert experience, they sang an exultant song about their appreciation of water to God.

Water scarcity continued after the Israelites entered Israel with Joshua and formed an agrarian society whose bounty or famine was regulated by rain. The Talmud teaches that God directly waters the Land of Israel while a messenger waters the rest of the world.[507] Israel is a semi-arid country with no major rivers. It receives modest rainfall, averaging less than four inches (100 millimeters) per year in the extreme south to 44 inches (1,128 millimeters) a year in the north.[508] (By comparison, New York City averages between 28 inches [710 millimeters] and 45 inches [1140 millimeters] of precipitation per year.[509]) Why is the one land in the world that God waters directly a land that receives far less water than many others? Since water is a sign of blessing, would not the Pacific Northwest or the rainforests of Brazil or Indonesia be more appropriate candidates for the Promised Land?

Water insecurity is by Divine design, to remind us that God is the ultimate Provider of all our needs. The Land of Israel contrasts with the land on both sides of the Nile, Euphrates, and Tigris rivers. In those river valleys, farmers can irrigate their crops year-round from a reliable water source. Yet until the twentieth century, most agriculture in Israel was rain-fed and not irrigated. The seven species that the Torah associates with the Land of Israel (grapes, olives, dates, pomegranates, figs, wheat, and barley) are all species that do not require irrigation.[510] The farmers who planted, tended, and harvested these crops depended on the winter rains to survive. In their acute need for rain each year, the Israelites depended on the God who provided it, a spiritual reality that was not present in the more water-abundant river valleys of nearby civilizations.

Today, Israel is working hard to address a recent water crisis spurred by a long-term drought induced by climate change. Reuse of wastewater for irrigation is a key method for increasing the supply of available water.[511] Desalination of Mediterranean seawater is becoming an increasing source of freshwater, yet requires a significant amount of energy to produce the water – energy currently supplied by burning fossil fuels. The world faces a growing water crisis particularly affecting the people of Africa, Southern Asia, and China. Indeed, insufficient safe drinking water is a leading cause of death in the world. Some 884 million people do not have access to safe drinking water sources.[512] A 2018 UN-Water report notes that "over two billion people live in countries experiencing high water stress."[513] The Torah's wisdom on water awareness is more relevant now than ever.

❧ MAKING BITTER WATERS SWEET ❧

Exodus 15:25 – God showed him [Moses] a piece of wood; he threw it into the water and the water became sweet. There He made for them a fixed rule, and there He put them to the test.

The Midrash shares the views of several rabbis about what type of wood was used to sweeten the water: "Rabbi Yehoshua says: a willow tree. Rabbi Eliezer HaModai says: an olive tree, there being no tree more bitter than an olive tree. Rabbi Yehoshua bar Karcha says: an ivy. Rabbi Nathan says: a cedar. Others say: He uprooted a fig and he uprooted a pomegranate."[514]

There are several ways to understand this teaching. At one level, the Midrash is a sort of Torah naturopathy, using items from nature to heal. God showed Moses the exact tree species that would sweeten bitter water. God created natural substances with healing properties that people with sufficient knowledge can use to promote healing. Maimonides, a rabbi and physician, expands upon this in his writings. In this, we see Divine-inspired wisdom of how to use things in nature for good.

Rabbi Eliezer HaModai says that God showed Moses the olive tree, since it has the most bitter wood. How do two bitter things make one sweet thing? This relates to homeopathy, an alternative medicine based on the view that "like cures like." While seemingly illogical, the bitter wood in the bitter water made the water sweet. Rabbi Shimon ben Gamliel says this is God's approach: "God heals bitter with bitter."

It may also be possible to explain the verse at a physical level. The water may have been alkaline, which made it bitter. If the wood were acidic, it would equalize the water's pH balance. On another level, this was a pure miracle that God performed for the Jewish people to provide them with fresh water in the desert. "The Holy One's way is to sweeten the bitter with bitter," according to Nachmanides.[515]

Even though in some places, human impact has made the waters too bitter to drink, the sweetening of the waters reminds us of the dictum of Rebbe Nachman of Breslov: "If you believe that you can destroy, then believe that you can repair."[516]

Rabbi Shmuel Simenowitz writes:

The power that major industries and corporations have used to cause environmental destruction can be harnessed to promote a cleaner, healthier future. Since 2018, Barron's has ranked America's 100 most sustainable companies.[517] The energy and tools needed for change are within our reach.

A distraught father, whose son was beginning to stray from the path of his forefathers, once brought his son to the Alter Rebbe, Shneur Zalman of Liadi. The Alter Rebbe asked the boy what he enjoyed doing. The boy responded that he liked riding horses. "And what qualities do you look for in a horse?" Rabbi Shneur Zalman asked him. "Speed," the boy replied. "And what if you are on a fast horse which takes a wrong turn in the road?" the sage continued. "You can get very lost in a hurry," was the boy's response. "And what if you turn the horse around?" the elderly sage pressed on. "You can get back just as fast." A slight smile crept across Rabbi Shneur Zalman's face as the boy nodded his head, indicating that he understood the Alter Rebbe's message.[518]

If we take the lesson of the bitter waters of Marah to heart, we can turn around our horses, currently galloping out of control toward oblivion. With the will to "return" on a path of responsible and sustainable stewardship, using the Tree of Life, the Torah, as our template, perhaps we, too, can come back just as fast, and be carried by the sweet waters of our ancestors to a cleaner future.[519]

❧ PALM TREES AND SOLAR ENERGY ❧

Exodus 15:27 – And they came to Elim, where there were twelve springs of water and seventy palm trees; and they encamped there beside the water.

Tamar, the Hebrew word for date palm, has the same *gematria,* or kabbalistic numbering, as *shemesh,* the Hebrew word for sun: 640.[520] The tops of some date trees actually look like a green sun with leaves radiating outward from a circular trunk. The date is one of the sweetest fruits with 60 to 80 percent sugar content by weight, which means that it is highly efficient at converting abundant desert sunlight into energy.[521] Modern solar panels mimic this photosynthesis by creating energy from sunlight.

Recent research into solar power explains how photosynthesis may contain the secret to sustainable power for future generations. According to a recent study, "Solar energy has great potential as a clean, cheap, renewable and sustainable energy source, but it must be captured and transformed into useful forms of energy similar to plants. An especially attractive approach is to store solar energy in the form of chemical bonds as performed in natural photosynthesis. Therefore, there has been a challenge in the last few decades to construct ... artificial photosynthetic systems, which are able to efficiently capture and convert solar energy and store it in the form of chemical bonds."[522]

In 1981, one of the leading rabbis in America, the Lubavitcher Rebbe, said about the US, "Very soon, the entire country should switch, first of all, to energy that can be generated from the sun's rays in the south [of the US], which should be supplied to the entire country… In fact, this can be practically implemented in such a manner as to provide more than enough, so that there is extra energy that can be supplied to other countries as well."[523]

❧ EATING FLESH ❧

Exodus 16:12 – I have heard the grumbling of the Israelites. Speak to them and say: "By evening you shall eat flesh, and in the morning you shall have your fill of bread; and you shall know that I the Lord am your God."

In recent times, factory farming has fed humankind's seemingly insatiable desire for meat. The act of kosher animal slaughter is a commandment and therefore has a blessing that precedes it. Yet, the vast majority of Jews will never say this blessing or fulfill this commandment themselves. Instead, throughout their lives, they rely on others who do so on their behalf. Each ritual slaughterer slaughters on behalf of thousands of people, which makes fulfilling the commandment of ritual slaughter with proper intent all the more difficult. Were the commandments intended to be heaped on the shoulders of one person because of consumer desires and mass production? By outsourcing this spiritual practice to a slaughterer, not only are we forgoing the opportunity to do it ourselves, but we are also disconnecting from the source of our food and the intentions behind the verse. If each person took responsibility for directly slaughtering the animals they consume, many might decide to forgo eating meat altogether.

Many rabbis through the ages have questioned and critiqued meat eating. This includes Rabbi Joseph Albo, Akeidat Yitzchak (Rabbi Isaac ben Moses Arama), and Kli Yakar. Kli Yakar writes, "It is far more appropriate for people not to eat meat." In our times, hundreds of contemporary rabbis have taken on a vegan or vegetarian lifestyle.[524]

Rabbinic laws permit causing pain to animals for human needs, like striking an ox to plow a field or a horse to move a wagon. But the suffering of factory-farmed animals is radically different from the context in which the rabbinic laws were made. In fact, a number of rabbis have suggested that even "kosher milk" could be technically unkosher. If 2 percent or more of the dairy cows in a herd have suffered life-threatening wounds from their cramped conditions, that would render them *"treif,"* or not kosher.[525]

♣ MANNA AND PORTION SIZE ♣

Exodus 16:18 – But when they measured it by the omer, he who had gathered much had no excess, and he who had gathered little had no deficiency: they had gathered as much as they needed to eat.

The Ha'amek Davar commentary explains that each person received the exact amount of manna they needed, with the measure of an *omer* being the average portion size.[526] Any excess "became infested with maggots and stank." Wasting food is wrong. We can learn from this the importance of serving suitable portion sizes at mealtimes.

Over 30 years, the typical size of American desserts increased by 70 percent, their calorie content by 79 percent,[527] and adult obesity rates by 200 percent.[528] On average, Americans waste a pound (450 grams) of food per person per day. The volume of discarded food is equivalent to the yearly use of 30 million acres (12 million hectares) of land, 780 million pounds (353 million kilograms) of pesticides, and 4.2 trillion gallons (16 trillion liters) of irrigated water.[529]

♣ MANNA AND FOOD SECURITY ♣

Exodus 16:19 – And Moses said to them, "Let no one leave any of it over until morning."

The rabbis convey a deep teaching about manna and dependence on God: "The students of Rabbi Shimon bar Yochai asked him, 'Why did the manna not descend to the Israelites once in a year?' He said to them, 'I will tell you a parable. What is this like? It is like a king who has one son. When he gave him his allowance once a year, his son would only come home once a year. So he gave him his allowance daily and his son had to greet him every day. So it is with Israel: A person with four or five children would worry and say, "Perhaps the manna will not descend tomorrow, and everyone will die of hunger." And so everyone would direct their hearts to their Father in Heaven.'"[530]

The Talmud is describing the phenomenon of food insecurity that has plagued humankind since creation. However, while food insecurity can create a greater dependence on God, food insecurity in the West today is considered a major cause of overeating. Uncertainty of food availability leads people (especially youth) to eat more than they need when it is available and is considered one among many factors leading to obesity and poor health.[531]

In discussing manna, the Torah stresses the importance of each family gathering only as much as they needed, which would have protected them from the risks of overeating while still ensuring a daily moment of gratitude to God.

❧ MANNA AND FOOD WASTE ❧

Exodus 16:21 – So they gathered it every morning, each as much as he needed to eat; for when the sun grew hot, it would melt.

One of the greatest causes of food waste is a failure in logistics, specifically in transporting the food from where it has been grown to where it is processed or eaten. At least 5 percent of food in India, for example, spoils on its way to the consumer, and far more if there is a significant delay (traffic or a train stoppage).[532] More specifically, ten million tons of grain spoil in storage in India each year, enough to feed 140 million people for one month.[533]

High food variety is one of the main causes of spoiling in the supply chain, while less variety leads to simpler stock management.[534] Perhaps this is also an environmental lesson to be learned from manna – people who are satisfied with a smaller range of foods do not need so much food transported from elsewhere. In contemporary society, demand for imported foods of great variety drives the transport of such foods, often across thousands of miles in energy-intensive refrigerated containers. These foods have high carbon footprints and higher rates of spoilage. Locally sourced, seasonal produce is a more sustainable solution.

In a related vein, Rashi comments, "The manna would melt into streams and the deer and rams would feed on it."[535] That is, the manna that the people did not eat was eaten by other mammals. It did not go to waste but was passed down the food chain. From this we might learn to compost food waste instead of throwing it in the garbage. The soil that emerges from compost enables us to fertilize our gardens to grow more crops and other plants.

❧ FEEDING THE BIRDS ❧

Exodus 16:26 – Six days you shall gather it; on the seventh day, the Sabbath, there will be none.

Rabbi David Golinkin relates a hasidic teaching of Rabbi Avraham Eliezer Hirshowitz: "Datan and Aviram went out on Friday night outside the camp and spread some manna, in order to make Moses a liar, since he said there would be no manna on Shabbat. They then said to the people: go out and see that there is manna in the fields! Therefore, some people went out to gather, but found nothing because the birds had eaten the manna which Datan and Aviram had strewn about."[536] There is a Jewish custom to feed birds outside one's home during the one Sabbath of the year when the story of the manna is read in synagogue. Rabbi Golinkin explains that this custom is based on the above teaching about the birds eating the manna. However, many rabbis state that the food must be left out before Shabbat, as there is a general prohibition of feeding non-domesticated animals on Shabbat itself.

This rabbinic prohibition of feeding wild birds on Shabbat can be puzzling. After all, shouldn't we feel sympathy for birds, especially in the cold winter when their natural food is scarce? However, recent research suggests that feeding wild birds can actually be to the detriment of native species. Bird feeding appears to favor introduced species over the native species and therefore swings the balance against native birds.[537] So while feeding the birds (before) Shabbat Shira is a nice custom and shows our appreciation of avian life, it appears that the custom to *not* feed wild birds every other Shabbat is also founded in deep ecological wisdom. It is also a sobering fact that over 20 billion chickens live in captivity and depend on humans to feed them.[538] In Europe, the population of domesticated chickens is greater than the combined population of the 144 most numerous wild bird species.[539] Remembering the birds eating manna can give us an opportunity to consider the fate of captive birds.

❧ RAW VS. ULTRA-PROCESSED FOODS ❧

Exodus 16:31 – The house of Israel named it manna; it was like coriander seed, white, and it tasted like wafers in honey.

Malbim comments that the Israelites "mistakenly thought it was only edible if prepared which gave it its name 'manna' and Moses informed them that it does not need preparation as there is no waste."[540] The word "manna" is also related to the Hebrew word for portion, implying that it was a portion of food.[541] While the Torah says about the manna that "they cooked it," Chizkuni explains, "that was the evil ones who cooked it," implying that the rest of the people did not cook it, but ate it raw and unprocessed.[542] Manna, the quintessential God-given food, was raw, fresh, vital, and came in limited, moderate portions. This can teach us to seek out similar types of foods.

Raw fruits and vegetables contain enzymes that reduce heart disease and provide multiple health benefits.[543] Professor T.H. Chan of the Harvard School of Public Health notes how the NOVA classification system distinguishes four categories of foods, from unprocessed to ultra-processed. "Depending on the degree of processing, many nutrients can be destroyed or removed…An ultra-processed food that contains an unevenly high ratio of calories to nutrients may be considered unhealthy. For example, research supports an association between a high intake of sugar-sweetened beverages and an increased risk of obesity, diabetes, and heart disease."[544]

❧ CAMPING AND FAMILY STRENGTH ❧

Exodus 17:1 – From the wilderness of Sin the whole Israelite community continued by stages as the Lord would command. They encamped at Rephidim, and there was no water for the people to drink.

Maimonides writes, "It was the wisdom of God to cause them to wander in the wilderness until they learned heroism – as it is known that camping in the desert and limiting the pampering of the body by bathing, and the like, generates strength of character, while the opposite yields a spirit of soft-heartedness – and it thereby generates people who will not be inferior or slaves."[545]

According to research on the impact of family camping holidays on youth:

> There is considerable evidence that family outdoor recreation helps in developing family strength and relationships. Outdoor programs often incorporate leisure activities that not only develop skills and require physical movement beneficial to health, but also teach perseverance, teamwork, and cooperation among family members. Further, outdoor recreation is important for healthy growth of youth. Most outdoor leisure activities take place in a variety of natural settings that are quite distinct from the constructed environment of the schoolyard or home. Outdoor recreation programs contain inherent challenges and offer opportunities for overwhelming mastery experiences that produce feelings of efficacy and have positive effects on family functioning. In addition, the feeling of collective efficacy through outdoor recreation can be generalized to other domains of family functioning, such as the ability to resolve conflict.[546]

This is the power of exposing ourselves and our families to nature!

Suggested Action Items

1. Use recycled paper products where possible – paper and paperboard products constitute the largest portion of municipal solid waste. Keep in mind that the greatest energy expenditure in papermaking comes from the pulping process used in new paper production.
2. Buy wood and lumber products certified by the Forest Stewardship Council. Like an organic label for food, FSC certification assures consumers that the wood products come from responsibly managed forests in which wildlife habitation and clean water are protected. It ensures that logging is done in an environmentally conscious and sustainable fashion.

3. Practice conscious consumerism by supporting Certified B Corporations. These 3,300 companies over 150 industries "balance purpose and profit. They are legally required to consider the impact of their decisions on their workers, customers, suppliers, community, and the environment."[547]

Torah portion of Yitro

❧ CORRUPTION AND CONSERVATION ❧

Exodus 18:21 – You shall also seek out from among all the people capable men who fear God, trustworthy men who spurn ill-gotten gain.

The Bekhor Shor commentary states that "trustworthy men" (literally "men of truth") means those who spurn flattery and don't act on just the literal facts, but on the bigger picture. Additionally, he explains that the trait of "spurning ill-gotten gain" is essential for truth to come to fruition – as corruption destroys truth.[548]

Research studies show a link between the level of corruption and the degree of environmental damage caused by a government. For example, in Cameroon, high levels of corruption have led to destruction of forests and selling of endangered species, along with underinvestment in sanitation and water projects, to produce short-term profits for high-ranking officials.[549]

Sustainable development today depends on us setting an example and teaching our children to be "capable, trustworthy people who fear God and spurn ill-gotten gain."

❧ LOCAL DECISION-MAKING ❧

Exodus 18:22 – Set these over them as chiefs of thousands, hundreds, fifties, and tens, and let them judge the people at all times. Have them bring every major dispute to you but let them decide every minor dispute themselves. Make it easier for yourself by letting them share the burden with you.

Rabbi Jonathan Sacks writes, "This is a significant devolution. It means that among every thousand Israelites, there are 131 leaders (one head of a thousand, ten heads of a hundred, twenty heads of fifty, and a hundred heads of tens). One in every eight adult male Israelites was expected to undertake some form of leadership role."[550] Jethro's advice promoted local, small-scale decision making that addressed people's specific needs and grievances.

In environmental governance, one of the biggest challenges is how to overcome the natural tendency of countries to manage social and ecological challenges in a heavily centralized, top-down, technocratic way. Central governance tends to apply fixes generally, without sufficient regard to local context or variation. When technical fixes are implemented without extensive input from local communities, including their social and ecological knowledge or practices, these fixes are likely to fail.[551]

For example, in the 1960s, the Green Revolution in Bali sought to increase rice production by abandoning the ancient water-temple irrigation system that was bound up with local religious practice. The result: yields actually declined. The ancient religious practice had ensured optimal timing for staggering irrigation between fields, ensuring dry periods when pests would not survive. Introducing Western-style irrigation to an Eastern community, without care to incorporate traditional knowledge, produced unnecessary damage.[552]

❧ NEW BEGINNINGS IN THE DESERT ❧

Exodus 19:2 – Having journeyed from Rephidim, they entered the wilderness of Sinai and encamped in the wilderness. Israel encamped there in front of the mountain.

The Midrash explains that the Torah was given in a place that was ownerless (the desert). Had the Torah been given in the Land of Israel, the Israelites could have said to the other nations of the world, "You have no portion in the Torah." Therefore, it was given in a place that was ownerless to teach that whoever wants it can come and partake of it.[553]

There is another beautiful understanding of why the Torah was given in a desert, one we can appreciate only when we consider the desert's paradoxical combination of harshness and ecology. Desert life is a way to start over. In the words of Deanne Stillman, who studied the impact of desert living:

> The desert is an escape hatch for all of us. Who hasn't just wanted to get away and start over? In the desert, you can do that every day... The desert doesn't care who you are or what you do... You get down to what counts very fast; in a land of mirage, the desert is a very honest place. Then there's the fact that the desert is filled with many wonders. Trees grow out of rocks. Frogs come out of the sand in a cloudburst. What creatures do to endure is amazing. Plenty of people in the desert are hanging on fiercely and yet just barely... They have been cast aside, banished almost, to a place that is misunderstood by many, regarded as a trash bin for outcasts. Their lives are fragile.[554]

According to this understanding, the desert is also a place of new opportunity, equality, and starting afresh.

♣ SPIRITUAL EATING ♣

Exodus 20:13 – You shall not murder. You shall not commit adultery. You shall not steal. You shall not bear false witness against your neighbor.

The rabbis say, "It is forbidden to derive benefit from this world without a blessing and one who does so is stealing from God... [from where do we learn this?] On the one hand it says 'The land is God's and all that is in it.'[555] And elsewhere, it is written 'The heavens are the heavens of God, but the land is given to humankind.'[556] This is no contradiction; the first statement is before someone makes a blessing and the second is after."[557]

In this rabbinical view, we steal from God when we misuse creation because we are only stewards of the planet, while God remains its ultimate owner. Every material pleasure that we derive from nature must be acquired with God's consent and elevated to a spiritual pleasure through the making of a blessing. The blessing expresses gratitude for the pleasure that is about to be partaken and prevents us from benefiting mechanically without taking a moment to appreciate God's generosity. Without this mindfulness, it is as if we are stealing from God.

In fact, psychologists recently observed that savoring our food can help us eat less and more healthily. In the words of one psychologist, "Rather than denying yourself the cake, enjoy it even more. But in smaller portions. Make the experience holy and intimate."[558] And what better way is there to savor our food than to thank God before and after eating?

☙ LOVE OF GOD AND MATERIAL DESIRE ❧
by Rabbi Yonatan Neril[559]

Exodus 20:14 – You shall not covet your neighbor's house: you shall not covet your neighbor's wife, or his male or female slave, or his ox or his donkey, or anything that is your neighbor's.

The Ten Commandments culminate with the command not to covet. Rabbi Yaakov Tzvi Mecklenburg explores this commandment, and in so doing offers a Torah approach to spiritual living and material consumption.[560] He relates this verse to another commandment that "you shall love the Eternal One your God with all your heart."[561] He asks, what is the significance of the word "all"? Why couldn't it have just taught "with your heart"? He answers that the Torah emphasizes loving God with all of one's heart to teach that a person should be totally committed to serving God and not split between love of God and love of physical pleasures. When a person is wholly in love with God, that person will not feel an attraction to material indulgence.

Rabbi Mecklenburg uses the metaphor of a cup, filled to the brim, with no room for anything else. So, too, a person full of love of God has no room for pure physicality. Such individuals feel so satiated in their core that their desire to gratify themselves from the physical world totally evaporates. Why indulge one's physical urge when one can experience spiritual bliss with the Creator of the universe?

Rabbi Mecklenburg does not seem to say that a Divine-aware life demands living like an ascetic or in poverty. Rather, a person should consume as a means to serving God. Such a person might live more modestly, while living comfortably and meeting their basic material needs. He criticizes consumption as an end in itself or as a means to self-gratification, which inevitably displaces the space in the cup for God's presence. When people use the physical world as a means to serve God, they will almost certainly consume less because they will realize what their true needs are.

When Rabbi Mecklenburg speaks about coveting, he is addressing a generation living in a pre-industrial, pre-consumer society. Those living in Biblical times might covet their neighbor's two-room house, donkey, or field – examples the Torah itself uses. Yet we live in a radically different time: modern, consumer-oriented, and highly technological. Many of us live in a materialistic world where coveting has become second nature, and even admired, as a form of personal initiative. In this material world, we covet and (over-)spend on the latest cell phones and luxury cars, cruise-ship vacations, and second homes – which all involve high levels of consumption.

Closeness to God isn't the only thing that may be lost when a person covets the physical. Rabbi Elchanan Samet of Yeshivat Har Etzion explains that in the view of Philo, a Greco-Jewish philosopher in first-century Alexandria, "The family, the land and all of humankind can ultimately be destroyed as a result of failure to suppress desires for various pleasures."[562]

What effect does one person's consumption have on the world at large? A recent study researched how many acres of biologically productive space the average US resident uses per year, in terms of food, water, energy, and other consumption. That is, how much land is necessary to support the lifestyle of one American? Over 108 acres.

With about eight billion people in the world, what is the average productive acreage per person? Fifteen acres.[563] That means the average American consumes over seven times what the earth can sustain. Multiply this by hundreds of millions of people in similarly developed nations and you can see how overconsumption is taking an environmental toll on the planet. Air and water pollution. Extinction of species. Climate change.

The Midrash states that God "caused [Israel] to hear the Ten Commandments since they are the core of the Torah and essence of the *mitzvot*, and they end with the commandment 'Do not covet,' since all of them depend on [this commandment], to hint that for anyone who fulfills this commandment, it is as if they fulfill the entire Torah."[564]

"Do not covet" is not a little addendum tacked on to the end of the Ten Commandments, but one of the central messages of Divine revelation. Finding spiritual satisfaction in the service of the Divine is an important means of weaning oneself from a life of physicality.

The commands "Love God with all your heart'" and "Do not covet" thus offer an alternative to a high-consumption, unsustainable future. We can begin to repair the world by improving ourselves. God offers no better way to do that than by filling our hearts with the love and light of the Divine.

❧ PRIORITIZING WHAT'S MOST IMPORTANT ❧

Exodus 20:20 – With Me, therefore, you shall not make any gods of silver, nor shall you make for yourselves any gods of gold.

Or HaChayim explains that a person making idols is really just worshiping the gold and silver.[565] Anthropologists recount how whole societies have been wiped out by their love of ornate religious items. Jared Diamond tells about such a colony, in medieval Greenland. It became so focused on amassing valuable walrus tusks that, during the short summer months when the men of Greenland should have been putting all their efforts into agriculture, men would go on expeditions to hunt and kill walruses so their tusks could be exchanged for "luxury goods" for their religious leaders and chiefs.[566] This was a critical element in the demise of the Greenland community, which depended on people to bale hay during the summer, for keeping livestock alive during the winter, and needed boats built for trading critical food products – not luxuries.

Today, giving to religious organizations is the largest subset of philanthropic giving in the US. In 2018, Americans gave $124 billion to religious organizations, which was 29 percent of the total of $427 billion in philanthropic giving.[567] While a tiny fraction of this giving promoted greening initiatives in churches, synagogues, and mosques, a much larger fraction was devoted to the construction of ornate houses of worship. At the same time, philanthropic giving to address climate change remains very low, since "staggeringly few foundations give the climate threat priority," as Larry Kramer, president of the Hewlett Foundation, wrote. "If we fail to keep global warming within tolerable limits, the cascading costs and effects will undo whatever has been done on other fronts. Simply put, if we fail on climate, we fail on everything."[568] The catastrophic destruction of houses of worship, along with residential houses, during the massive 2018 wildfires in Paradise, California shows how fragile both our human structures and our climate are. Our spiritual investment is not fragile, though, and can fuel our future work to protect all of God's creation.

Suggested Action Items

1. Be inspired by the Israelites camping in the wilderness of Sinai: plan a family or community camping trip! Whether it is a day trip to the local park or a week in the wild, nature is sure to excite and inspire you.
2. Remember the tenth commandment – *Do not covet… anything that is your neighbor's* – when you next visit a friend. Learn to be grateful for their happiness, rather than jealous of their success or envious that they own something you do not.
3. Think about what fills your spiritual cup and identify one thing that you had planned to buy but do not need; now replace it with an act that benefits others, and brings you closer to God.

Torah portion of Mishpatim

✤ VALUING EYES AND NATURE ✤

Exodus 21:24–25 – Eye for eye, tooth for tooth, hand for hand, foot for foot, burn for burn, wound for wound, bruise for bruise.

Rashi explains that this means that the person who causes physical damage to another must pay the "market value" of an eye, a tooth, a hand, etc.[569]

Calculating costs of damage done to people and nature is something that economists struggle with to this day. Environmental economists call nature's processes "ecosystem services." A 2018 study by the World Wildlife Fund valued them at $125 trillion total per year.[570] Consider just the value of sunlight that we receive every day – its value in growing crops, powering solar energy production, and reducing home heating costs!

❧ AN ANIMAL BILL OF RIGHTS ☙

Exodus 21:28 – When an ox gores a man or a woman to death, the ox shall be stoned and its flesh shall not be eaten, but the owner of the ox is not to be punished.

The Mishnah states that an ox that gores a human is tried before a court of 23 judges (just like its owner), as is a wolf, lion, leopard, cheetah, or snake that kills a human.[571] Meanwhile, a bull that kills a human in a bullfighting stadium is not sentenced to death as the verse states "an ox that gores," not "an ox that is caused to gore."[572] Professor Israel Rosenson explains that the Mishnah is creating a sort of "bill of rights" for animals, comparable to human rights.[573] Many people consider bullfighting, with a bull and a human bullfighter, or any forced fighting between two animals, to be a form of animal abuse. The concept of anti-cruelty laws to protect animals dates at least to the 1800s, and animal "rights" in the secular world has been discussed seriously since the second half of the twentieth century.[574] The Torah has been discussing and defending these rights for 3,500 years.

❧ RESPECTING PUBLIC SPACE ☙

Exodus 21:33 – When a man opens a pit, or digs a pit and does not cover it, and an ox or a donkey falls into it.

Rashi explains that the verse is discussing the person who digs a pit in the public thoroughfare.[575] The Midrash mentions a story of a man who is throwing rocks from his field into the public thoroughfare and a wise man passes by and asks, "Why are you throwing rocks from land that is not yours into land that is yours?" The man laughs at him. After some time, the man is forced to sell his field and is walking in the public thoroughfare when he trips over one of his own rocks. Now he understands![576]

The Torah wants us to understand that the public space is the only space that is truly ours. Today that would include the atmosphere and the ocean. When we pollute the air and the ocean, we are polluting our own "land."

❧ SHEPHERDS AND FARMERS IN CONFLICT ❧

Exodus 22:4 – When a man lets his livestock loose to graze in another's land, and so allows a field or a vineyard to be grazed bare, he must make restitution for the impairment of that field or vineyard.

The need for decisive laws on compensation for farmers is no less important today than in the past. Clashes between farmers and nomadic herdsmen have occurred for millennia, beginning with the first children of Adam and Eve. (Cain, a farmer, killed Abel, a herdsman.) Domestic cattle stray into farmland and eat crops. Conflicts occur, which are generally unpunished by local law enforcers. According to the Global Terrorism Index 2017 report, "tensions and violence have increasingly flared between herders and farmers with some estimates suggesting that in Nigeria alone up to 60,000 people have been killed in clashes since 2001."[577] Some governments recommend restricting cattle to ranches rather than moving them around the country for grazing. However, this approach does not honor the culture and tradition of nomads. An alternative solution is to mark out grazing routes that are acceptable to both farmers and herdsmen.[578]

❧ SWAPPING DEBTS FOR NATURE ❧

Exodus 22:24 – If you lend money to My people, to the poor among you, do not act toward them as a creditor; exact no interest from them.

The Maharal of Prague teaches that the Hebrew word for loan, *malveh*, also means "to escort."[579] Interest-free loans promote unity, connecting with other people's needs, and sympathizing with the pain of the needy. Rabbi Matis Weinberg explains that God's ideal is a world of no interest, where there's no debt, with only the investors themselves being equal stakeholders in any endeavor. He contrasts this with the Western model of debt and interest where "the disattached capitalist develops a rat-race mentality and at times is constrained to forfeit the satisfaction of meaningful relationships."[580] Rabbi Daniel Kohn notes that taking control of another person's money is about power and not relationship. An interest-based society is cold blooded, without the context of an overarching relationship with the One to whom all belongs.[581]

Furthermore, Rashi explains the simple meaning of the verse: if you see that the borrower cannot repay, do not behave as a lender acting forcefully to retrieve his debt.[582] In developing countries, high levels of national debt often lead to a short-term approach to ecology and specifically to high levels of deforestation in order to pay back the loans with interest.[583] The situation is the opposite when lending nations swap debt for "nature" – in other words, write off debt in exchange for the debtor country enacting and upholding conservation laws. This is precisely in fulfillment of the obligation "not to act toward them as a creditor." Over the past three decades such swaps have generated over $1 billion in funding for conservation activities globally.[584] This is a "win-win" result protecting the interests of both the developing nation and the world as a whole.

❧ THE SOUL OF AN ANIMAL ❧

Exodus 22:28–29 – You shall not put off the skimming of the first yield of your vats. You shall give Me the first-born among your sons. You shall do the same with your cattle and your flocks: seven days it shall remain with its mother; on the eighth day you shall give it to Me.

According to Dr. Richard Schwartz, "This precept shows the desire of the Torah to spare the feelings of living creatures (acknowledging the stress to calf and mother of premature separation) and to instill a spirit of compassion in people."[585] Rabbi Elie Munk writes concerning the above precept: "For the sages of the Midrash, this waiting period is symptomatic of the Divine compassion for the mother; it would be cruel to tear away her young so soon after birth."[586] The Book of Proverbs states, "The righteous one knows the soul of their animal."[587] The Midrash understands this as referring to God, who commanded that a calf, lamb, or kid remain with its mother for its first seven days of life.[588]

Compare this with the practice of modern dairy farms where calves are generally separated from their mothers within the first 24 hours after birth. The majority of the milk thus enters the food market and not the stomachs of the calves. This early maternal isolation leads to higher stress levels in both the calves and mothers.[589]

☘ FORBIDDEN MILK ☘

Exodus 22:30 – You shall be holy people to Me: you must not eat flesh torn by animals in the field; you shall cast it to the dogs.

This verse alludes to forbidding meat from an animal that is injured to the extent that it is unlikely to live for another 12 months. Rabbi David Rosen explains that industrially farmed animals and their milk may be forbidden under this category due to the way that they are treated. He states one example where "examination of the internal organs of the animals, especially in the dairy industry … actually renders them non-kosher. If they are non-kosher then their products are non-kosher and their milk becomes non-kosher."[590]

☘ HELPING ANIMALS IN DISTRESS ☘

Exodus 23:4 – When you encounter your enemy's ox or donkey wandering, you must take it back to him. When you see the donkey of your enemy lying under its burden and would refrain from raising it, you must nevertheless raise it with him.

From here we see the extra moral obligation to avoid the suffering of animals. Shadal explains that the words "when you encounter" indicate an obligation to return the animal only when we are close by. However, in the next verse about unloading an animal, we are commanded to help when "we see it" – we must come to help even when we see it from a distance.

We can learn from this how much the Torah cares about the suffering of animals. When the animal is just lost and not in pain, we only need to help when we are close by. However, when the animal is in pain, collapsed under a heavy load, then we are commanded to come to its aid even when we are far off.[591] In our days, when we rarely witness in person the suffering of the farmed animals we eat, is it enough to see the animal suffering on a YouTube video (at a distance)? Will this sufficiently motivate us to alleviate the animal's suffering?

Concern for animal welfare is an intrinsic part of Torah morality. The Torah's laws of justice embrace all of God's creatures. Laws on the treatment of animals include assisting others to unload their donkey (even on Shabbat), and not plowing with animals of different species next to each other (so that one animal is not at a disadvantage in strength or in access to food). These laws show the level of sensitivity that God demands of us regarding treatment of animals. The Torah also teaches that animals must be allowed to rest on Shabbat, that a person must not eat until their animals are fed, and that it is forbidden to sell an animal to a cruel person.

Today, chicken sheds and cow enclosures in industrial egg and dairy production fall far short of this standard. According to some rabbinic authorities, this even makes their eggs and milk non-kosher.[592]

❧ A SABBATH FOR ANIMALS ❧

Exodus 23:12 – Six days you shall do your work, but on the seventh day you shall cease from labor, in order that your ox and your donkey may rest, and that your bondman and the stranger may be refreshed.

Rashi asks, "Does this mean to give [the ox] rest and to permit it to tear up and eat grass from the earth? Or does it mean that one must confine the animals indoors [refrain from work as categorized for humans]?" And he answers, "[Confining them indoors] would not be rest but discomfort to them!"[593] From here we see that the rabbis understood that Shabbat should also be a rest for the animals, in their own way – being allowed to rest in their pasture. This is not just for the financial benefit of their owners, but for them as creatures in their own right. The Torah makes clear that domestic animals have a right to rest one day a week.

Malbim expresses this in even stronger terms and writes, "Rest is the opposite of unease, physical or mental... Therefore the Torah is talking about the sort of rest appropriate for an ox, which is to graze in a field... this is what the ox considers rest, both in a physical sense and internally."[594]

Needless to say, most chickens, cows, goats, sheep, and pigs in factory farms are kept in cramped conditions from birth to death. Not only do they not get a Sabbath day once a week, they do not enter a restorative, natural environment at all in their lives.

The Torah teaches that the Divine mandate of Shabbat includes allowing our animals to experience rest and contentment on the seventh day. Rabbi Samson Raphael Hirsch comments on this verse: "The Sabbath is a school for teaching the recognition of every other creature beside oneself as being equally a child and object of the same Creator; and this freeing of all creatures from the mastery of the human being is one of the objectives of the Sabbath."[595]

❧ THE TRAGEDY OF THE COMMONS ❧

Exodus 24:7 – Then he took the record of the covenant and read it aloud to the people. And they said, "All that the Lord has spoken we will faithfully do!"

The Hebrew verse states literally, "We will do and we will understand!" The Talmud tells of a man who asks the sage, Rava, why the Israelites preceded "We will understand" with "We will do." After all, the normal way is to understand first and then to decide whether or not to act.

Rava explained that one must act according to the Torah's laws without a complete understanding, because we must trust that God would only lead us on the right path.[596] Where a whole group or nation must make a decision, such as in the acceptance of the Torah, acting on trust is even more imperative as it is unlikely that everyone will fully understand.

Ecological economics speaks about the "tragedy of the commons," a situation in a shared-resource system where individuals act independently, according to their own self-interest. In so doing, they behave contrary to the common good by depleting or spoiling a resource through their collective actions.[597] The classic, historical example is of many shepherds grazing sheep on a collective field (the commons). Each shepherd tries to maximize his or her grazing of sheep, even though overgrazing is ultimately to the long-term detriment of all. Professor Elinor Ostrom of Indiana University was awarded the Nobel Prize in Economics for characterizing the ways that cooperative agreements allow communities to break out of the "tragedy of the commons" dynamic.[598] A group of sheep owners sharing one field for grazing might agree collectively that it would be sensible to leave the field fallow for a period of time in order to regrow its grass.

If everyone could be trusted to cooperate, it would be in their combined best interests to leave enough grass to regrow (or in the case of fishing, enough fish to breed). But in the absence of cooperation, many individuals will consume the complete stock of grass or fish. In this situation, the best outcome would be achieved if each individual would "do and then understand." In other words, their long-term best interests are achieved only when each person acts against their own short-term self-interest. At Sinai, the Israelites were modest enough to admit that they might not be able to see the whole picture and its long-term implications. When given good advice by those we trust, sometimes we need to "do" before we fully understand.

Suggested Action Items

1. Realize your responsibility as a custodian of God's world and make a habit of cleaning up some litter on the street each day. Alternatively, organize a neighborhood clean-up day. As you invest time and energy, remind yourself that you are fulfilling God's intention for humans to guard and protect the creation.
2. When building a house or other structure, try to include green design. See http://www.greenbuilding.com/ for more information.
3. Find out where you can safely dispose of electronic devices and batteries. The use of these objects of human ingenuity and craftsmanship makes you responsible for disposing of them carefully.
4. Petition local stores to limit products made with palm oil sourced from the rainforests, since tree burning to clear land for palm-oil plantations causes rainforest loss.
5. When you see a wandering animal, return it to its owner. Help all animals, even if the owner is someone with whom you don't always see eye-to-eye. If you see injured birds or small wildlife, contact a wildlife rescue center or agency.

Torah portion of Terumah

❧ A HOLY BALANCE ❧

Exodus 25:3 – And these are the gifts that you shall accept from them: gold, silver, and copper.

The Tabernacle to house the Tablets of Testimony was built from five materials from each of the following categories: inanimate minerals (gold, silver, copper, lapis lazuli, and other stones), animals (blue and purple wools, goats' hair, ram, and *tachash* skins), and plants (fine linen, acacia wood, crimson silk,[599] spices for the oil, and spices for the incense). As Rabbi Yanki Tauber writes, "In the 'small world' that is a person, the inanimate element is our capacity for self-negation ('May my soul be as dust to all') – our capacity for devotion, servitude, and deed. Plant and animal life represent the capacity for growth and development in our emotional and intellectual life."[600]

That the Tabernacle comprised an equal number of mineral, plant, and animal materials may suggest that, to God, ultimate holiness is achieved through maintaining a balance in the universe. In our world today, this could translate to people engaging in sustainable efforts in technology and energy (from minerals for cell phones to solar panels for heating), agriculture (from crops for feeding to trees for housing), and animal husbandry (from livestock for meat and dairy to wildlife for maintaining our natural ecosystems).

❧ GOD IN NATURE ❧

Exodus 25:4 – Blue, purple, and crimson yarns, fine linen, goats' hair.

Rabbi Tuvia Aronson writes:

> Rabbi Moshe Cordevero explains that the Tabernacle represents the Divine Presence dwelling within the created world. The Divine name reflecting this aspect of God is *Elohim*. In Hebrew numerology that word equals 86. *HaTeva*, the natural world, also equals 86.[601] Another relevant word equaling 86 is *kos*, cup. Just as a cup holds wine, the natural world contains Divine energy.[602] So, after the magnitude of

experiencing God at Mount Sinai, the Torah teaches us to maintain a connection with God by seeing the natural world as the Divine clothing.

Rabbi Isaac ben Judah Abarbanel quotes the historian Josephus who was alive when the Second Temple stood. Josephus writes, "Behold, one who searches will find that everything that was made in the Tabernacle was in the image of natural things... And since the hangings are made up of four parts, it hints to the four elements, because linen hints to earth because flax grows in the ground; purple wool hints at water because it was dyed using a certain fish; sky-blue wool hints at air; and scarlet wool hints to the element of fire."[603]

❧ THE NARWHAL AND THE TABERNACLE ❧

Exodus 25:5 – Tanned ram skins, [tachash] dolphin skins, and acacia wood.

Rabbeinu Bachaya cites the Talmud that the *tachash* was an animal with one horn in the middle of its forehead.[604] Rabbi Aryeh Kaplan believes the *tachash* was a narwhal – a marine-mammal relative of the beluga whale – which has a single tusk, actually a tooth on its forehead. Narwhals are occasionally found off the South Sinai coast, far from their primary habitat of cold northern ocean. During the sixteenth century, Queen Elizabeth I received a carved and bejeweled narwhal tusk worth £10,000 (approximately $3.5 million in 2018 money).[605]

An estimated 50,000–170,000 narwhals survive today. They are near threatened status, and several sub-populations appear to be in decline. In an effort to support conservation, the European Union established an import ban on their tusks in 2004 (although it was lifted in 2010). The US has forbidden imports on their tusks since 1972 under the Marine Mammal Protection Act.[606]

❧ SUSTAINABLE FORESTRY FOR THE TABERNACLE ❧

by Rabbi Yonatan Neril[607]

Exodus 25:10 – They shall make an ark of acacia wood, two and a half cubits long, a cubit and a half wide, and a cubit and a half high.

When building the Tabernacle, the Israelites were instructed to use acacia wood. Where did this wood come from? The Midrash teaches that when Jacob went down to Egypt, he received a prophecy that his descendants would be redeemed from there and be commanded to build a Tabernacle in the desert. Jacob instructed his children to plant acacia trees in Egypt. Over the hundreds of years of slavery, those saplings grew into large, mature trees. Before the Exodus, the Israelites cut down those trees and brought them with them through the Sea of Reeds into the desert.[608] When the Israelites built the Sanctuary out of these trees, the trees sang jubilantly before God, as it says in Psalms, "then all the trees of the forest will sing with joy before God."[609]

This may be the earliest reference to sustainable forest management. Under many circumstances, we should not cut down trees – to prevent erosion, protect wildlife habitat, and preserve an important source of oxygen for humans to breathe. But for building the Tabernacle, using trees was not only planned and permitted, it was a source of joy. Perhaps we can learn what the Torah considers an appropriate use of our resources, a kind of "Torah litmus test" for ethical resource use.

According to horticulturalist James Duke, "The acacia tree is extremely hardy and tolerates hot, arid climates; it is extremely drought resistant and can survive with less than four inches (100 millimeters) annual rainfall and long, erratic dry seasons; it grows fairly well in shallow soil."[610] The Tabernacle was built from one of the hardiest trees, and teaches us that a Torah life is built on stamina and resilience to outside pressures, whether religious persecution or environmental threats. In addition, the Midrash explains that God specified use of acacia wood for the construction of the Sanctuary, rather than wood from fruit-bearing trees, to teach us the importance of preserving fruit trees.[611]

Nowadays, we use trees in myriad ways – for homes, furniture, paper, and packaging. The ecological threat comes from people currently cutting down 15 billion trees per year and only replenishing five billion.[612] The global tree count has fallen 46 percent from the start of human civilization.[613] Much of the cutting, like in the Amazon rainforest, is to clear land for unsustainable cattle ranching, single-crop soybean fields, and huge palm-oil plantations.

In the building of the Tabernacle, we can find the ultimate example of trees used for a higher goal. According to the sages, these trees were in relationship with people for thousands of years, from the Garden of Eden to the moment they were cut for the Sanctuary.[614] They became the pillars of the Sanctuary of God, which the Torah describes as the dwelling place of the Divine Presence amidst the Israelites, and which existed as a center for Divine worship for over 400 years.[615]

❧ HUMBLE INSIDE ❧

Exodus 25:11 – Overlay it with pure gold – overlay it inside and out – and make upon it a gold molding round about.

Rabbi Samson Raphael Hirsch explains the significance of the gold covering the Ark: "The Holy Ark is made out of three boxes – the middle of wood, the outer and inner of gold. The Ark – symbolizing the Torah scholar, the receptacle of Torah – must be incorruptible and pure, both inside and outside, but he must view himself only as wood, not gold."[616]

How often do we think of ourselves as invincible human beings, protected by a "golden" protective surface and free to use and abuse the environment, disposing of endless single-use plastics and pumping huge quantities of carbon into the atmosphere? A key message from the wood of the Ark is to remember that, on the inside, we are as exposed as a tree to the forces of nature, climate, and pollution.

Suggested Action Items

1. Limit your intake of meat as part of a commitment to reduce deforestation. If and when you buy meat, choose locally produced, grass-fed, free range, organic meat from a source you trust.
2. Before buying something new, stop and consider why you are buying it. If it is for a holy purpose, go ahead. If it is to fill a void that might not be God-focused, think again.
3. Reconsider your gift-giving habits. Purchase products that are locally sourced, responsibly made, fair trade, and/or multi-use. Consider making a meaningful donation in the recipient's name.
4. To commemorate the wood used in building the Tabernacle, plant a tree in Israel, in your local park, and/or in the Amazon rainforest. Does your region have an urban-forests-themed nonprofit? Many organizations around the world have tree-planting projects, to which you can also donate from afar.

Torah portion of Tetzaveh

❧ THE 2,000-YEAR-OLD OLIVE TREE ❧

Exodus 27:20 – You shall further instruct the Israelites to bring you clear oil of beaten olives for lighting, for kindling lamps regularly.

Eda Goldstein writes:

> The old olive tree is often seen to have several young shoots springing up all around it from its roots unlike most other trees where the saplings tend to grow further away from the parent. These young shoots are often so plentiful that King David used the olive tree as a metaphor for being fruitful and having children: "Your children shall be like olive shoots round about your table."[617] The olive tree is incredibly resistant, able to withstand drought, disease, and even fire. It's able to live for hundreds, or even thousands, of years. An olive tree above the village of Deir Hanna, in the north of Israel, is reputed to be over 2,000 years old.[618]

As time goes on, the original olive tree dies and becomes hollow, and the new generation of trees becomes incorporated into the original tree, actually growing inside its trunk. That's why the olive tree has a uniquely twisted trunk. It's not one tree growing in disarray, but generations of trees meshed together and growing as one.[619] King David's blessing of "Your children shall be like olive shoots round about your table" means that one's children will carry on the legacy of the parents and sustain life for many generations.

❧ NATURE AS OUR JUDGE ❧

Exodus 28:15 – You shall make a breastpiece of decision, worked into a design; make it in the style of the ephod: make it of gold, of blue, purple, and crimson yarns, and of fine twisted linen.

The breastpiece was a mark of judgment and consisted of five separate components, "gold, of blue, purple, and crimson yarns, and of fine twisted linen."[620] Chida (Rabbi Chayim Yosef David Azulai) explains,

"Five materials to represent the two witnesses and three judges [in a Torah court of law]."[621] The rabbis state that the breastplate of law came to atone for misjudgments by the Torah courts.[622]

It is noteworthy that the five components of the breastplate of law comprise five separate aspects of nature: gold represents the inanimate world of minerals; the blue coloring for the blue wool derives from the sea snail; the purple wool derived from sheep represents land mammals; the crimson silk derives from the silkworm, which itself is the young of the flying silk moth; and the linen represents plant life as it comes from flax. It is as if to say that humans are to be judged by their impact on the inanimate world and on plant and animal life on land, in the sea, and in the sky.

A famous Talmudic passage states, "When a person comes before the Heavenly Tribunal, they will be asked six questions, 'Did you do business honestly? Did you fix times for Torah learning? Did you help others find their spouses? Did you anticipate redemption? Did you engage in wisdom? Did you have fear of Heaven?'"[623]

Perhaps the five species mentioned in this verse will be the judges and witnesses to our lives on earth, asking:

- Did we do business honestly – and responsibly – not polluting our world or exploiting our workers or animals?
- Did we fix times for learning timeless wisdom (including ecological Torah teachings), rather than focusing mostly on earning a living?
- Did we help sustain life in this world, by helping others find supportive community, or by protecting species from extinction?
- Did we anticipate redemption and bring about a better future for the world, not just focus on our immediate concerns?
- Did we really try to understand our impact on this earth, or did we plod on unaware of the damage we were creating for future generations?
- Did we have fear of Heaven, thinking about the universe, God, and what God wants for creation, or did we just think about ourselves?
- In summary, did we leave a world that was better than when we entered it?

How fitting that plant and animal life and the environment – through their survival – are to be the judges and witnesses of the sustainability of our lives.

❧ ALL THAT IS GOLD DOES NOT GLITTER ❧

by Shimshon Stüart Siegel[624]

Exodus 28:22 – On the breastpiece make braided chains of corded work in pure gold.

All that glitters is not gold.[625] The Tabernacle is the center of the Israelite camp, the locus of the Divine Presence on earth and the precursor of King Solomon's Temple in Jerusalem. Appropriately, the instructions feature a long list of rare metals, fine skins and fabrics, precious gems, and gold. A lot of gold.

The Torah mentions gold nearly 50 times in the description of the Tabernacle, far more than any other material.[626] Gold covers most of the Tabernacle and its furniture, including the Holy Ark, which is topped with two solid gold cherubs. The High Priest, who leads the service of the Tabernacle, is draped in gold: gold chains, gold bells, gold rings, gold settings for precious stones. Gold threads even weave through the fabric of his garments.[627] A solid gold head-plate crowns the ensemble.

Such a finely adorned sanctuary and spiritual leader would not be out of place in our own time. Our society has a passion for gold and jewelry. We mark significant life transitions with jewelry. We regard finery as a symbol of sophistication, love, and inherent worth.

But today, behind many gold rings are mountains of toxic waste and trails of destruction. According to the US Environmental Protection Agency, hard rock mining – which includes, but is not limited to, the mining of gold – releases almost half of all toxic pollution in the US with a clean-up cost in the tens of billions of dollars.[628] Gold mining uses toxic chemicals, releases harmful elements previously bound up in the rock ore, and consumes massive amounts of water. Here are just a few examples of problems associated with gold mining:

The planet's bulk gold deposits have nearly been depleted, so many of today's mines use a process known as heap leaching. To produce one ounce of gold, around 100 tons of ore and rock must be mined from the earth. Next a cyanide-solution is poured over the mound to separate the gold from the rock so the miners can collect the remaining microscopic gold particles.[629] Cyanide use is effective and cheap, but accidental spills harm wildlife and pollute river systems around the mine.[630] In 2000, a mine reservoir in Romania broke its dam, causing a toxic waste spill that polluted a tributary of the Danube River. That accident, the second that year, was described as the worst environmental disaster in Europe since the 1986 Chernobyl nuclear reactor accident in Ukraine.[631]

The United Nations Development Program's Global Mercury Project states that between 30 and 40 percent of all human-made mercury pollution comes from small scale or "artisanal" gold mining, a situation that the Project describes as "of grave ecological significance."[632] These mines use mercury to separate the gold from ore and then distill the mercury off to purify the gold. They then dispose of the mercury, often into the local streams. In this way, artisanal gold mining releases up to 1,000 tons of mercury a year – the largest source of mercury pollution on earth.[633]

These devastating mercury releases from mining camps extend beyond streams into soil and vegetation, and also contaminate fish, making it a major contributor to the long-range transport of mercury throughout the world. Mercury exposure is a major health issue for the indigenous populations who practice artisanal gold mining, including native tribes in the Amazon basin, Africa, Indonesia, Philippines, Laos, and China. According to estimates, more than ten million people may participate in artisanal gold mining, including up to 500,000 women and children directly exposed to mercury during mining operations. Many of these miners and their families have little or no access to health services.[634]

Injustice. Pollution. Poison. Waste. This is the legacy of today's gold. Yet the Torah prescribes the clothing of the priests "for honor and splendor." The exquisite golden appointments of the High Priest and the Tabernacle concentrated gold's power on a singular aim – creating a space for God's presence in the midst of humanity. It would be impossible for this sacred craftsmanship to be done with dirty gold. In fact, the Tabernacle was made, in good part, out of reused and recycled materials. The Israelites donated the materials for the Tabernacle as part of a process of spiritually rectifying and elevating the wealth taken from Egypt.[635] Through the building of the Tabernacle, we learn that all of our possessions should be sourced and used conscientiously, especially the most precious.

The High Priest's pure gold head-plate bore the engraved words, "Holy to the Lord." Gold that originates in injustice and destruction and is used to satisfy individual desires does not reflect this holy potential. Such adornments serve our vanity, but do not promote our awareness of the Divine, or the unity of our world. The time has come to follow the Torah's example by ensuring that we attain and use our gold with a pure conscience.

Of course, even ethical mining leaves a mark on the earth. Recycling and reusing old precious metals and gems is the most environmentally friendly way to attain new, personalized jewelry.[636] A grassroots movement of boutique jewelry artists uses recycled materials. Many of us have collections of old jewelry from parents and grandparents that, all too often, sit unused in jewelry boxes or safe-deposit boxes. Recycling and reusing these beloved heirlooms creates precious new pieces that honor the memory of the past while promoting a viable and ethical future.

The ultimate challenge is the cultivation of a holy, honorable, and harmonious relationship with gold. Let us reevaluate our perceived need for gold and ask ourselves if the jewelry we buy truly reflects our values. As we adorn ourselves with gold, are we aware of the destruction it is causing to the earth, as well as the harm to villagers and animals near the gold mines? As we celebrate our happiest occasions with traditional gifts of gold jewelry, are we linking our joy to God's joy over the fullness of the earth?

The Torah demands that, if we are to use gold, we should adorn ourselves not just in splendor, but with honor and holiness.

❧ NATURE'S POWER TO INSPIRE ❧

Exodus 28:31 – You shall make the robe of the ephod of pure blue.

The blue color was from a sea snail. It was so rare, it became the color for royal garb and hence the priests' and high priests' clothing. Rabbi Abraham Isaac Kook reminds us why such important garments should come from what may seem like a lowly creature: "When we contemplate physical creation as a whole, we realize that it is all one organism, since the parts are linked in varying gradations to each other. We see this in every plant, in every living being…The realization dawns on us that if it were not for the lower beings, the uncouth and the unseemly, the higher beings could not have emerged in their splendor, their esteem, and their luminous quality. We are continually becoming more aware of the Integration and Unity of Existence."[637]

Kli Yakar explains further, based on the Talmud, "The blue reminds us of the sea."[638] A recent study shows that looking out to sea has beneficial effects on peace of mind.[639] If the blue coat of the High Priest can inspire us to think about life by reminding us of the sea, how much more so can the sea itself induce such thoughts! Nature can inspire us, relax us, revitalize us, and connect us with each other.

❧ SUSTAINABLE CLOTHING ❧

Exodus 29:29 – The sacral vestments of Aaron shall pass on to his sons after him, for them to be anointed and ordained in.

The Torah describes in great length and detail the eight special garments of the High Priest, which were to be made by hand by embroiderers, weavers, and artisans. Indeed, the clothing of the High Priest is the focus of more Torah verses than any other item aside from the Sanctuary. It is therefore fitting that these garments would not be thrown out upon his death but rather would be used and reused from generation to generation.

The Torah states that Aaron's holy garments were to be passed on to and worn by his sons.[640] When Aaron dies, later on in the Torah, God says to Moses and Aaron, "Strip Aaron of his vestments and put them on his son, Eleazar. There Aaron shall be gathered unto the dead."[641] Despite the fact that Aaron wore these garments for about 40 years in the desert, including while conducting animal sacrifices and sprinkling blood and ash, they were not discarded upon his passing, but worn by his son, Eleazar. These garments were likely worn thousands of times, over multiple generations, and repaired when torn.

We would do well to learn from the long-term use of clothing by the high priests of Israel. In Britain today, the average piece of clothing is worn seven times before being thrown out.[642] Some $3.4 billion in clothing is purchased each summer in Britain alone for one-time use at weddings, barbecues, and festivals.[643] Only 1 percent of the materials from discarded clothing are recycled.[644]

Our use and reuse of clothing has global impacts. Today, clothing accounts for around 10 percent of global greenhouse gas emissions.[645] Many garments could be worn hundreds of times, repaired, and then worn some more. Donating our used clothes to charity shops, or sharing them with friends and relatives, can reduce lifecycle emissions by over 50 percent (5 percent of global total emissions).[646]

Suggested Action Items

1. Educate yourself on gold mining's harmful impact on human rights and the environment. Then sign on to Earthworks' "No Dirty Gold" campaign at https://earthworks.org/campaigns/no-dirty-gold/.

2. Reflect carefully when purchasing a gold ring or other item. Does your purchase express your values? Contemplate recycling a family heirloom. For example, melt down or resize your grandmother's gold ring to create a ring that fits your taste and purpose. Or acquaint yourself with organizations that adopt ethical mining and manufacturing practices. They include companies which follow the Kimberley Process Certification Scheme, join the Ethical Metalsmiths community, or have Fairtrade Gold or Fairmined certification.[647]

3. Before shopping for new clothing, consider buying used clothing to minimize the environmental and human costs of manufacturing garments. Another option is renting a fancy dress or suit – even wedding dress; online clothing rental sites are increasing in popularity all over the world.

Torah portion of Ki Tisa

❧ WEALTH – FOR WHAT PURPOSE? ❧

by Shimshon Stüart Siegel[648] and Rabbi Yonatan Neril

Exodus 30:12 – When you take a census of the Israelite people according to their enrollment, each shall pay the Lord a ransom for himself on being enrolled, that no plague may come upon them through their being enrolled.

God commands Moses to take a census of the Israelites by collecting a silver coin from each adult. The silver is used for a holy purpose – to make the sockets that hold the wooden planks of the Tabernacle that will be God's sanctuary among the people.[649] The verse links this census to God protecting the people from a plague. Today, we may not pay to be counted in a religious census, but we do pay taxes to support public health programs that should help protect us from plagues like the COVID-19 pandemic.

The Midrash commentary says God showed Moses a half-shekel (an ancient Near Eastern coin) made of fire and said, "Like this one shall they give."[650] Rabbi Noam Elimelech of Lizhensk says money is like fire; it can be used to create, protect, and nourish, or it can be used to harm and destroy.[651] People today are seeking wholeness and healing, but trying to find these through ever-increasing consumption of consumer products and profit-driven media. Modern-day overconsumption is a significant driver of ecological impacts, partly because many "must have" products – like cell phones – are made with materials mined in ways that devastate local environments.

In Biblical times, Egypt was noted for its prosperity – massive pyramids and palaces, heavily adorned with gold and precious materials. Egypt's wealth came partly from the bounty of nature – the Nile's yearly flooding made fertile soil for crops that fed vast populations – and partly from the scourge of slavery. The nation's wealth was at times used for good – feeding many during famine – but also for slave-built, massive construction projects that only deified wealth and the kings and queens whose power ordained their construction. There are counterparts of this

Biblical history around the world today, when cheap and even "slave" laborers in certain countries are abused to feed the material appetites of powerful nations. One example is hazelnut workers in Turkey, which supplies 70% of the world's hazelnuts, including to companies like Ferrero, Nestlé, and Godiva. The minimum wage that workers receive is not enough to keep families above the country's poverty line.[652]

Leaving the land of wealth-worship behind was only the first step for the Israelites in their journey to freedom. God intended that through the Exodus, Israel would create a new paradigm of materialism in the world. The Torah rejects worship of material things and charges us with the mission of transforming the way society views wealth. The construction of the Sanctuary was the first time that rectification of the material was attempted on a national level. God commands Moses to collect the half-shekel specifically in the context of a census. The Hebrew words, *Ki Tisa*, often translated as "when you count [the people]," literally mean "when you lift." God elevates each of us in Divine service when we dedicate ourselves, and our wealth, to spiritually and materially further righteousness in the world.

❧ STRIVING TO DO BETTER ❧

Exodus 32:14 – And the Lord renounced the punishment He had planned to bring upon His people.

The incident of the Golden Calf teaches us that God is prepared to forgive us if we repent. In the words of King Solomon, "There is no one who is completely righteous and never sins."[653] No one is perfect or is expected to be perfect, but each of us can continually strive to improve our ways. By doing so, we actually raise ourselves to a higher level of spiritual awareness and physical action than we achieved before the sin, according to the Sefat Emet commentary.[654]

The "reducetarianism" movement does not seek "perfect" behavior but encourages people at least to reduce their meat and dairy intake, and their impact on the planet's limited food resources. The philosophy is that veganism is too much of a stretch for most people who enjoy meat, fish, dairy, and eggs, even those people who care deeply for animals and the planet. The more reasonable goal of reducing consumption of animal products – achievable even for die-hard carnivores – is based on the idea that even small, incremental changes are enough to cause a significant shift in the way we tackle the big issues of environmental protection, animal welfare, and world hunger.[655]

❧ THE MATTER DEPENDS ON ME ❧

Exodus 32:32 – Now, if You will forgive their sin [well and good]; but if not, erase me from the book which You have written!

The Talmud describes the scene of Moses defending the Israelites before God, with Moses stating, "this matter depends on me!" Rabbi Abahu teaches that "Moses grabbed God, as it were, by the collar as one might grab a fellow, and said, 'God, I will not let go of You until You forgive this people!'"[656]

According to the Zohar, Moses was a reincarnation of Noah, and this episode served as reparation for how Noah acted in a similar situation. The word *mecheni*, erase me, contains the same letters as the Hebrew phrase *mi No'ach*, meaning "from Noah." While Noah didn't plead with God on behalf of his generation to save them from the Flood, Moses stood up for the people that God threatened to destroy after the Golden Calf, saying that should God wipe out His people, He should also erase Moses' name from God's book.[657]

The American rock band R.E.M. had a famous song, "It's the End of the World as We Know It (and I Feel Fine)." For many people, the ecological crisis simply does not matter to them. Rabbi Sharon Brous writes that if we truly believe that "this climate change matter depends on me," then perhaps we would be motivated, like Moses, to hold our leaders by the collar and say to them, "we will not let go until you solve this problem!"[658] Citizen's Climate Lobby provides one such example, as they have been mobilizing to promote bipartisan climate action at a governmental level.[659] Through different strategies, including civil disobedience, Extinction Rebellion succeeded in its goal of the British government declaring a "climate emergency" in 2019.[660]

❧ GRAZING AND SUSTAINABILITY[661]

Exodus 33:3 – A land flowing with milk and honey. But I will not go in your midst, since you are a stiff-necked people, lest I destroy you on the way.

The Torah often describes the Land of Israel as "a land flowing with milk and honey." The Talmud interprets this to mean: "milk flows from the goats [udders], and honey flows from the dates and the figs."[662] From this, one can understand the significance of goats and shepherding to ancient Israel's society.

Some herders would take their flocks to graze for six months at a time, between Passover and the beginning of winter, while others would keep their flocks in pasture year-round.[663] Professor Gedaliah Alon, in his noted history of Mishnaic and Talmudic times, writes that some herders raised flocks of sheep and goats in great numbers.[664] Yet goats and sheep are voracious herbivores, and the rabbis in the times of the Mishnah and Talmud witnessed how these animals could devour field crops.

In response, the Mishnah prohibited raising goats and sheep in agriculturally productive parts of Israel.[665] This enactment was likewise adopted by the rabbis in Babylonia for the Jewish community there, which in the times of the Talmud replaced Israel as the most sizable Jewish community in the world.[666] Further, the Talmud prohibited freely grazing oxen and cows as well.[667]

From the patriarchs and the tribes of Israel, to Moses and King David, the Bible is replete with a rich history of shepherding and livestock raising. Nevertheless, the Mishnaic decree addressed the need to stop goats from harming farmers' crops by preventing Jews from raising them in settled parts of Israel. If the rabbis were prepared to contravene thousands of years of Biblical tradition by forbidding herding, this should serve as a lesson to contemporary humankind about the need to limit the raising of livestock in massive numbers, when we are aware of the environmental damage that this causes.

As Yale's Global Forest Atlas notes, "Cattle ranching is the largest driver of deforestation in every Amazon country, accounting for 80 percent of current deforestation rates. Amazon Brazil is home to approximately 200 million head of cattle, and is the largest exporter in the world, supplying about one-quarter of the global market. Approximately

280,000 square miles (450,000 square kilometers) of deforested Amazon in Brazil are now in cattle pasture."[668]

In the coronavirus pandemic of 2019–20, a new disease infected people in Wuhan, China, before rapidly spreading across the globe. Contemporary scientists are beginning to see a connection between such pandemics and human impacts on the environment. When humans cut down forests and destroy the habitat of animals, the surviving animals move to new territories where they encounter new diseases, some of which may be transferred to humans.[669] For example, 27 outbreaks of the Ebola virus were found to have a strong association with nearby cutting down of forests.[670] Close to 75 percent of all emerging infectious diseases have jumped from an animal to a human, according to researchers. When people destroy ecosystems, pathogens like viruses that emerge from nature have fewer and fewer non-humans to infect.[671] In the interconnected earth on which we live, deforesting the world's rainforests can have unforeseen and major consequences.

❧ SLEEPING CLOSE TO NATURE ❧

Exodus 33:7 – And Moses took the tent and pitched it for himself outside the camp, distancing [it] from the camp, and he called it the tent of meeting, and it would be that anyone seeking the Lord would go out to the tent of meeting, which was outside the camp.

The Torah describes Moses as a man of great humility,[672] and this is exemplified in his pitching his own tent instead of ordering others to do so for him, and sleeping in a lowly position, close to the ground. Nature can truly humble people. Whether Moses slept in a tent outside the camp because he was humble, or whether he became humble through sleeping close to nature, he certainly sets an example for humankind about how to get closer to God by spending time closer to nature. The Hebrew word "to camp," *lechanot*, shares the same root as the word for "grace," *chen*. We grace a place when we camp there, if we tread lightly.

☙ LEADERSHIP AND TOUGH LOVE ❧

Exodus 34:3 – No one else shall come up with you, and no one else shall be seen anywhere on the mountain; neither shall the flocks and the herds graze at the foot of this mountain.

In the words of Abarbanel, "The first tablets were given in public and the evil eye gripped them. The second tablets were not given in public and the evil eye did not grip them."[673] The "evil eye" is the harmful negative energy that is created when one looks at something with envy or ill feeling.[674] Abarbanel is saying that the public giving of the Law was unpopular with the masses as they judged the laws negatively amongst themselves. Only when the second set of tablets was given, in private, did the laws have gravitas because the general public were not present to slander them.

Divine inspiration sometimes requires deep solitude. New concepts of how to live, including how to protect the environment, are not always embraced at large – but the power of laws that care for God's creation can lead to public understanding and acceptance. Today, laws that limit carbon emissions to save humanity and all species often come with unpopular short-term costs. Nonetheless, they may also be just what society needs to sustain future generations.

☙ LEGACIES THAT LAST GENERATIONS ❧

Exodus 34:7 – He [God] does not remit all punishment but visits the iniquity of parents upon children and children's children, upon the third and fourth generations.

These days, people manufacture many products with unregulated, toxic chemical byproducts that can persist as pollutants for multiple generations. Some are even passed on from nursing mothers, in their milk, to their babies.[675] In addition, plastics made today can last in the environment for hundreds of years. What can we do as individuals, communities, nations, and the world as a whole so that we do not foist our environmental mistakes onto our children, grandchildren, and their descendants?

Suggested Action Items

1. Dedicate some of your wealth in service of something that will elevate you and make God's presence manifest in your daily life, such as supporting work to reveal the connection between religion and ecology.

2. Avoid calf-based sins: reduce your beef intake and eat a soy, bean, nut, or vegetable burger instead. Limiting your beef intake will benefit both the planet and your health.

3. Pitch a tent in your backyard or nearest national park. Praying and playing in nature are scientifically proven to boost your mood and can help you connect with God in new ways![676]

Torah portion of Vayak-hel

♣ THE SABBATH AND ECOLOGY ♣

by Rabbi Yonatan Neril[677]

Exodus 35:2 – On six days work may be done, but on the seventh day you shall have a Sabbath of complete rest, holy to the Lord; whoever does any work on it shall be put to death.

So impactful is this commandment, today most of the world's population enjoys a "weekend" that can be traced back to this command.

Rabbi Norman Lamm writes:

> Perhaps the most powerful expression of the Bible's concern for man's respect for the integrity of nature as the possession of its Creator, rather than his own preserve, is the Sabbath... The six workdays were given to man in which to carry out the commission to "subdue" the world, to impose on nature his creative talents. But the seventh day is a Sabbath; man must cease his creative interference in the natural order (Jewish law's definition of *melakha* or work), and by

this act of renunciation demonstrate his awareness that the earth is the Lord's and that man therefore bears a moral responsibility to give an accounting to its Owner for how he has disposed of it during the days he "subdued it"…A new insight into Jewish eschatology: not a progressively growing technology and rising GNP, but a peaceful and mutually respectful coexistence between man and his environment."[678]

On Shabbat, traditionally observant Jews stop working, stop traveling, stop creating. The Ten Commandments teach us that on Shabbat, "You shall not perform any kind of creative work."[679] Rabbi Hirsch, in his commentary on this verse, explains that physical exertion is not one of the basic criteria of the term "creative work." According to the Torah, if one lifts a heavy piece of furniture on Shabbat, one is not guilty of violating the prohibition against work, even though such an activity is not necessarily in keeping with the spirit of Shabbat. If, however, one plucks a leaf off a tree or plants a seed in the earth, then one has violated the mandate not to perform work on Shabbat. A study of Torah law reveals that the definition of work on Shabbat is an activity in which a person transforms anything in the environment for his or her own use, such as for food, clothing, or shelter.[680]

Rabbi Abraham Joshua Heschel taught, "To set apart one day a week for freedom, a day on which we would not use the instruments which have been so easily tuned into weapons of destruction, a day for being with ourselves, a day of detachment from the vulgar, of independence of external obligations, a day on which we stop worshipping the idols of technical civilization, a day on which we use no money, a day of armistice in the economic struggle with our fellow men and the forces of nature – is there any institution that holds out greater hope for man's progress than the Sabbath?"[681]

Observance of Shabbat – taking a day each week to refrain from the transformation of nature – has the potential to alter a person's feeling of creative and technological control over nature. In early nineteenth-century Germany, Rabbi Samson Raphael Hirsch senses the profound relevance of Shabbat for industrial society, exclaiming, "Sabbath in our time! To cease for a whole day from all business, from all work, in the frenzied hurry-scurry of our time!... The pulse of life would stop beating and the world perish! The world perish? On the contrary, it would be saved."[682] This message of Shabbat is sorely needed in today's Western society. The mentality and lifestyle of "doing" without regard to "being," of transforming the natural world without taking time to reflect on the value of that transformation, is taking an environmental toll on the planet. A society that never rests nor reflects is the same society that over-extracts and over-consumes. This mastery of the earth without sufficient contemplation of its consequences has produced ecological destruction on the local, regional, and global level.

Air and water pollution. Species loss. Climate change. These are problems not of the environment, but of a society bent on doing and producing seven days a week. A *New York Times Magazine* article commented on American lifestyles, saying, "A nation of remarkably productive, often well-paid workers... are becoming increasingly reluctant to pause from their labors and refresh their souls." Meanwhile, the countries with the largest percentage of people working 60 hours a week or more in their main job are Turkey (23.3 percent) and South Korea (22.6 percent). On Shabbat, we are to walk on the earth without asserting our mastery over it, in order to acknowledge the sovereignty of the Creator. In this way, we will remember that we are only the custodians of the earth with the responsibility "to work it and to guard it."[683]

❧ THE FIRE INSIDE ❧

Exodus 35:3 – You shall kindle no fire throughout your settlements on the Sabbath day.

The verse is a reminder to connect to the other fires of creation on Shabbat, by slowing down and checking in with our body and its biological flame. Today we almost endlessly connect to the bright glow from our cell phone screens, but far less to the glow of Divine fire, the passion that comes from living in a more spiritual way.

Physical fire consumes – in these times of extreme climate change, fire consumes forests and homes with equal voraciousness. Divine fire does the opposite – it can create anew from the ashes of suffering and loss. Physical fire absorbs oxygen from the air and consumes carbon-based fuel. Divine fire replenishes our souls with inspiration and light. The

Torah demands a sustainable model of fire, both physical and Divine. When we focus on our spiritual energy, we create far more light, while burning up less of our planet's energy resource.

❧ LOVING IS GIVING ❧

Exodus 35:22–24 – Men and women, all whose hearts moved them, all who would make an elevation offering of gold to the Lord, came bringing brooches, earrings, rings, and pendants – gold objects of all kinds. And everyone who had in his possession blue, purple, and crimson yarns, fine linen, goats' hair, tanned ram skins, and dolphin skins, brought them; everyone who would make gifts of silver or copper brought them as gifts for the Lord; and everyone who had in his possession acacia wood for any work of the service brought that.

Why was it important for the Israelites to give of their own possessions for the building of the Sanctuary? An important insight comes from Rabbi Eliyahu Dessler[684] who asks, "Does loving lead to giving, or does giving lead to loving? Do I love you so I give to you, or the more I give, the more I love?" He answers, "The more you give, the more you love."

In fact, the word for love in Hebrew – *ahava* – is from the root *hav*, which means to give. A parent loves a child more than the child loves the parent, because the parent has given so much to the child. So, too, with God: to feel a strong love for God, we have to give something to God, be it material possessions, our time, our thoughts. This is the source for sacrifice. A sacrifice, or self-sacrifice, is needed to build our relationship with God.

What is true for our love of God is true for our love of humankind and nature: to truly love, we must give up something of value to us. Otherwise, we'll forever remain in a state of indifference. If we don't love our common earth home enough, it may be because we are not sufficiently involved in giving to it by truly caring for it.

❧ WORKING WITH OUR HANDS ❧

Exodus 35:25 – And all the skilled women spun with their own hands, and brought what they had spun, in blue, purple, and crimson yarns, and in fine linen.

This verse teaches that the craftswomen contributed fabrics to the Sanctuary, the work of their own hands. Today, the well-documented

"IKEA effect" demonstrates that people assign a greater financial and emotional value to objects that they have helped construct for their own use.[685] Urbanization has cut us off from nature, negatively affecting us and the environment as we are less involved in growing our own food or working to sustain the natural world around us.[686] A greater love of nature will come to us only if we choose to walk, work with our hands, play, and even pray outside more often.

❧ THE CENTRALITY OF CREATION ❧

Exodus 37:17–21 – He made the lampstand of pure gold. He made the lampstand – its base and its shaft – of hammered work; its cups, calyxes, and petals were of one piece with it. Six branches issued from its sides: three branches from one side of the lampstand, and three branches from the other side of the lampstand. There were three cups shaped like almond-blossoms, each with calyx and petals, on one branch; and there were three cups shaped like almond-blossoms, each with calyx and petals, on the next branch; so for all six branches issuing from the lampstand. On the lampstand itself there were four cups shaped like almond-blossoms, each with calyx and petals, on the next branch; so for all six branches issuing from the lampstand.

Rabbi Ellen Bernstein points out that there is substantial ecological detail in the description of the Sanctuary and its vessels. In Ezekiel's vision of the Temple, it is written:

> As I came back, I saw trees in great profusion on both banks of the stream. "This water," he told me, "runs out to the eastern region, and flows into the Arabah; and when it comes into the sea, into the sea of foul waters, the water will become wholesome. Every living creature that swarms will be able to live wherever this stream goes; the fish will be very abundant once these waters have reached there. It will be wholesome, and everything will live wherever this stream goes. Fishermen shall stand beside it all the way from En-gedi to En-eglaim; it shall be a place for drying nets; and the fish will be of various kinds [and] most plentiful, like the fish of the Great Sea. But its swamps and marshes shall not become wholesome; they will serve to [supply] salt. All kinds of trees for food will grow up on both banks of the stream. Their leaves will not wither nor their

fruit fail; they will yield new fruit every month, because the water for them flows from the Temple. Their fruit will serve for food and their leaves for healing."[687]

Rabbi Bernstein writes:

It's not that the earth is God's temple, but that the Sanctuary, the temple-like structure the Israelites build for God, is actually a testament to the earth – to the whole of creation. The supreme value of creation is sealed into the architecture of the Sanctuary. The ancient rabbis noticed that the Sanctuary is a microcosm of creation. Here are a few parallels:

- Two cherubs were positioned in the Sanctuary to guard the Ark. Two cherubs were positioned just outside Eden to guard the garden.
- A candelabrum rich in floral detail – with calyxes, petals, branches, and blossoms suggesting the tree of life – stood in the midst of the Sanctuary; the tree of life stood in the midst of the garden of Eden.
- The work of the human being in the garden of Eden was described with two words: to *serve* and to *guard*. The only other place these two words occur as a pair is in relation to the Levites, whose work was to serve God in the Sanctuary.

The rabbis noticed how even the colors of the linen and the clothes of the priests recall the creation: blue for the heavens, purple for the seas, scarlet for fire. The pomegranates on the High Priest's robe signified lightning and the bells around the bottom edge of his robe, ringing when he walked, suggested thunder. You begin to see an arc that hints at the centrality of creation in Torah – that begins in Genesis with the first creation and ends in Exodus with the Sanctuary, an architectural ode to creation."[688]

❧ COPPER AND CORONAVIRUS ❧

Exodus 38:8 – He made the laver of copper and its stand of copper, from the mirrors of the women who performed tasks at the entrance of the Tent of Meeting.

The laver, used for washing the hands of the priests before their service, was made of copper. So, too, was the snake that Moses was commanded to fashion in the desert to save the people from snake bites.[689] Rabbi David Seidenberg writes, "The washbasin and the base it stood on were made of copper, or possibly bronze; both are called *nechoshet* in the Torah. It turns out that copper is a powerful antiviral and antibacterial substance: viruses and bacteria that land on a copper surface break down and die.[690] Bronze has enough copper in it to do the same thing…I don't think it's an accident that the metal of the washbasin was copper. The copper kept the water not just holy but clean and pure."[691]

Scientists found that coronavirus was not able to survive on copper surfaces for more than four hours, while it could remain on plastics and stainless steel for three days. Of ten surface types tested, copper performed the best.[692]

Suggested Action Items

1. Celebrate Shabbat with clothes made of environmentally friendly materials, like organic cotton, responsible wool, hemp, or recycled polyester. This helps us prevent pollution and build a balanced relationship with the natural world.

2. Before Shabbat, unplug electric appliances that need not be left on during the day: microwaves, stereos, or computers, for example. Get in the habit of only plugging in electrical appliances when you need them. Learn more about appliances on standby electricity, also known as vampire power or phantom power.

3. On Shabbat, think about how you live in the natural world – as a master and consumer, steward and guardian. What do you like about your relationship to the natural world?

4. Instead of giving standard gifts, honor children on milestone occasions with a more meaningful present. Choose an item that has Fair Trade certification, meaning the producers and traders have met the Fairtrade Standards designed to address injustices in trade. You can also purchase a locally made gift that benefits someone in your community. Another idea is donating to charity in the recipient's name or gifting a membership to an environmental organization.

Torah portion of Pekudei

❧ GOD IS IN THE DETAILS ❧

by Rabbi Eliezer Shore, PhD[693]

Exodus 38:21 – These are the records of the Tabernacle, the Tabernacle of the Pact, which were drawn up at Moses' bidding – the work of the Levites under the direction of Ithamar son of Aaron the priest.

The Torah outlines the details of the components of the Tabernacle, apparently just summarizing the information presented twice in the preceding chapters.[694] This section begins with an accounting of all the material that went into the project and concludes with a further recounting of the Tabernacle's parts as they are finally erected into a single structure by Moses.[695] Considering how incredibly sparing the Torah is with words, it seems strange that the Torah should spend so much time simply reiterating what was said before.[696] Why wasn't it enough for the Torah to simply state: "And the people did what Moses commanded, and Moses assembled the Tabernacle"? Perhaps the answer lies in the nature and purpose of the Tabernacle and its relationship to creation.

According to the Midrash, the Tabernacle was also a microcosm of the universe. Each of its vessels corresponded to another part of creation: the tent of the Tabernacle paralleled the firmament, the candelabrum paralleled the sun and moon, the laver for washing paralleled the ocean, and so on through the days of creation.[697]

Thus the meaning of the Torah's precise recounting of the Tabernacle's construction may not lie in the specific verses themselves, but in their overall effect. The Torah is telling us that details – no matter how small – are actually of supreme importance. We tend to think of revelation as a grand event – the splitting of the sea, the thunder of Sinai – yet the verses detailing the Tabernacle's construction suggest that a revelation of God can also be born out of attention to the smallest details.

These passages tell us that through the precise alignment of details, something infinitely greater than the parts can be revealed. Furthermore, these passages reflect a deep ecological way of thinking. Today, even individuals with little environmental awareness realize that life-threatening changes are occurring on a global level. Yet few of us, as individuals, feel we can make the wide-scale changes needed to avoid such catastrophes. We are left making donations to "green" organizations and supporting the appropriate politicians. What else can we do?

A small book that quickly became a national bestseller in the US is titled *50 Simple Things You Can Do to Save the Earth*.[698] Numerous similar books have followed.[699] All of them bear the same message – that our smallest actions can have global repercussions, and that by becoming sensitive to even the smallest details of our lives, we can, as a whole, help to rectify the world.

People in the US use approximately 100 billion plastic shopping bags annually.[700] Most land in garbage dumps where they will never completely biodegrade, and may end up in the ocean.[701] The average US office worker uses 10,000 sheets of printing/copying paper per year, of which 45 percent end up in the trash by the end of the day. If just those printed items not needed the next day were replaced by digital copies, it would save the equivalent of 133 million trees and keep more than 1.8 billion cubic feet of paper out of landfills.[702]

The place to begin perfecting the world is the Tabernacle of our own lives – our homes and workplaces (which sometimes are the same location). Early in its inception, the environmental movement coined the term: "Think globally, act locally." This means that while our eyes and hearts must remain on the larger picture, the repair of the world begins in locales closest to us, with the smallest details of our lives. This is a Torah way of thinking, which recognizes the importance of details in the redemption of the world. As Maimonides teaches, "Every individual must think of himself and of the world as a whole, as if their merits and demerits were balanced. By committing one sin, he pushes himself and the entire world to the side of demerit, thereby destroying himself; whereas by doing one *mitzva*, he pushes himself and the entire world to the side of merit, and brings upon him deliverance."[703]

❧ ECOLOGICAL AUDITS ❧

Exodus 38:21 – These are the records of the Tabernacle, the Tabernacle of the Pact, which were drawn up at Moses' bidding – the work of the Levites under the direction of Ithamar son of Aaron the priest.

Rashi explains that the next ten verses of the Torah serve as a complete audit of all the metals donated to the Tabernacle.[704] Audits are critical in public works as well as in environmental conservation. Governments routinely carry out biodiversity audits to understand wildlife trends inside their borders, and the data from such audits can guide policies to protect the environment.[705] The global effort to address climate change began with the auditing required in the UN Framework Convention on Climate Change in 1992.[706]

❧ EVERYTHING HAS ITS PLACE ❧

Exodus 39:43 – And when Moses saw that they had done all the tasks – as God had commanded, so they had done – Moses blessed them.

Why repeat "had done" here? According to Kli Yakar, this reflects the repetition in creation where God stated at the conclusion of each day that it was "good," and at the end of the week, "And God saw all that He had made, and found it very good."[707]

Some things can be good by themselves, but when combined with other creations, they don't remain "good." In creation, as with the Tabernacle, not only was each element good in its own right, it was equally good when combined with all the other components. The message is that creation, just like the Tabernacle, is a divine balance of components that work perfectly together. In the same way that the Tabernacle would not have been "blessed" had it not been completed, so too, creation is not blessed unless it is complete.

It is clear that such a state requires active human involvement to promote balance and sustainability. May we be blessed to care for creation so that the Creator, humanity, and all life on earth experience it as being "very good."

Suggested Action Items

1. Discuss simple ways to protect the planet with your family. These can include always carrying a reusable shopping bag to prevent using plastic bags; reducing water use by turning off the tap while washing dishes; planting trees in your local park; walking instead of driving; and starting a compost bin in your neighborhood. Choose some ideas and start implementing them.

2. Before you buy new clothing, research companies which create clothes from sustainable materials. More businesses are experimenting with bamboo, water-efficient fibers, ethically-sourced, or pesticide-free cotton, responsible wool – even polyester made from recycled plastic bottles.[708]

3. Spend time looking at clouds. Appreciate their diverse shapes, colors, and speeds. Meditate on whether clouds remind you of God and how the Heavens are part of your prayers, as cloud cover is part of the health of our planet.

4. Share your discoveries and efforts to help the environment with others and encourage them to try similar lifestyle changes. You can share directly or even through social media. Join and become involved in a local or international organization working to sustain our planet. The Interfaith Center for Sustainable Development is one such organization. You can also reach out to your elected officials and urge them to initiate and continue critical environmental policies and programs.

5. Write a short review for *Eco Bible* on Amazon: https://www.amazon .com/review/create-review/.

Biographical Details of Jewish Scholars and Teachers throughout the Ages Noted in This Work

Listed alphabetically according to last name, acronym, or name of major work

Abarbanel, Rabbi Isaac ben Judah – 15th century, Portugal and Spain, commentator on the Bible

Akeidat Yitzchak, Rabbi Isaac ben Moses Arama – 15th century, Spain, author of the Akeidat Yitzchak, a collection of philosophical sermons on the Torah

Albo, Rabbi Yosef – 15th century, Spain, author of Sefer HaIkarim, a seminal book on Jewish philosophy

Alexandri, Rabbi – 3rd century, Israel, rabbi in the Talmud

Alon, Gedaliah, PhD – 20th century, Israel, historian

Aronson, Rabbi Tuvia – contemporary, Israel, Jewish ecological thinker

Artson, Rabbi Bradley, PhD – contemporary, US, Dean at Ziegler School of Rabbinic Studies of AJU

Bachaya, Rabbeinu, Rabbi Bachaya ben Asher ibn Halawa – 13th–14th century, Spain, leading Spanish commentator on the Torah

Bekhor Shor, Rabbi Joseph ben Isaac Bekhor Shor – 12th century, France, one of the Tosafot authors (see below) and commentator on the Torah

Benstein, Jeremy, PhD – contemporary, Israel, Jewish ecological author and cofounder of the Heschel Center for Sustainability

Berman, Rabbi Phyllis – contemporary, US, author and activist

Bernstein, Rabbi Ellen – contemporary, US, Jewish ecological author

Breitowitz, Rabbi Yitzchak – contemporary, US and Israel, lecturer, Ohr Somayach

Breslover Rebbe, Rebbe Nachman of Breslov – 18th century, Ukraine, founder of the Breslov hasidic movement and proponent of the benefits of Jewish meditation

Brous, Rabbi Sharon – contemporary, US, Ikar Synagogue

Carmell, Rabbi Aryeh – 20th–21st century, England, co-author of Mikhtav Me'Eliyahu, the philosophical teachings of his teacher, Rabbi Dessler (see below)

Chafetz Chayim, Rabbi Yisrael Meir (HaKohen) Kagan – 19th–20th century, Belarus/Poland, leading European rabbi

Chananel, Rabbeinu, Chananel ben Chushiel – 11th century, Tunisia, author of a seminal commentary on the Talmud

Chida, Rabbi Chayim Yosef David Azulai – 18th century, Israel and Europe, prolific writer on Jewish law and Midrash

Chizkuni, Rabbi Chizkiyahu ben Rabbi Mano'ach – 13th century, France, commentator on the Torah

Da'at Mikra – contemporary, Israel, rabbinical commentary on the Torah published by Mosad HaRav Kook and edited by Rabbis Yehuda Elitzur, Amos Hakham, Sha'ul Yisra'eli and Mordechai Breuer.

Da'at Zekeinim – 12th–13th century, Europe, commentary on the Torah by the rabbis who authored the Tosafot (commentary on the Talmud)

Eiger, Rabbi Shlomo – 19th century, Eastern Europe, son of Rabbi Akiva Eiger, a distinguished expert on Jewish law, who became a Hasid

Eisenberg, Evan – contemporary, New York, author of *The Ecology of Eden*

Feinstein, Rabbi Moshe – 20th century, US, leading Orthodox rabbi

Gerstenfeld, Manfred, PhD – contemporary, Israel, former Chairman of the Steering Committee of the Jerusalem Center for Public Affairs

Glasser, Rabbi Fivel Yedidya – contemporary, Israel, Jewish educator

Golinkin, Rabbi David – contemporary, Israel, President of the Schechter Institutes, Inc.

Greenberg, Rabbi Natan – contemporary, Israel, head of the Bat Ayin Yeshiva

Grossman, Jonathan, PhD – contemporary, Israel, professor of Biblical Studies, Bar Ilan University, Tel Aviv

Hattin, Rabbi Michael – contemporary, Israel, faculty of Pardes Institute of Jewish Studies

Heschel, Rabbi Abraham Joshua – 20th century, US, theologian, professor, and author of books on Jewish philosophy

Hirsch, Rabbi Samson Raphael – 19th century, Germany, one of the founders of Modern Orthodoxy who propounded the need for studying secular as well as religious texts

Hirshowitz, Rabbi Avraham Eliezer – early 20th century, Ukraine, author of a seminal book on Jewish traditions

Hochman, Rabbi Mordechai – contemporary, Israel, head of a Jewish learning institution

Ibn Ezra, Rabbi Abraham ibn Ezra – 12th century, Spain, commentator on the Bible

Jacobson, Rabbi Yosef Yitzchak – contemporary, US, author and speaker

Judah the Prince, Rabbi (also simply called Rabbi) – 2nd century, Israel, compiler of the Mishnah

Kaplan, Rabbi Aryeh – 20th century, US, prolific writer on Torah, Kabbalah, and science

Kasher, Rabbi Menachem Mendel – 20th century, Israel, author of a cross reference of the Torah with the Oral Law

Ketav VeHaKabbalah, Rabbi Yaakov Tzvi Mecklenburg – 19th century, Germany, commentator on the Torah

Kli Yakar, Rabbi Shlomo Efraim Luntschitz – 16th century, Eastern Europe, author of a seminal Torah commentary

Kohn, Rabbi Daniel – contemporary, Israel, rabbi of Bat Ayin

Kook, Rabbi Abraham Isaac HaKohen, HaRaAYaH – 19th–20th century, Israel, Chief Rabbi of Palestine in the 1920s, author of *Orot*, philosophical Jewish writings, and founder of modern religious Zionism

Kotzker Rebbe, Rabbi Menachem Mendel of Kotzk – 19th century, Poland, founder of Ger hasidut, inspirational hasidic leader

Lamm, Rabbi Norman, PhD – 20th–21st century, US, emeritus Chancellor of Yeshiva University

Maggid of Mezeritch, Rabbi Dov Ber ben Avraham – 18th century, Ukraine, early leader of the hasidic movement in Europe

Maimonides, Rambam, Rabbi Moshe ben Maimon – 12th century, Spain, author of a seminal work on Jewish law, the Mishneh Torah and a seminal philosophical work, *The Guide to the Perplexed*

Malbim, Rabbi Meir Leibush – 19th century, Eastern Europe, commentator on the Bible

Maor VaShemesh, Rabbi Kalonymus Kalman Epstein – 18th–early 19th century, Poland, hasid and author of books on Jewish ethics

Marks, Rabbi Gil – 20th century, U.S, author

Marzouk, Evonne – contemporary, US, founding director of Canfei Nesharim

Mei Shilo'ach, Rabbi Mordechai Yosef Leiner, the Ishbitzer Rebbe – 19th century, Poland, hasidic commentator on the Torah

Mekhilta, Mekhilta d'Rabbi Yishmael – 2nd century, Israel, commentator on the Book of Exodus

Melchior, Rabbi Michael – contemporary, Israel, active interfaith and peace activist, emeritus Chief Rabbi of Norway

Midrash Tanchuma – 5th–9th century, Babylon, early collection of commentaries on the Torah

Mikhtav Me'Eliyahu, Rabbi Eliyahu Eliezer Dessler – 20th century, UK, author of a seminal book on Jewish philosophy

Munk, Rabbi Elie – 20th century, France, author

Nachmanides, Ramban, Rabbi Moshe ben Nachman – 13th century, Spain, scholar of Jewish law and philosophy and commentator on the Torah

Netziv, Rabbi Naftali Tzvi Yehuda Berlin – 19th century, Russia, commentator on the Torah

Neuman, Rabbi Avi – contemporary, Israel

Noam Elimelech, Rabbi Elimelech of Lizhensk, 18th century, Poland, founding rabbi of the hasidic movement and author of the Noam Elimelech commentary on Torah

Onkelos – 1st–2nd century, Israel, author of the earliest translation of the Torah into Aramaic

Or HaChayim, Rabbi Chayim ben Moshe ibn Attar – 18th century, Morocco, commentator on the Torah

Pirkei d'Rabbi Eliezer, published 9th century, Italy with some content attributed to Rabbi Eliezer ben Hyrkanus (2nd century, Israel), early Torah commentary in midrashic style

Pri Tzadik, Rabbi Tzadok HaKohen Rabinowitz of Lublin – 19th century, Eastern Europe, author of Pri Tzadik commentary on the Torah

Radak, Rabbi David Kimchi – 12th–13th century, France, Biblical commentator and philosopher

Ralbag, Rabbi Levi ben Gershon – 14th century, France, scholar of Jewish law and philosophy

Rashbam, Rabbi Shmuel ben Meir – 11th–12th century, France, grandson of Rashi

Rashi, Rabbi Shlomo ben Yitzchak – 11th century, France, author of the most fundamental commentary on the Bible and Talmud

Rava, Abba ben Yosef bar Chama – 4th century, Babylonia, rabbi of the Talmud

Reish Lakish, Rabbi Shimon ben Lakish – 3rd century, Roman Palestine/ Israel, leading rabbi

Riskin, Rabbi Shlomo, PhD – contemporary, Israel, Chief Rabbi of Efrat and founder and chancellor emeritus of Ohr Torah Stone institutions

Riva, Rabbi Yitzchak ben Asher HaLevi – 12th century, France, Biblical commentator

Rosen, Rabbi David, CBE, KSG – contemporary, Israel, International Director of Interreligious Affairs AJC

Rosenson, Israel, PhD – contemporary, Israel, professor of physics and religious ecologist

Sacks, Rabbi Lord Jonathan, PhD – contemporary, UK, author of commentaries on the weekly Torah portion, and contemporary Jewish philosophy, emeritus Chief Rabbi of the UK and Commonwealth

Samet, Rabbi Elchanan – contemporary, Israel, faculty of Yeshivat Har Etzion

Schneider, Sarah Yehudit – contemporary, Israel, founding director of A Still Small Voice

Sefat Emet, Rabbi Yehuda Aryeh Leib Alter – 19th century, Poland, hasidic rabbi and expert on Jewish law whose Torah commentary is known as the Sefat Emet

Seidenberg, Rabbi David, PhD – contemporary, US, scholar of Jewish thought

Shadal, Rabbi Samuel David Luzzatto – 19th century, Italy, Biblical commentator and philosopher

Shore, Rabbi Eliezer, PhD – contemporary, Israel, teacher and writer on hasidism and Jewish spirituality

Siegel, Shimshon Stüart – contemporary, US, Jewish ecological thinker and co-director at Sonoran Desert Inn and Conference Center

Siegelbaum, Rebbetzin Chana Bracha – contemporary, Israel, founding director of Midreshet B'erot Bat Ayin

Siftei Chakhamim, Rabbi Shabbethai ben Joseph Bass, 17th–18th century, Eastern Europe, author of a commentary on Rashi

Simenowitz, Rabbi Shmuel – contemporary, US, farmer and speaker

Sinclair, Rabbi Yedidya – contemporary, Israel, Jewish educator and author

Soloveitchik, Rabbi Joseph Ber, PhD – 20th century, US, head of Rabbi Isaac Elchanan Theological Seminary at Yeshiva University

Taragin, Rabbi Moshe – contemporary, Israel, teacher at Yeshivat Har Etzion

Targum Yonatan, Rabbi Jonathan ben Uzziel, 2nd century, Babylon, Aramaic translation of the Bible

Tauber, Rabbi Yanki – contemporary, US, hasidic scholar and writer

Toldot Yitzchak, Rabbi Isaac Karo, 15th–16th century, Spain and Turkey, author of Toldot Yitzchak and uncle and teacher of Rabbi Joseph Karo, author of the Shulchan Arukh

Tur Ha'Arokh, Rabbi Jacob ben Asher – 13th–14th century, Spain, compiler of an important early code of Jewish law, the Tur, and a commentator on the Torah

Waskow, Rabbi Arthur – contemporary, US, founding director of Shalom Center and Jewish ecological author

Weinberg, Rabbi Matis – contemporary, US and Israel, author and teacher

Weiner, Rabbi Benjamin – contemporary, US, Jewish Community of Amherst

Wiesel, Elie – 20th–early 21st century, Romania and US, author and Nobel Laureate

Wolbe, Rabbi Shlomo – 20th–21st century, Israel, prominent Orthodox rabbi

Yalkut Shimoni – 13th century, Germany, compilation of late midrashim

Zarum, Rabbi Raphael, PhD – contemporary, UK, dean of the London School of Jewish Studies

Glossary

Babylonian Talmud (BT) – An elucidation of the Mishnah, compiled from works written between the 3rd and 5th centuries in Babylonia. It is the primary source of Jewish law and philosophy. Also known as the Gemara or Shas.

Hasid (pl. Hasidim), hasidut (hasidism), hasidic (adjective) – A Hasid is a follower of a stream of Orthodox Judaism (Hasidut) founded in 18th-century Eastern Europe by Rabbi Yisroel ben Eliezer (the Ba'al Shem Tov). Hasidut deals with a range of spiritual concepts such as God, the soul, and the Torah, making them understandable and applicable.

Jerusalem Talmud (JT) – An elucidation of the Mishnah, compiled from works written between the 3rd and 4th centuries in Israel (predominantly from the Galilee region as Jews were not permitted in Jerusalem at that time).

Kabbalah – Jewish mysticism. The most fundamental kabbalistic text, the Zohar, was first published by Moses de León (13th century, Spain), although many attribute it to Rabbi Shimon bar Yochai (2nd century, Israel).

Midrash (pl. midrashim) – The term means "study" and refers to an ancient form of Biblical interpretation that "plays" with the Hebrew meaning of words and understands them through their use in other, often seemingly unconnected, passages of the Torah.

Mishnah – The first written compilation of the Jewish "Oral Law" that was passed down by word of mouth from Moses. It was finally transcribed by Rabbi Judah the Prince (3rd century, Israel) in order to prevent it from being forgotten following the destruction of the Second Temple.

"The rabbis" – A generic term for the rabbis of the Mishnah, Talmud and frequently includes the chain of Orthodox rabbis up until the 19th century.

Notes

1. Sefer HaBahir 31.

2. Rabbi Jonathan Sacks, *The Dignity of Difference: How to Avoid the Clash of Civilizations* (London: Continuum, 2003), 207.

3. Midrash Genesis Rabbah 1:1.

4. Midrash Exodus Rabbah 47:4.

5. Rabbi Samson Raphael Hirsch, commentary to Numbers 8:11, in *The Pentateuch*, vol. 4: Numbers (Gateshead, England: Judaica Press, 1989).

6. Ethics of the Fathers 1:17.

7. "Best Selling Book," Guinness World Records, https://www.guinnessworldrecords.com/world-records/best-selling-book-of-non-fiction. This figure is primarily for copies sold of the Christian Bible and Hebrew Bible.

8. Daniel Silliman, "The Most Popular Bible of the Year Is Probably Not What You Think It Is," *The Washington Post*, August 28, 2015, accessed April 20, 2020, https://www.washingtonpost.com/news/acts-of-faith/wp/2015/08/28/the-most-popular-bible-of-the-year-is-probably-not-what-you-think-it-is/.

9. David Van Biema, "The Case for Teaching the Bible," *Time* magazine, March 22, 2007, accessed April 20, 2020, http://content.time.com/time/magazine/article/0,9171,1601845,00.html.

10. Claire Gecewicz and Dennis Quinn, "U.S. Churchgoers Are Satisfied with the Sermons They Hear," Pew Research Center, January 28, 2020, https://www.pewresearch.org/fact-tank/2020/01/28/u-s-churchgoers-are-satisfied-with-the-sermons-they-hear-though-content-varies-by-religious-tradition/.

11. Phillip Goff, Arthur Farnsley, and Peter Thuesen, *The Bible in American Life, A National Study by the Center for the Study of Religion and American Culture* (Indianapolis: Indiana University–Purdue University, 2014).

12. Numbers 10:35.

13. Rabbi Abraham Isaac Kook, "On Torah for its Own Sake," *Orot HaTorah II* (Jerusalem: Sifriat Hava, 2005), §1.

14. Rabbi Daniel Kohn, oral teaching, Yeshivat Sulam Yaakov, Jerusalem, May 2011.

15. Rashbam, commentary to Genesis 37:2.

16. Gus Speth, "Shared Planet: Religion and Nature" program, BBC Radio 4, London: BBC, October 1, 2013 as cited in Rod Oram, "Reviewing the Global

Economy: the UN and Bretton Woods Systems," *Policy Quarterly* 13, no. 1 (February 2017): 20–25, https://doi.org/10.1080/09692290.2019.1635513.

17. Pew Research Center Forum on Religion & Public Life, "The Global Religious Landscape, December 18, 2012, https://www.pewforum.org/2012/12/18/global-religious-landscape-exec/.

18. Pew Research Center, "Religious Landscape Study," 2014, https://www.pewforum.org/religious-landscape-study/.

19. "Believers, Sympathizers, and Skeptics: Why Americans Are Conflicted about Climate Change, Environmental Policy, and Science," November 21, 2014, online at http://publicreligion.org/site/wp-content/uploads/2014/11/2014-Climate-Change-FINAL1.pdf.

20. Talk at Vayehi Ohr Conference, Hebrew University of Jerusalem, April 5, 2009.

21. Babylonian Talmud, Tamid 32a.

22. Rabbi Jonathan Sacks, *The Dignity of Difference: How to Avoid the Clash of Civilizations* (London: Continuum, 2003), 207.

23. Edward O. Wilson, *The Creation: An Appeal to Save Life on Earth* (New York: W.W. Norton & Company, 2006), 3–5.

24. Midrash Leviticus Rabbah 4:6.

25. As quoted by Rabbi Moshe Luria, Bahir Beit Ganzei, *Pitchei Tefillah*, part 2, 15.

26. Part of this section on Noah is from Yonatan Neril, "Countering Destruction: Lessons from Noach," Canfei Nesharim, a branch of Grow Torah, February 19, 2004, http://canfeinesharim.org/countering-destruction-lessons-from-noach-longer-article/.

27. *Eitz Yosef* commentary to Midrash Tanchuma, Parshat Noach, §5.

28. Pirkei d'Rabbi Eliezer, ch. 22.

29. Midrash Genesis Rabbah 31:5.

30. Rabbi Samson Raphael Hirsch, commentary to Genesis 6:11, *The Pentateuch*: vol. 1: Genesis (Gateshead, England: Judaica Press, 1989), 138.

31. Midrash Genesis Rabbah 31

32. Mark Maslin, *Global Warming, A Very Short Introduction* (Oxford: Oxford University Press, 2004).

33. "History of the IPCC," Intergovernmental Panel on Climate Change, accessed March 1, 2020, https://www.ipcc.ch/about/history/.

34. Julie Turkewitz, Manny Fernandez, and Alan Blinder, "In Houston, Anxiety and Frantic Rescues as Floodwaters Rise," *The New York Times*, August 27, 2017, https://www.nytimes.com/2017/08/27/us/hurricane-harvey-texas.html?_r=0.

35. Eugene Linden, "How Scientists Got Climate Change So Wrong," *The New York Times*, November 8, 2019, https://www.nytimes.com/2019/11/08/opinion/sunday/science-climate-change.html.

36. Gerardo Ceballos, Paul R. Ehrlich, Peter H. Raven, "Vertebrates on the Brink as Indicators of Biological Annihilation and the Sixth Mass Extinction,"

Proceedings of the National Academy of Sciences, June 2020, 201922686; DOI: 10.1073/pnas.1922686117.

37. Rabbi Samson Raphael Hirsch, commentary to Genesis 1:1.

38. Midrash Ecclesiastes Rabbah 7:13.

39. As cited in Rabbi Norman Lamm, *Derashot Ledorot: A Commentary for the Ages – Genesis* (Jerusalem: OU Press and Maggid Books, 2012), and Rabbi Norman Lamm, *Faith and Doubt* (Brooklyn: KTAV Publishing House, 1986), 175.

40. Psalms 19:1.

41. Rabbi David Rosen, "Jewish Ethics, Animal Welfare, and Veganism: A Panel of Rabbis and Experts," interview, Jewish Eco Seminars Productions, January 2018, https://www.youtube.com/watch?v=UHIyXrN1JAI.

42. Rabbi Shalom Berezovsky, *Netivot Shalom* (Jerusalem: Yeshivat Beit Avraham Slonim, 2000), Numbers 41.

43. Genesis 1:31.

44. Midrash Genesis Rabbah 3:7.

45. Michael Greshko, "What Are Mass Extinctions, and What Causes Them?" National Geographic, https://www.nationalgeographic.com/science/prehistoric-world/mass-extinction/.

46. Midrash Genesis Rabbah 5:7.

47. "Ice, Snow, and Glaciers and the Water Cycle," Water Science School, US Geological Survey, accessed February 18, 2020, www.usgs.gov/special-topic/water-science-school/science/ice-snow-and-glaciers-and-water-cycle?qt-science_center_objects=0#qt-science_center_objects.

48. Eric Rignot et al., "Four Decades of Antarctic Ice Sheet Mass Balance from 1979–2017," *Proceedings of the National Academy of Sciences* 116, no. 4, January 2019, 1095–1103, https://doi.org/10.1073/pnas.1812883116.

49. Tur Ha'Arokh on Genesis 1:11.

50. Radak on Genesis 1:22. See also Midrash Genesis Rabbah 97:3 and Babylonian Talmud, Berakhot 20a which relate to Genesis 48:16 on the use of the Hebrew root containing fish, *dag*, as meaning "to reproduce and proliferate."

51. "UN Report: Nature's Dangerous Decline 'Unprecedented'", United Nations, May 6, 2019, https://www.un.org/sustainabledevelopment/blog/2019/05/nature-decline-unprecedented-report/ citing IPBES Global Assessment Report on Biodiversity and Ecosystem Services.

52. Karina Acevedo-Whitehouse and Amanda L. J. Duffus, "Effects of Environmental Change on Wildlife Health," *Philosophical Transactions of the Royal Society B, Biological Sciences* 364, no. 1534, November 2009, 3429–3438, https://doi.org/10.1098/rstb.2009.0128.

53. Kenneth Rosenberg et al., "Decline of the North American Avifauna," *Science*, 2019, https://www.birds.cornell.edu/home/wp-content/uploads/2019/09/DECLINE-OF-NORTH-AMERICAN-AVIFAUNA-SCIENCE-2019.pdf.

54. Rabbi Isaac Karo, Toldot Yitzchak commentary to Genesis 1:28.

55. Rabbi Gil Marks, *Olive Trees and Honey* (Hoboken, NJ: Wiley Publishing Co., 2005), viii.

56. This is adapted from "Genesis and Human Stewardship of the Earth," Yonatan Neril, February 24, 2014, content produced by Canfei Nesharim, a branch of Grow Torah. It is available at http://canfeinesharim.org/genesis-and-human-stewardship-of-the-earth/.

57. Genesis 1:26.

58. Ibid., 1:28.

59. Midrash Genesis Rabbah (Vilna Edition), 8:12. Artscroll Rashi to Genesis 1:26 notes, "The Maharal explains in Gur Aryeh to Genesis 1:26 that 'the verse uses *v'yirdu* for "ruling," from the root *resh-dalet-heh*, rather than the more common *mashal*, so that it can be expounded as if it were from the root *yud-resh-dalet*, "declining, degenerating," as well.'"

60. Rashi on Genesis 1:26.

61. *Midrash Rabbah: Genesis,* Rabbi Dr. Harry Freedman and Maurice Simon trans. (London: Soncino Press, 1983).

62. *Climate Change 2014: Synthesis Report. Contribution of Working Groups I, II and III to the Fifth Assessment, A Report of the Intergovernmental Panel on Climate Change,* Rajendra K. Pachauri and Leo Meyer eds, IPPC, 2014, https://www.ipcc.ch/site/assets/uploads/2018/05/SYR_AR5_FINAL_full_wcover.pdf.

63. "Missing Link in Coronavirus Jump from Bats to Humans Could Be Pangolins, Not Snakes," American Chemical Society, March 26, 2020, https://www.acs.org/content/acs/en/pressroom/newsreleases/2020/march/missing-link-in-coronavirus-jump-from-bats-to-humans-could-be-pangolins-not-snakes.html.

64. Rabbi Zev Wolf Einhorn in his commentary (Perush Maharzav) to the Midrash explains that this midrash is explaining the different grammatical uses of the verb "to rule" in verses 26 and 28. In verse 26, before the human being has been created, God says about them, "*v'yirdu*," in the future tense, meaning "and they shall rule over." Verse 27 reads "And God created Man..." Verse 28 contains God's blessing to people, in the imperative form "*urdu*," meaning "rule over." The Midrash, however, reads the latter verse differently. The lettering can also be read "*v'yeiradu*," in the passive form meaning "they [people] will be ruled over [by animals]."

65. Rabbi David Sears, "Selections From 'A Vision of Vegetarianism and Peace'," in *The Vision of Eden: Animal Welfare and Vegetarianism in Jewish Law and Mysticism*, Rabbi David Cohen ed., David Sears trans. https://www.jewishveg.org/DSvision.html.

66. Rabbi Abraham Isaac Kook, "Selections From 'A Vision of Vegetarianism And Peace'," in *The Vision of Eden: Animal Welfare and Vegetarianism in Jewish Law and Mysticism*, Rabbi David Cohen and Jonathan Rubenstein eds. (California: CreateSpace Independent Publishing Platform, 2nd edition, 2014), 246.

67. Ibid., §§1–7.

68. Rabbi Elchanan Samet. "The Story of Creation and Our Ecological Crisis," Yeshivat Har Etzion VBM, 2002, https://www.etzion.org.il/en/story-creation -and-our-ecological-crisis.

69. Rashi on Genesis 1:30.

70. Cara Giaimo, "Crocodiles Went Through a Vegetarian Phase, Too," *The New York Times*, June 27, 2019, https://www.nytimes.com/2019/06/27/science /crocodiles-vegetarian-teeth.html.

71. Nachmanides on Genesis 1:4.

72. Isaiah 11:2.

73. Rashi on Genesis 2:5.

74. Rabbi Daniel Kohn, Jerusalem, 2012.

75. Rabbi Abraham Isaac Kook, *Gold from the Land of Israel*, Chanan Morrison ed. (California: CreateSpace Independent Publishing Platform, 2017), 216–217. Adapted from Rabbi Abraham Isaac Kook, *Orot HaKodesh, Volume II* (Jerusalem: Mosad HaRav Kook, 1937), 563–564.

76. Rabbi Jonathan Sacks, "The Stewardship Paradigm," January 14, 2014, http:// rabbisacks.org/tu-bshvat/.

77. Genesis 2:15.

78. Psalms 24:1.

79. Rabbi Samson Raphael Hirsch, commentary on Genesis 1:26. The commentaries on this verse by Radak, Nachmanides, and Ralbag also shed light on this point.

80. Leviticus 19:19, Deuteronomy 22:6–7, and 20:19–20.

81. "Mercury and Air Toxics Standards," US Environmental Protection Agency, accessed June 7, 2020, https://www.epa.gov/mats.

82. University of California – San Diego, "Climate Change and Deforestation Will Lead to Declines in Global Bird Diversity, Study Warns," *ScienceDaily*, June 5, 2007, www.sciencedaily.com/releases/2007/06/070604205627.htm.

83. *Climate Change 2014: Synthesis Report Summary for Policymakers*, Rajendra K. Pachauri and Leo Meyer eds., Geneva, IPCC, 2014, https://www.ipcc.ch/site /assets/uploads/2018/02/AR5_SYR_FINAL_SPM.pdf.

84. Midrash Ecclesiastes Rabbah 7:13.

85. Rabbi Samson Raphael Hirsch, *The Nineteen Letters of Ben Uziel* (New York: BN Publishing, 2011), 30.

86. Rabbi Arthur Waskow, "Torah and the Climate Crisis" webinar, May 2019.

87. Martin Buber, *I and Thou* (London: A&C Black, 1937).

88. Genesis Rabbah 17:4.

89. Hoseah 11:10.

90. Pirkei d'Rabbi Eliezer 21.

91. Rabbi David Seidenberg, "Crossing the Threshold: God's Image in the More-Than-Human World," PhD thesis, Jewish Theological Seminary, 2004, 164.

92. Babylonian Talmud, Eruvin 100b.

93. Proverbs 6:6.

94. Genesis 2:16–17.

95. Rabbi Tzadok HaKohen Rabinowitz of Lublin, "Section 8: Genesis," in *Pri Tzadik.*

96. Susan (Sarah Yehudit) Schneider, *Eating as Tikun* (Jerusalem: A Still Small Voice, 1996), 18.

97. Or HaChayim commentary to Genesis 3:17.

98. Pirkei d'Rabbi Eliezer 14.

99. Rashi on Genesis 2:21 and Midrash Genesis Rabbah 8:1.

100. Rashi on Genesis 3:18.

101. Haigen Xu et al., "The Distribution and Economic Losses of Alien Species Invasion to China," *Biological Invasions* 8, October 2006, 1495–1500, https://doi .org/10.1007/s10530-005-5841-2.

102. Costanza Ceccanti et al., "Mediterranean Wild Edible Plants: Weeds or 'New Functional Crops'?" *Molecules* 23, no. 9, September 2018, 2299, https://dx .doi.org/10.3390%2Fmolecules23092299.

103. Clearly this must be subject to a full toxin analysis to ensure that they are nutritious and not harmful.

104. Rabbi Shlomo Riskin, oral teaching, Yeshivat Hamivtar, Migdal Oz, November 2009.

105. Ihab Mikati et al., "Disparities in Distribution of Particulate Matter Emission Sources by Race and Poverty Status," *American Journal of Public Health* 108, no. 4, April 1, 2018, 480–485, https://doi.org/10.2105/AJPH.2017.304297.

106. Kanta Kumari Rigaud et al., "Groundswell: Preparing for Internal Climate Migration," World Bank Group, 2018, https://openknowledge.worldbank.org /handle/10986/29461.

107. John Podesta, "The Climate Crisis, Migration, and Refugees," The Brookings Institution, July 25, 2019, https://www.brookings.edu/research/the-climate -crisis-migration-and-refugees/.

108. Rashi on Genesis 6:16.

109. Jim Ippolito and Mahdi Al-Kaisi, "The Dirt on Soil Loss from the Midwest Floods," Colorado State University, April 16, 2019, https://source.colostate.edu /the-dirt-on-soil-loss-from-the-midwest-floods/.

110. Babylonian Talmud, Sanhedrin 108b.

111. https://en.wikipedia.org/wiki/List_of_ammonium_nitrate_disasters.

112. *World Green Building Trends 2018: Smart Market Report*, Steven A. Jones ed. (Bedford: Dodge Data Analytics, 2018) https://www.worldgbc.org/sites /default/files/World%20Green%20Building%20Trends%202018%20SMR %20FINAL%2010-11.pdf.

113. Radak on Genesis 6:18.

114. US Census Bureau. World Population 1950–2050. https://www.census.gov /library/visualizations/2011/demo/world-population--1950-2050.html.

115. "Living Planet Report–2018: Aiming Higher," M. Grooten. and R.E.A. Almond eds., WWF, Gland, Switzerland, https://www.wwf.org.uk/sites/default /files/2018-10/wwfintl_livingplanet_full.pdf.

116. This content was produced by Canfei Nesharim, a branch of Grow Torah. It is available at http://canfeinesharim.org/noach-a-paradigm-for-environmental -consciousness/.

117. Midrash Genesis Rabbah 30:7.

118. Babylonian Talmud, Sanhedrin 108b based on Genesis 6:16.

119. Midrash Aggadah, v. 29.

120. Malbim on Genesis 6:21.

121. Nachmanides on Genesis 7:23.

122. Matthew Savoca, "The Bad News Is That Fish Are Eating Lots of Plastic. Even Worse, They May Like It," *The Washington Post*, April 9, 2017, https://www .washingtonpost.com/national/health-science/the-bad-news-is-that-fish-are -eating-lots-of-plastic-even-worse-they-may-like-it/2017/09/01/54159ee8-8cc6 -11e7-91d5-ab4e4b76a3a_story.html.

123. Sanae Chiba et al., "Human Footprint in the Abyss: 30 Year Records of Deep-Sea Plastic Debris," *Marine Policy* 96, October 2018, 204–212, https://doi .org/10.1016/j.marpol.2018.03.022.

124. "The New Plastics Economy: Rethinking the Future of Plastics," World Economic Forum, 2016, http://www3.weforum.org/docs/WEF_The_New _Plastics_Economy.pdf.

125. Babylonian Talmud, Sanhedrin 108b and Midrash Genesis Rabbah 38:4.

126. "Gerardo, Ceballos, Paul R. Ehrlich, Peter H. Raven, "Vertebrates on the Brink as Indicators of Biological Annihilation and the Sixth Mass Extinction," Proceedings of the National Academy of Sciences, June 16, 2020, 117 (24) 13596–13602, https://doi.org/10.1073/pnas.1922686117.

127. Jinxing He et al., "Quantifying the Effects of Climate and Anthropogenic Change on Regional Species Loss in China," *PLOS One* 13, no. 7, July 25, 2018, https://doi.org/10.1371/journal.pone.0199735.

128. Part of this section is from Yonatan Neril, "Countering Destruction: Lessons from Noach," Canfei Nesharim, a branch of Grow Torah, February 19, 2004, http://canfeinesharim.org/countering-destruction-lessons-from-noach -longer-article/.

129. Rabbi Samson Raphael Hirsch on Genesis 9:13.

130. Nachmanides on Genesis 9:12.

131. Rabbi Shlomo Riskin, "The 'Noah Covenant' with Mankind," *Arutz Sheva*, October 31, 2018, http://www.israelnationalnews.com/Articles/Article.aspx /8340.

132. Ibid.

133. Hannah Ritchie and Max Roser, "CO$_2$ and Greenhouse Gas Emissions,"

Our World in Data, revised December 2019, https://ourworldindata.org/co2
-and-other-greenhouse-gas-emissions#co2-in-the-atmosphere.

134. CO₂ Earth, accessed June 21, 2020, https://www.co2.earth/.

135. Zeke Hausfather, "Analysis: Why Scientists Think 100% of Global Warming Is Due to Humans," Carbon Brief, December 13, 2017, https://www.carbonbrief .org/analysis-why-scientists-think-100-of-global-warming-is-due-to-humans.

136. Footnote 43 to Zohar, Noah 72b.

137. Rashi on Genesis 9:20 citing Genesis Rabbah 26:3.

138. Rashi on Genesis 6:13, citing Genesis Rabbah 31:7.

139. Bijumon Kurian, "Farmers Plant 200,000 Seedlings to Replace Lost Crops after Kerala Floods," Fairtrade Foundation, November 27, 2018, https://www .fairtrade.org.uk/Media-Centre/Blog/2018/November/Farmers-become -earth-builders-after-Kerala-floods.

140. *Torah of the Earth*, vol. 1, Arthur Waskow ed., Evan Eisenberg, "The Mountain & the Tower," 30–33.

141. Manfred Gerstenfeld, *The Quality of the Environment* (Israel: The Jerusalem Institute for Research, 2002), 48.

142. Jeremy Benstein, *The Way Into Judaism and the Environment* (Vermont: Jewish Lights Publishing, 2008), 64–66.

143. Shadal on Genesis 11:6.

144. Jared Diamond, *Collapse* (London: Penguin, 2005), 274.

145. "Top Chain Restaurants Worldwide," Restaurant Engine, accessed June 17, 2020, https://restaurantengine.com/top-chain-restaurants-worldwide/.

146. "UN Agency Sounds Alarm: Dwindling Agrobiodiversity 'Severe Threat' to Food Security," UN News, November 14, 2019, https://news.un.org/en/story /2019/11/1051411.

147. Jared Diamond, *Collapse: How Societies Choose to Fail or Succeed* (New York: Viking, 2009), 489.

148. Midrash Genesis Rabbah 39:1.

149. Rabbi Yosef Y. Jacobson, "The Burning Palace," Chabad, September 11, 2002, www.chabad.org/library/article_cdo/aid/59473/jewish/The-Burning -Palace.htm.

150. Rabbi Jonathan Sacks, *Radical Then, Radical Now* (London: Continuum, 2000), 49–53.

151. Alexandria Symonds, "Amazon Rainforest Fires: Here's What's Really Happening," *The New York Times*, August 28, 2019, https://www.nytimes.com /2019/08/23/world/americas/amazon-fire-brazil-bolsonaro.html.

152. Rabbeinu Bachaya on Genesis 26:1.

153. Midrash Genesis Rabbah 64:2. Famine occurs in the time of Isaac in Genesis 26:12, and in the time of Jacob in Genesis 41:56.

154. See Seder Olam for the dates that Abraham went to Egypt and the date that Jacob left for Egypt.

155. Stephen Devereux, "Famine in the Twentieth Century," IDS *Working Papers* 105, January 2000.

156. IPCC, "Climate Change and Land, An IPCC Special Report on Climate Change, Desertification, Land Degradation, Sustainable Land Management, Food Security, and Greenhouse Gas Fluxes in Terrestrial Ecosystems," Summary for Policymakers, IPCC, 2019, https://www.ipcc.ch/site/assets/uploads/2019 /08/4.-SPM_Approved_Microsite_FINAL.pdf.

157. Seth Borenstein and Jamey Keaten, "UN Climate Report: Change Land Use to Avoid a Hungry Future," Phys.org, August 8, 2019, https://phys.org/news /2019-08-climate-hungry-future.html.

158. This content was produced by Canfei Nesharim, a branch of Grow Torah. It is available at http://canfeinesharim.org/lech-lecha-joining-together-for -justice-in-the-land/.

159. Ha'amek Davar on 13:6 and Rabbi Samson Raphael Hirsch on Genesis 13:6 in *The Pentateuch*, Efraim Oratz ed., Gertrude Hirschler trans. (New York: Judaica Press, 1986). This idea has a precedent in Pesikta Rabati 83.

160. Onkelos on Genesis 13:6. Ibn Ezra also translates *yachdav* as *yachid* – united, and not *yachad* – together.

161. Ralbag on Genesis 14:3.

162. Rashi on Genesis 13:10.

163. Guy Pe'er and Uriel N. Safriel, *Climate Change Israel National Report: Impact, Vulnerability and Adaptation* (Israel: Blaustein Institute for Desert Research, Ben-Gurion University of the Negev, October 2000).

164. Israel Water Authority, "Saving the Dead Sea," accessed June 18, 2020, http:// www.water.gov.il/Hebrew/Water-Environment/Dead-Sea/DocLib1/saving -dead-sea-eng.pdf.

165. This is distinct from clay, which is referred to as *chomer*. Onkelos translates *chemar* into Aramaic as *chemra*, which is understood by language scholars to refer to bitumen or asphalt. See Marcus Jastrow, *Dictionary of the Targumim*, 1926, accessed January 3, 2020, https://www.sefaria.org.il/Jastrow%2C_%D7%97 %D6%B5%D7%99%D7%9E%D6%B8%D7%A8%D6%B8%D7%90?lang=he. See also Safa Ivrit, "Chimer and Chomer." https://www.safa-ivrit.org/form /khomer.php.

166. "Bitumen," Energy Education, University of Calgary, last modified June 25, 2018, https://energyeducation.ca/encyclopedia/Bitumen.

167. Rabbi Aryeh Kaplan writes, "Even now asphalt is found in the Dead Sea region. The Romans referred to it as Mer Apheltitus, the Asphalt Sea, as it was known to cast up lumps of asphalt. Rabbi Aryeh Kaplan, *The Living Torah*, commentary to Genesis 14:10, 65. Josephus, *The Wars of the Jews* 4:8:4; Tacitus, *Histories* 5:6.

168. Asaf Oron et al., "Early Maritime Activity on the Dead Sea: Bitumen Har-

vesting and the Possible Use of Reed Watercraft," *Journal of Maritime Archaeology* 10, no. 1, April 2015, 65–88, https://doi.org/10.1007/s11457-015-9135-2.

169. Genesis 14:11.

170. "What Are the Oil Sands?", Canadian Association of Petroleum Producers, accessed March 1, 2020, https://www.capp.ca/oil/what-are-the-oil-sands/.

171. Stephen Leahy, "This Is the World's Most Destructive Oil Operation – and It's Growing," *National Geographic*, April 11, 2019, https://www.nationalgeographic .com/environment/2019/04/alberta-canadas-tar-sands-is-growing-but -indigenous-people-fight-back/.

172. Lisa Song, "Why Tar Sands Oil Is More Polluting and Why It Matters," *Reuters*, May 22, 2012, https://www.reuters.com/article/idUS201043482520120522.

173. Elizabeth Mcgowan And Lisa Song, "The Dilbit Disaster: Inside the Biggest Oil Spill You've Never Heard Of," InsideClimate News, Jun 26, 2012, https:// insideclimatenews.org/content/dilbit-disaster-inside-biggest-oil-spill-youve -never-heard.

174. Genesis Rabbah 42:7, quoted by Rashi on Genesis 14:10.

175. Jacobson et al., "100% Clean and Renewable Wind, Water, and Sunlight All-Sector Energy Roadmaps for 139 Countries of the World," Joule 1, 108–121 September 6, 2017, Elsevier Inc. http://dx.doi.org/10.1016/j.joule.2017.07.005.

176. Maharal, Netivot Olam, Netiv HaOsher 1:4.

177. See Rashi on Genesis 13:7.

178. Abraham ibn Ezra, "God Everywhere" (1089–1164).

179. Jeremy Benstein, *The Way Into Judaism and the Environment* (Vermont: Jewish Lights Publishing, 2006), 142, citing Elie Wiesel.

180. Rabbi Mordechai Hochman, "Footnote 1 based on the Midrash," in "The Bird That Brings Life to the Carcasses," Yeshiva Beit El, published Kislev 5, 5770, https://www.yeshiva.org.il/midrash/12714.

181. Rabbeinu Chananel on Genesis 18:4.

182. Job 14:7–9.

183. Psalms 1:3.

184. Moises Velasquez-Manoff, "Can Humans Help Trees Outrun Climate Change?" *The New York Times*, April 25, 2019, https://www.nytimes.com/2019 /04/25/climate/trees-climate-change.html?searchResultPosition=7.

185. William R.L. Anderegg et al., "Hydraulic Diversity of Forests Regulates Ecosystem Resilience during Drought," *Nature* 561, no. 7724, September 2018, https://doi.org/10.1038/s41586-018-0539-7.

186. Radak on Genesis 18:7.

187. Responsa Igrot Moshe, Even Ha'Ezer, vol. iv 92. Quoted in "The Environment in Jewish Thought and Law," Saul Stokar, *Sviva Israel* (2018), 28.

188. Midrash Tanchuma Vayeira 23:1.

189. Keoni Everington, "Taoyuan's Zhongli District Has Worst Acid Rain in

Taiwan," *Taiwan News*, August 19, 2019, https://www.taiwannews.com.tw/en/news/3764930.

190. "Acid Rain Program," US EPA, accessed June 22, 2020, https://www.epa.gov/acidrain/acid-rain-program.

191. This content was produced by Canfei Nesharim, a branch of Grow Torah. It is available at http://canfeinesharim.org/wp-content/uploads/2014/05/Parsha-vayera-sin-of-sedom-Rabbi-Cherlow-sourcesheet.pdf.

192. Genesis 13:10.

193. Deuteronomy 29:22.

194. Genesis 6:13.

195. Ibid., 19:29.

196. Ezekiel 16:49.

197. Mishnah Avot 5:10.

198. Deuteronomy 20:19.

199. Genesis 19:28.

200. Rashi on Genesis 19:28.

201. Chizkuni on Genesis 19:25.

202. "Impacts of Acid Rain on Soils," *Air Pollution UK*, accessed May 16, 2019, http://www.air-quality.org.uk/16.php.

203. William K. Stevens, "To Treat the Attack of Acid Rain, Add Limestone to Water and Wait," *The New York Times*, January 31, 1989, https://www.nytimes.com/1989/01/31/science/to-treat-the-attack-of-acid-rain-add-limestone-to-water-and-wait.html.

204. Jean Tirole, "Some Economics of Global Warming," *Rivista di Politica Economica* 98, no. 6, November 2008, 9–42.

205. Malbim on Genesis 21:33.

206. "Article 6" in "Treaty of Peace between the State of Israel and the Hashemite Kingdom of Jordan," Israel Ministry of Foreign Affairs, October 26, 1994, https://mfa.gov.il/mfa/foreignpolicy/peace/guide/pages/israel-jordan%20peace%20treaty.aspx.

207. Rabbeinu Bachaya on Genesis 23:4.

208. Eldad Keynan, "Private vs. Public Burials: Differences and Time Span," The Bible and Interpretation, The University of Arizona, October 2010, http://www.bibleinterp.com/articles/burial357907.shtml#sdfootnote9sym. Citing Jerusalem Talmud, Mo'ed Katan 1:5, 80d; Sanhedrin 6:10, 23d.

209. Aysel Uslu, Emin Barış, and Elmas Erdoğan, "Ecological Concerns over Cemeteries," *African Journal of Agricultural Research* 4, 13, December 2009, 1505–1511.

210. Sam Sokol, "Squeezed for Burial Space, Jerusalem Prepares an Underground City of the Dead," *The Times of Israel*, October 26, 2019, https://www.timesofisrael.com/squeezed-for-burial-space-jerusalem-prepares-an-underground-city-of-the-dead/.

211. Yair Altman, "Shortage of 1.5 Million Graves in the Center of Israel" (in Hebrew), *Israel Hayom*, March 23, 2020, https://www.israelhayom.co.il/article /744597.

212. Genesis 3:19.

213. Tanchuma, Pekudei 3.

214. Rabbi Matis Weinberg, *Frameworks: Genesis* (Boston: Foundation for Jewish Publications, 1st edition, 1998), 100–101.

215. Martin Buber, *I and Thou* (London: A&C Black, 1937).

216. J. Donald Hughes and J.V. Thirgood, "Deforestation, Erosion, and Forest Management in Ancient Greece and Rome," *Journal of Forest History* 26, no. 2, April 1982, 60–75, https://doi.org/10.2307/4004530.

217. Babylonian Talmud, Ta'anit 23a.

218. "Dreams to Action: Beginning a Meaningful Conversation with Young Leaders," UN Environment Programme, published April 23, 2019, https:// www.unenvironment.org/news-and-stories/story/dreams-action-beginning -meaningful-conversation-young-leaders.

219. Lydia Denworth, "Children Change Their Parents' Minds about Climate Change," *Scientific American*, May 6, 2019, https://www.scientificamerican .com/article/children-change-their-parents-minds-about-climate-change/ ?redirect=1.

220. David Crouch, "The Swedish 15-Year-Old Who's Cutting Class to Fight the Climate Crisis," *The Guardian*, September 1, 2018, https://www.theguardian.com /science/2018/sep/01/swedish-15-year-old-cutting-class-to-fight-the-climate -crisis.

221. Babylonian Talmud, Chulin 63a.

222. Job 35:11.

223. Knut Schmidt Nielsen, *Animal Physiology: Adaptation and Environment* (Cambridge: Cambridge University Press, 5th ed., 1997).

224. Jonathan Kingdon, *East African Mammals: An Atlas of Evolution in Africa, Volume 1* (Chicago: University Of Chicago Press, 1984).

225. Rebbetzin Chana Bracha Siegelbaum, "Discovering the Camel Connection: Nature in the Parasha: Parashat Chayei Sarah," *Women on the Land*, November 11, 2014, http://rebbetzinchanabracha.blogspot.com/2014/11/discovering-camel -connection.html.

226. This content was produced by Canfei Nesharim, a branch of Grow Torah. It is available at http://canfeinesharim.org/parshat-chayei-sarah-praying-in -the-fields/.

227. Genesis 24:63.

228. Babylonian Talmud, Berakhot 26b, citing use of the same Hebrew root word in Psalms 102:1.

229. Ibid., 34b.

230. Ibid.

231. Rabbi Nachman of Breslov, Likutei Moharan 1:52.

232. Shiur on Likutei Moharan, part 2, teaching 11. Rabbi Greenberg is the Rosh Yeshiva of the Bat Ayin Yeshiva. This shiur is available in audio form at www .bat-ayin.org.

233. Citing Babylonian Talmud, Avodah Zarah 11a.

234. Babylonian Talmud, Avodah Zarah 11a.

235. Israel Central Bureau of Statistics, "Agricultural Statistics Quarterly July–September 2019," https://www.cbs.gov.il/en/publications/Pages/2020 /Agricultural-Statistics-Quarterly-July-September-2019.aspx.

236. This content was produced by Canfei Nesharim, a branch of Grow Torah. It is available at http://canfeinesharim.org/the-conflict-of-yaakov-and-esav/.

237. Etz Chayim, Heikhal HaNikudim (Sha'ar 8, ff.).

238. Genesis 1:2.

239. Ibid., 25:32.

240. Arizal, Likutei Torah on Parshat Vayishlach.

241. "U.S. Environmental Footprint Factsheet," Center for Sustainable Systems, University of Michigan, accessed December 12, 2019, http://css.umich.edu /factsheets/us-environmental-footprint-factsheet.

242. Genesis 27:4–14.

243. Rabbi Raphael Zarum, oral class, Limmud Festival UK, December 26, 2019, based on Rabbi Henau, *Nechmad Lemareh*, commentary on Genesis Rabbah 63:10.

244. Rabbi Yonatan Neril and Rabbi Yedidya Sinclair, "We Are How We Eat: A Jewish Approach to Eating and Food," produced by Canfei Nesharim (now a branch of Grow Torah), February 24, 2014, http://canfeinesharim.org/we -are-how-we-eat-a-jewish-approach-to-food-and-sustainability-long-article/.

245. Genesis Rabbah 21, Midrash Tanchuma, Pinchas 13; Midrash Genesis Rabbah (Vilna edition), 63:12, citing Mishnah, Shabbat 24:3.

246. Rabbi Samson Raphael Hirsch, commentary to Genesis 25:30.

247. Cited in Rabbi Tzadok HaKohen, Kitzur Kuntras Eit HaOchel, §9.

248. Likutei Moharan 1, 62:5.

249. Rabbi Shlomo Wolbe, *Alei Shor* (Jerusalem, 1998).

250. Rabbi Nathan (Sternhartz) of Breslov, *Chayey Moharan*, #515, Rabbi Avraham Greenbaum trans.

251. Babylonian Talmud, Chagigah 27a.

252. Chapter 3, Mishnah 4.

253. Rabbi Tzadok HaKohen, *Pri Tzadik*, Treatise on the Time of Eating, §6.

254. "Increased Food Intake Alone Explains the Increase in Body Weight in the United States," Boyd Swinburn et al., oral presentation, 17th European Congress on Obesity, May 2009, news abstract online at http://www.medicalnewstoday .com/articles/149553.php. The researchers consider this increased food consumption to be the leading cause of the obesity epidemic.

255. "Luxus Consumption: Wasting Food Resources through Overeating," By Dorothy Blair and Jeffery Sobal, *Agriculture and Human Values*, vol. 23, Number 1, 2006, 63–74, https://doi.org/10.1007/s10460-004-5869-4.

256. "Global Greenhouse Gas Emissions Data," US EPA, accessed June 21, 2020, https://www.epa.gov/ghgemissions/global-greenhouse-gas-emissions-data.

257. HaKetav VeHaKabbalah on Genesis 25:34.

258. Genesis 18:8.

259. Carlo Petrini, *Slow Food Nation: Why Our Food Should Be Good, Clean, and Fair* (New York: Rizzoli Publications, 2013).

260. Carl Honoré, *In Praise of Slow: How a Worldwide Movement Is Challenging the Cult of Speed* (Toronto: Vintage Canada, 2004).

261. Mark N. Wexler, Judy Oberlander, and Arjun Shankar, "The Slow Food Movement: A 'Big Tent' Ideology," *Journal of Ideology* 37, no. 1 (January 2017).

262. Genesis 25:27.

263. Rashi on Genesis 26:12, citing Midrash Genesis Rabbah ad loc.

264. Jeff Jenness, Joe Dooley, Jose Aguilar-Manjarrez, and Claudia Riva, *African Water Database*, Rome: FAO, 2007, www.fao.org/3/a1170e/a1170e.pdf.

265. Andrew J. Kondash, Nancy E. Lauer and Avner Vengosh, "The Intensification of the Water Footprint of Hydraulic Fracturing," Science Advances 4, no. 8, August 2018, DOI: 10.1126/sciadv.aar5982.

266. Rabbi David Seidenberg, "How Fracking Conflicts with Kabbalah," *Forward*, July 16, 2013, https://forward.com/opinion/180507/how-fracking-conflicts-with-kabbalah/.

267. This content was produced by Canfei Nesharim, a branch of Grow Torah. It is available at http://canfeinesharim.org/parshat-toldot-digging-the-wells-the-importance-of-protecting-our-natural-resources/.

268. Deuteronomy 20:19.

269. Genesis 26:18–22.

270. Morgan Gass and Helena Freire Haddad, "Revolutionizing Sustainable Agriculture," Northwestern University Center for Water Research, September 19, 2019, https://water.northwestern.edu/2019/09/19/get-water-blog-2-revolutionizing-sustainable-agriculture/.

271. Colin Kelley et al., "Climate Change in the Fertile Crescent and Implications of the Recent Syrian Drought," *Proceedings of the National Academy of Sciences of the United States of America* 112, no. 11, 2015, 3241–3246. www.jstor.org/stable/26462026.

272. Elizabeth M. Gallagher, Stephen J. Shennan, and Mark G. Thomas, "Transition to Farming More Likely for Small, Conservative Groups with Property Rights, but Increased Productivity Is Not Essential," *Proceedings of the National Academy of Sciences* 112, no. 46 (November 2015): 14218–14223, https://doi.org/10.1073/pnas.1511870112.

273. Genesis 26:33.

274. Ibid., 26:28.

275. Ibid., 25:27.

276. Ibid.

277. Kli Yakar on Genesis 28:27.

278. The Interfaith Center for Sustainable Development, www.interfaithsustain.com.

279. Ibn Ezra on Genesis 28:11 based on the Zohar 1:72.

280. Genesis Rabbah 68.

281. Rabbi Daniel Kohn, oral teaching, 2013.

282. Proverbs 3:24.

283. Gaétan Chevalier et al., "Earthing: Health Implications of Reconnecting the Human Body to the Earth's Surface Electrons," *Journal of Environment and Public Health* 3, January 2012, https://doi.org/10.1155/2012/291541.

284. Richard Louv, *Last Child in the Woods: Saving Our Children from Nature-Deficit Disorder* (Chapel Hill, NC: Algonquin Books, 2005).

285. Gregory Bratman et al., "Nature and Mental Health: An Ecosystem Service Perspective," *Science Advances*, July 24, 201, vol. 5, no. 7, eaax0903 DOI: 10.1126/sciadv.aax0903.

286. Maimonides, Mishneh Torah, Matanot Aniyim 9:13.

287. Hannah Ritchie, "How Much of the World's Land Would We Need In Order To Feed the Global Population with the Average Diet of a Given Country?" Our World in Data, October 3, 2017, https://ourworldindata.org/agricultural-land-by-global-diets.

288. Rabbi Avi Neuman, "Parshat Vayeitzei: Ya'akov and Going Out," December 31, 2013. This content was produced by Canfei Nesharim, a branch of Grow Torah. It is available at http://canfeinesharim.org/parshat-vayeitzei-yaakov-and-going-out/.

289. Genesis 29:1.

290. Sforno on Genesis 29:1.

291. "Per Capita Living Space in China in Urban and Rural Areas from 2002 to 2017," Statista and National Bureau of Statistics of China, CEIC, August 2018, https://www.statista.com/statistics/225016/per-capita-living-space-in-china-in-urban-and-rural-areas/.

292. Anne Thiel and Xiufang Sun, "China's Logging Ban Impacts Not Just Its Own Forestry Industry, but Others around the World As Well," Forest Trends, March 14, 2016, https://www.forest-trends.org/blog/chinas-logging-ban/.

293. Malbim on Genesis 31:18.

294. Henning Steinfeld and Simon Mack, "Livestock Development Strategies," FAO, accessed June 5, 2019, http://www.fao.org/3/V8180T/v8180T0a.htm.

295. This content was produced by Canfei Nesharim, a branch of Grow Torah. It is available at http://canfeinesharim.org/parshat-vayishlach-small-vessels/.

296. Genesis 32:25, Babylonian Talmud, Chulin, 91a. Midrash Aggadah – Buber

on 32:25. Rashi on 32:25. The Gur Aryeh (Maharal of Prague) on 32:24 says these were two or three very small vessels. Ba'alei Tosafot on 32:25 understood *levado* as hinting at *lekado*, "for his vessels."

297. Orchot Tzadikim on Genesis 32:24.

298. Victor Lebow, "Price Competition in 1955," *The Journal of Retailing* (Spring 1955), 7.

299. John Kenneth Galbraith, *The Affluent Society* (Boston: Houghton Mifflin, 1958).

300. Likutei Moharan (Jerusalem: Breslov Research Institute) §54c.

301. Rashi on Genesis 33:11.

302. Tanchuma Vayishlach 3 and Genesis Rabbah.

303. Rabbi Matis Weinberg, *Frameworks: Genesis* (Boston: Foundation for Jewish Publications, 1 edition, 1998) 193–194.

304. Ecclesiates 5:10.

305. Kurt Cobb, "Greed Explained: J. Paul Getty, Aristotle and the Maximum Power Principle," Resource Insights, December 21, 2014, http://resourceinsights .blogspot.com/2014/12/greed-explained-j-paul-getty-aristotle.html.

306. From class given at Yeshivat Sulam Yaakov, Jerusalem, 2012.

307. Yeonjin Lee, MA and Ichiro Kawachi, "The Keys to Happiness: Associations between Personal Values regarding Core Life Domains and Happiness in South Korea," PLOS ONE 14, no. 1 (January 2019), https://doi.org/10.1371/journal .pone.0209821.

308. This content was produced by Canfei Nesharim, a branch of Grow Torah. It is available at http://canfeinesharim.org/the-conflict-of-yaakov-and-esav/.

309. Genesis Rabbah 67:6, cited by Rashi on Genesis 27:39.

310. "Deepwater Horizon Joint Investigation Team Releases Final Report," The Bureau of Ocean Energy Management, Regulation and Enforcement, September 14, 2011, https://www.boem.gov/sites/default/files/boem-newsroom/Press -Releases/2011/press0914.pdf.

311. Igal Berenshtein et al., "Invisible Oil beyond the *Deepwater Horizon* Satellite Footprint," *Science Advances*, February 12, 2020, vol. 6, no. 7, eaaw8863 DOI: 10.1126/sciadv.aaw8863.

312. Lisa Friedman, "Ten Years after Deepwater Horizon, U.S. Is Still Vulnerable to Catastrophic Spills," *The New York Times*, April 19, 2020, https://nyti.ms /2KiHaSg.

313. Christopher Helman, "A Decade after Deepwater Horizon, Oil Still Flows from This Prolific Patch in the Gulf of Mexico," Forbes, April 23, 2020, https:// www.forbes.com/sites/christopherhelman/2020/04/23/a-decade-after -deepwater-horizon-oil-still-flows-from-this-prolific-patch-in-the-gulf-of -mexico/#167b85d043a9.

314. David Gelles et al., "Boeing Was 'Go, Go, Go' to Beat Airbus with the 737

Max," *The New York Times*, March 23, 2019, https://www.nytimes.com/2019/03
/23/business/boeing-737-max-crash.html?searchResultPosition=6.

315. Babylonian Talmud, Shabbat 33b.

316. World Food Programme, "What is 'Blockchain' and How Is It Connected
to Fighting Hunger?" *Medium*, March 6, 2017, https://insight.wfp.org/what-is
-blockchain-and-how-is-it-connected-to-fighting-hunger-7f1b42da9fe.

317. "Statistics on China–Africa Trade in 2018," Ministry of Commerce People's
Republic of China, January 26, 2019, http://english.mofcom.gov.cn/article
/statistic/lanmubb/AsiaAfrica/201901/20190102831255.shtml.

318. Nicholas Muller, "The Chinese Railways Remolding East Africa," *The
Diplomat*, January 25, 2019, https://thediplomat.com/2019/01/the-chinese
-railways-remolding-east-africa/.

319. This content was produced by Canfei Nesharim, a branch of Grow Torah.
It is available at http://canfeinesharim.org/parshat-vayeishev-shepherd
-consciousness-and-the-post-industrial-jew/.

320. Genesis 37:2.

321. Ibid., 47:3.

322. The following ideas are based on and adapted from Rabbi Abraham Isaac
Kook, *Ein Eyah* vol. 4, 144–145 and *Orot HaKodesh* vol. 3, 267, 269–274; vol. 2,
439–441 (Jerusalem: Mosad HaRav Kook Publishers, 2000).

323. Orot HaKodesh, vol. 3, 270.

324. Likutei Moharan, part 2, Torah 25.

325. Genesis 34.

326. Jared Diamond, *Collapse* (London: Penguin, 2005), 497.

327. Midrash Genesis Rabbah 84.

328. Ibid., 77:2.

329. Genesis 37:24.

330. Ibid., 37:7.

331. Oral class at Yeshivat Hamivtar, November 2009.

332. Genesis 47:11.

333. "Trends in Global Export Volume of Trade in Goods from 1950 to 2018,"
Statista, July 2019, https://www.statista.com/statistics/264682/worldwide
-export-volume-in-the-trade-since-1950/.

334. "The Carbon Footprint of Global Trade," OECD and International Transport
Forum, 2015, https://www.itf-oecd.org/sites/default/files/docs/cop-pdf-06
.pdf.

335. Rabbi Michael Melchior, oral teaching, Jerusalem, May 15, 2005. See also
Rabbeinu Bachaya on Genesis 40:7.

336. Rabbi Abraham Isaac Kook, Orot HaKodesh II, 444, http://www.ravkook
.net/universalism.html.

337. Dr. Jonathan Grossman, "Two Dreams and Two Solutions," Parashat

Hashavua Study Center, Bar-Ilan University, December 21, 2011, https://nanopdf
.com/download/two-dreams-and-two-solutions_pdf.

338. "Bread Waste Is Off the Scale," *Toast*, March 24, 2020, https://www.toastale
.com/bread-waste/.

339. "Key Facts on Food Loss and Waste You Should Know!" FAO, accessed
February 13, 2020, twosides.info/includes/files/upload/files/UK/Myths_and
_Facts_2016_Sources/18-19/Key_facts_on_food_loss_and_waste_you
_should_know-FAO_2016.pdf.

340. Madeline Puckette, "Better Than Organic: Sustainability and Wine," Wine
Folly, Folly Enterprises, May 18, 2016, https://winefolly.com/tips/beyond
-organic-certified-sustainable-wine/.

341. Likutei Tefillot 2:21.

342. Bekhor Shor on Genesis 41:1.

343. Gilbert F. White, "The Environmental Effects of the High Dam at Aswan,"
Environment: Science and Policy for Sustainable Development, July 2010, 30:7, 4–40,
https://doi.org/10.1080/00139157.1988.9930898.

344. Declan Walsh and Somini Sengupta, "For Thousands of Years, Egypt
Controlled the Nile. A New Dam Threatens That," *The New York Times*, February
9, 2020, https://www.nytimes.com/interactive/2020/02/09/world/africa/nile
-river-dam.html.

345. This content was produced by Canfei Nesharim, a branch of Grow Torah.
It is available at http://canfeinesharim.org/parshat-mikeitz-the-song-of-the
-land-a-torah-teaching-for-the-western-environmentalist/.

346. Genesis 41:2–4.

347. In rabbinic terminology, "The Place" is one of the names of God.

348. Likutei Moharan, part 2, §63.

349. "Rabbi Michael Melchior on God, Land & People – Caring for People &
Nature," Jewish Eco Seminars, February 14, 2018, video, 1:04:07, https://www
.youtube.com/watch?v=FgfRShMyiOY&feature=youtu.be.

350. Rabbi Matis Weinberg, *Frameworks: Genesis* (Boston: Foundation for
Jewish Publications, 1 edition, 1998), 250.

351. J.Y. Simms, "The Economic Impact of the Russian Famine of 1891–92," *The
Slavonic and East European Review* 60, no. 1, January 1982, 63–74.

352. "Number of Cattle Worldwide from 2012 to 2020," Statista, April 2020,
https://www.statista.com/statistics/263979/global-cattle-population-since
-1990/.

353. Mary Beth de Ondarza, "Energy," Milkproduction.com, DeLaval, September 29, 2000, www.milkproduction.com/Library/Scientific-articles/Nutrition
/Energy/; and "How Much Meat Can You Expect from a Fed Steer?" SDSU
Extension, December 20, 2018, https://extension.sdstate.edu/how-much-meat
-can-you-expect-fed-steer.

354. "Global Land Use for Food Production," Hannah Ritchie, Our World in

Data, October 3, 2017, https://ourworldindata.org/agricultural-land-by-global
-diets.

355. Babylonian Talmud, Tamid 32a.

356. Klaus Deininger et al., *Rising Global Interest in Farmland: Can It Yield Sustainable and Equitable Benefits?* (Washington: The World Bank, 2011).

357. "Global Hunger Continues to Rise, New UN Report Says," World Health Organization, September 11, 2018, https://www.who.int/news-room/detail/11 -09-2018-global-hunger-continues-to-rise---new-un-report-says.

358. Malbim on Genesis 41:48.

359. Rashi on Genesis 41:48.

360. "Principles," Transition Network, accessed June 29, 2020, https:// transitionnetwork.org/about-the-movement/what-is-transition/principles-2/.

361. Levush Ha'Orah on Rashi Genesis 41:50.

362. Rashi on Genesis 41:50, citing Babylonian Talmud, Ta'anit 11a.

363. Jerusalem Talmud, Ta'anit 1:6.

364. Shulchan Arukh, Orach Chayim 240:12.

365. Genesis 1:28.

366. Shulchan Arukh, Even Ha'Ezer, 1:5. For a fuller treatment of this topic, see Jeremy Cohen, *"Be Fertile and Increase, Fill the Earth and Master It"* (Ithaca, NY: Cornell University Press, 1989), 124–165.

367. From class given at the Bat Ayin Yeshiva, winter 2006.

368. Ba'al HaTurim and Maharim on Genesis 41:50.

369. Deuteronomy 33:13.

370. Adapted from David L. Goldblatt, "Parshat Vayigash: Lessons from Yosef's Foresight and Restraint," Canfei Nesharim, a branch of Grow Torah, Dec. 31, 2013, http://canfeinesharim.org/parshat-vayigash-lessons-from-yosefs-foresight -and-restraint/.

371. Likutei Moharan, part 2, §63.

372. Riva on Genesis 45:6.

373. Kipling Balkcom et al., "Managing Cover Crops in Conservation Tillage Systems," in *Managing Cover Crops Profitably,* 3rd ed. (College Park: Sustainable Agriculture Research & Education, 2007).

374. O.A. Opara-Nadi, "Conservation tillage for increased crop production," in *Soil Tillage in Africa: Needs and Challenges; FAO Soils Bulletin 69* (Rome: Food and Agriculture Organization, 1993), www.fao.org/3/t1696e/t1696e09.htm.

375. Kathryn Reid, "Africa Hunger, Famine," World Vision, October 24, 2019, https://www.worldvision.org/hunger-news-stories/africa-hunger-famine -facts.

376. Genesis 46:1.

377. Da'at Zekeinim on Genesis 45:20.

378. Rabbeinu Bachaya on Genesis 46:32.

379. Riva on Genesis 47:6.

380. Exodus 10:24.

381. Ibn Ezra on Genesis 46:34.

382. Alexandra Touseau et al., "Diet of Ancient Egyptians Inferred from Stable Isotope Systematics," *Journal of Archaeological Science*, vol. 46, June 2014, 114–124.

383. Ha'amek Davar on Genesis 47:17.

384. "Becoming a Vegetarian," *Harvard Women's Health Watch*, Harvard Health Publishing, last modified October 23, 2018, https://www.health.harvard.edu /staying-healthy/becoming-a-vegetarian.

385. This content was produced by Canfei Nesharim, a branch of Grow Torah. It is available at http://canfeinesharim.org/parshat-vayigash-lessons-from -yosefs-foresight-and-restraint/.

386. Genesis 49:22. See Babylonian Talmud, Chagigah 13b, on how the ox instructs about great wisdom.

387. From his email Torah commentary on Vayigash, 5767/2006. Rabbi Greenbaum is the founder and director of the Azamra Institute for Jewish Learning.

388. Genesis 47:13–19.

389. Ibid., 47:19.

390. Paolo F. Ricci et al., "Precaution, Uncertainty and Causation in Environmental Decisions," *Environment International* 29, no. 1, April 2003, 1–19, https:// www.ncbi.nlm.nih.gov/pubmed/12605931.

391. Kirk Semple, Rachel Knowles, and Frances Robles, "Bahamas Relief Efforts Frustrated as Dorian Pulls Away," *The New York Times*, September 3, 2019, https:// www.nytimes.com/2019/09/03/world/americas/bahamas-hurricane-dorian .html.

392. "Life-Sustaining Properties of Water," WithCarbon, October 24, 2013, https://www.withcarbon.com/2013/10/24/life-sustaining-properties-of -water/.

393. Malbim on Genesis 49:9.

394. "The Ecological Role of Lions," ALERT, February 20, 2020, http://lionalert .org/page/article-ecological-role-of-lions.

395. This content was produced by Canfei Nesharim, a branch of Grow Torah. It is available at http://canfeinesharim.org/parshat-vayechi-eating-holy-food -in-a-holy-way/.

396. Genesis 49:11.

397. Midrash Genesis Rabbah 98:9; Rashi on Genesis 49:11, s.v. *osri lagefen iro.*

398. Babylonian Talmud, Ketubot 111b.

399. Genesis 49:13.

400. Rashi on Genesis 49:13, s.v. *vehu lechof aniyot.*

401. Babylonian Talmud, Megillah 6b.

402. Genesis 49:15.

403. Rashi on Genesis 49:15, s.v. *vayar menucha ki tov.*

404. Michael Pollan, *The Omnivore's Dilemma* (New York: Penguin, 2006), 239.

405. Radak on Genesis 49:17.

406. Linda B. Glaser, "Snakes Act as 'Ecosystem Engineers' in Seed Dispersal," *Cornell Chronicle*, February 7, 2018, https://news.cornell.edu/stories/2018/02/snakes-act-ecosystem-engineers-seed-dispersal.

407. Midrash Exodus Rabbah §10.1. Rabbi David Stein, *A Garden of Choice Fruit* (Pennsylvania: Shomrei Adamah, 1991), 10.

408. Beth Greenwood, "What Are the Duties of a Shepherd?" *The Houston Chronicle*, Hearst Newspapers, last modified June 28, 2018, https://work.chron.com/duties-shepherd-23576.html.

409. Job 38:1, 8–11, 28–30, 39, 41; 39:1, 4–5, 8, 13, 19, 27–28, 40:3–4. As quoted in Rabbi David Stein, *A Garden of Choice Fruit* (Pennsylvania: Shomrei Adamah, 1991), 50.

410. Or HaChayim on Genesis 49:27, citing 1 Samuel 9:1–2.

411. "Arabian Wolf," Wikipedia, https://en.wikipedia.org/wiki/Arabian_wolf#Range_and_conservation.

412. "Gray Wolves," Defenders of Wildlife, accessed April 11, 2019, https://defenders.org/ecological-role-wolves.

413. Kim Murray Berger, Eric M. Gese, and Joel Berger, "Indirect Effects and Traditional Trophic Cascades: A Test involving Wolves, Coyotes, and Pronghorn," *Ecology* 89, no. 3, March 2008, 818–828, http://trophiccascades.forestry.oregonstate.edu/sites/trophic/files/Murray%20et%20al%202008.pdf.

414. Daniel Fortin et al., "Wolves Influence Elk Movements: Behavior Shapes a Trophic Cascade in Yellowstone National Park," *Ecology* 86, no. 5, 2005, 1320–1330, https://doi.org/10.1890/04-0953.

415. Erin Wilson and Elizabeth Wolkovich, "Scavenging: How Carnivores and Carrion Structure Communities," *Trends in Ecology and Evolution* 26, no. 3, March 2011, 129–135, https://doi.org/10.1016/j.tree.2010.12.011.

416. Rabbi Yaakov Tzvi Mecklenburg, HaKetav VeHaKabbalah commentary to Exodus 1:9.

417. Alan Edouard Samuel et al., "Ancient Egypt," Encyclopædia Britannica, accessed April 17, 2020, https://www.britannica.com/place/ancient-Egypt.

418. Declan Walsh and Somini Sengupta, "For Thousands of Years, Egypt Controlled the Nile. A New Dam Threatens That," *The New York Times*, February 9, 2020, https://www.nytimes.com/interactive/2020/02/09/world/africa/nile-river-dam.html.

419. "97% of Population Growth to Be in Developing World," Consultancy.uk, June 24, 2015, https://www.consultancy.uk/news/2191/97-percent-of-population-growth-to-be-in-developing-world.

420. Bradley A. Thayer, "Considering Population and War: A Critical and Neglected Aspect of Conflict Studies," October 27, 2009, https://royalsocietypublishing.org/doi/full/10.1098/rstb.2009.0151.

421. "List of Wars by Death Toll," Wikipedia, accessed May 30, 2019, https://en.wikipedia.org/wiki/List_of_wars_by_death_toll.

422. Kate Jones et al., "Global Trends in Emerging Infectious Diseases," *Nature*, vol. 451, February 21, 2008, https://doi.org/10.1038/nature06536.

423. Shulkhan Arukh, Even Ha'Ezer 1:5. For a fuller treatment of this topic, see Jeremy Cohen, *"Be Fertile and Increase, Fill the Earth and Master It"* (Ithaca, NY: Cornell University Press, 1989), 124–165.

424. In Rabbi Ellen Bernstein, *The Promise of the Land: A Passover Haggadah* (Millburn, NJ: Behrman House, 2020), 23.

425. See Genesis 14:10, 6:14, and 11:3.

426. John Schwartz, "Where's Airborne Plastic? Everywhere, Scientists Find," *The New York Times*, June 11, 2020, https://www.nytimes.com/2020/06/11/climate/airborne-plastic-pollution.html.

427. Rashi on Exodus 2:16.

428. Brian Beckers, Jonas Berking, and Brig Schütt, "Ancient Water Harvesting Methods in the Drylands of the Mediterranean and Western Asia," *Journal for Ancient Studies* 2, September 2013, 145–164.

429. Yoshihide Wada et al., "Global Depletion of Groundwater Resources," *Geophysical Research Letters* 37, no. 20, October 2010. This is about 25 percent of total seawater rise.

430. Midrash Exodus Rabbah 2:2.

431. Kli Yakar on Exodus 3:1.

432. Psalms 8:4–10.

433. Likutei Moharan 2:63.

434. Alon Tal, *All the Trees of the Forest: Israel's Woodlands from the Bible to the Present* (New Haven: Yale University Press, 2013), 175–179.

435. Gioietta Kuo, "When Fossil Fuels Run Out, What Then?" Millennium Alliance for Humanity and Biosphere, May 2019, https://mahb.stanford.edu/library-item/fossil-fuels-run/.

436. C. Nathan Bergeron, "Internal Heat in Chinese Medicine," accessed June 9, 2020, https://cnathanbergeron.com/internal-fire-in-chinese-medicine-2/.

437. Rabbi Bradley Artson, "Is There Only One Holy Land?" in *Ecology & the Jewish Spirit: Where Nature and the Sacred Meet*, Ellen Bernstein ed. (Woodstock, VT: Jewish Lights Publishing, 2008), 42.

438. Rashi on Exodus 6:6, Artscroll Rashi (New York: Mesorah Publications, 1994), footnote 6.

439. G.E. Miller, "The U.S. is the Most Overworked Developed Nation in the World," 20somethingfinance, last modified January 13, 2020, https://20somethingfinance.com/american-hours-worked-productivity-vacation/.

440. Alastair Marsh, "Virus Exposes Gig Economy 'Exploitation' ESG Investors Ignored," Bloomberg Green, March 27, 2020, https://www.bloomberg

.com/news/articles/2020-03-27/virus-exposes-gig-economy-exploitation-esg
-investors-ignored.

441. Cynthia Fuchs Epstein et al., *The Part Time Paradox: Time Norms, Profes-sional Lives, Family, and Gender* (New York: Routledge, 1998), 134.

442. Ibn Ezra on Samuel II 22:12.

443. Dr. Stephen Mortlock, "The Ten Plagues of Egypt," *The Biomedical Scientist*, January 7, 2019, https://thebiomedicalscientist.net/science/ten-plagues-egypt. See also Joel Ehrenkranz and Deborah Sampson, "Origin of the Old Testament Plagues: Explications and Implications," *Yale Journal of Biology and Medicine* 8, no. 1 (2008), 31–42.

444. S.I. Trevisanato, *The Plagues of Egypt: Archaeology, History, and Science Look at the Bible* (NJ: Gorgias Press, 2005).

445. Rabbi Yitzchak Breitowitz, "Learning Faith and Gratitude through Our Relationship to Hashem's Creation," Canfei Nesharim, January 29, 2014, http://canfeinesharim.org/learning-faith-and-gratitude-through-our-relationship-to-hashems-creation/.

446. Malbim on Exodus 7:18.

447. "What Is a Dead Zone?" National Oceanic and Atmospheric Admin-istration, US Department of Commerce, accessed February 2, 2019, https://oceanservice.noaa.gov/facts/deadzone.html.

448. B.Y. Queste et al., "Physical Controls on Oxygen Distribution and Denitri-fication Potential in the North West Arabian Sea," *Geophysical Research Letters*, 45, 4143–4152, April 27, 2018, https://agupubs.onlinelibrary.wiley.com/journal/19448007.

449. Jenny Howard, "Dead Zones, Explained," *National Geographic*, July 31, 2019, https://www.nationalgeographic.com/environment/oceans/dead-zones/.

450. Dominik Doehler, "What Passover Teaches Us about the Environmental Crisis," *The Jewish Journal*, April 5, 2019, https://jewishjournal.com/commentary/blogs/296977/what-passover-teaches-us-about-the-environmental-crisis/, based on an interview with Yonatan Neril.

451. Ligaya Mishan, "Frogs Are Disappearing. What Does That Mean?" *The New York Times*, October 18, 2018, https://www.nytimes.com/2018/10/18/t-magazine/frogs-extinction-food-fertility.html.

452. Rachel Grant and Timothy Halliday, "Predicting the Unpredictable; Evidence of Pre-Seismic Anticipatory Behaviour in the Common Toad," *Journal of Zoology* 281, no. 4, July 2010, https://zslpublications.onlinelibrary.wiley.com/doi/abs/10.1111/j.1469-7998.2010.00700.x.

453. Likutei Moharan 3. Perhaps the meaning is that a frog has an insightful bird's-eye view of what is coming.

454. Simon N. Stuart et al., "Status and Trends of Amphibian Declines and Extinctions Worldwide," *Science* 306, no. 5702, December 2004, https://science.sciencemag.org/content/306/5702/1783.

455. Laurie J. Vitt et al., "Amphibians as Harbingers of Decay," *BioScience* 40, no. 6 (June 1990): 418.

456. Lei Li et al., "Discovery of Novel Caeridins from the Skin Secretion of the Australian White's Tree Frog, *Litoria caerulea*," *International Journal of Genomics*, July 11 2018, https://www.hindawi.com/journals/ijg/2018/8158453/.

457. "The cane toad and other members of the Bufonidae family produce secretions widely used in traditional folk medicine, but endangered family members, like Panama's golden frog, *Atelopus zeteki*, may disappear before revealing their secrets." Candelario Rodríguez et al., "Toxins and Pharmacologically Active Compounds from Species of the Family Bufonidae (Amphibia, Anura)," *Journal of Ethnopharmacology*, February 2017, https://www.sciencedirect.com/science/article/abs/pii/S037887411632373X?via%3Dihub.

458. Midrash Tanchuma, Va'eira 14 (quoted by Rashi on Exodus 8:2: And the frogs (lit. frog) came up – "Really there was only one frog, but when they struck at it, it was split into many swarms. This is a midrashic explanation of the usage of the singular noun here" (cf. Babylonian Talmud, Sanhedrin 67b; Midrash Exodus Rabbah 10:4).

459. Matthew P. Hill, Sarina Macfadyen, Michael A. Nash, "Broad Spectrum Pesticide Application Alters Natural Enemy Communities and May Facilitate Secondary Pest Outbreaks," *PeerJ* vol. 5, December 19, 2017, https://peerj.com/articles/4179/.

460. Eric M. Gese, *Demographic and Spatial Responses of Coyotes to Changes in Food and Exploitation* (Logan: National Wildlife Research Center, 2005), 271–285.

461. Rabbi Akiva, Babylonian Talmud, Sanhedrin 67b.

462. Yalkut Shimoni, Tehillim 889.

463. Babylonian Talmud, Pesachim 56a. Perhaps this suggests that we would be wise to listen to the frogs if humankind is to live "forever and ever."

464. The chief disciple of the Ba'al Shem Tov.

465. John Vidal, "Destroyed Habitat Creates the Perfect Conditions for Coronavirus to Emerge," *Scientific American*, Ensia, March 18, 2020, https://www.scientificamerican.com/article/destroyed-habitat-creates-the-perfect-conditions-for-coronavirus-to-emerge/.

466. Rabbi Zalman M. Schachter-Shalomi and Netanel Miles-Yepez, *A Hidden Light: Stories and Teachings of Early HaBaD and Bratzlav Hasidism* (Santa Fe: Gaon Books, 2011), 235.

467. Commentary to 9:8.

468. This content was produced by Canfei Nesharim, a branch of Grow Torah. It is available at http://canfeinesharim.org/parshat-vaera-the-earth-is-the-lords/.

469. Exodus 9:29.

470. Chizkuni on Exodus 9:27.

471. Exodus 9:27.

472. Sforno on Exodus 9:29.

473. Exodus, commentary by Amos Chacham, trans. by the author (Jerusalem: Mosad HaRav Kook Publishers, 1991), 246.

474. Vladimir Jabotinsky, *A Pocket Edition of Several Stories, Mostly Reactionary* (Tel Aviv: Jabotinsky Institute, 1984).

475. United Nations Environment Programme, *Global Environmental Outlook 4* (Malta: Progress Press, 2007).

476. Rashi on Exodus 9:7, based on Onkelos.

477. Numbers 12:3.

478. Midrash Tanchuma 12:2.

479. Rabbi Daniel Kohn, oral class, Yeshivat Sulam Yaakov, Jerusalem, February 2011.

480. Cecil McKithan, "Drake Oil Well," *National Register of Historic Places. Inventory – Nomination Form.* Pennsylvania Historical and Museum Commission, March 1978, accessed July 8, 2011.

481. "Deepwater Horizon Oil Spill," Wikipedia, https://en.wikipedia.org/wiki/Deepwater_Horizon_oil_spill.

482. Jeff Desjardins, "The World's Deepest Oil Well Is Over 40,000 Feet Deep," *Business Insider*, March 22, 2017, https://www.businessinsider.com/worlds-deepest-oil-well-2017-3.

483. Exodus 9:15.

484. Malbim on Exodus 9:27.

485. Lawrence Torcello, "Yes, I Am a Climate Alarmist. Global Warming Is a Crime against Humanity," *The Guardian*, April 29, 2017, https://www.theguardian.com/commentisfree/2017/apr/29/climate-alarmist-global-warming-crime-humanity.

486. *Rabbi Nachman's Stories*, Rabbi Aryeh Kaplan trans. (Jerusalem: Breslov Research Institute, 1985), 279.

487. Adam R. Martin et al., "Regional and Global Shifts in Crop Diversity through the Anthropocene," PLOS ONE, February 6, 2019, https://journals.plos.org/plosone/article?id=10.1371/journal.pone.0209788.

488. Rashi on Exodus 10:3, based on Onkelos.

489. Ihab Mikati et al., "Disparities in Distribution of Particulate Matter Emission Sources by Race and Poverty Status," *American Journal of Public Health* 108, no. 4, April 2018, 480–485, https://ajph.aphapublications.org/doi/10.2105/AJPH.2017.304297.

490. Wangpeng Shi et al., "Unveiling the Mechanism by which Microsporidian Parasites Prevent Locust Swarm Behavior," PNAS 111, no. 4, January 2014, 1343–48, https://www.ncbi.nlm.nih.gov/pmc/articles/PMC5844406/.

491. Antoaneta Roussi, "Why Gigantic Locust Swarms Are Challenging Governments and Researchers," Nature, March 12, 2020, https://www.nature.com/articles/d41586-020-00725-x.

492. Bob Berwyn, "Locust Swarms, Some 3 Times the Size of New York City,

Are Eating Their Way across Two Continents," March 22, 2020, Inside Climate News, https://insideclimatenews.org/news/20032020/locust-swarms-climate -change.

493. The report was requested by the White House and based on a National Academy of Sciences climate study.

494. Arthur Waskow and Phyllis Berman, *Freedom Journeys – The Tale of Exodus and Wilderness across Millennia* (Vermont: Jewish Lights, 2011), 62.

495. Ibid., 63.

496. This content was produced by Canfei Nesharim, a branch of Grow Torah. It is available at http://canfeinesharim.org/wp-content/uploads/2014/05/Parsha -Bo-taking-notice-in-our-time-Rabbi-Judelman-dvartorah.pdf.

497. Psalms 148:1–10.

498. Babylonian Talmud, Berakhot 17a.

499. Braita of Rabbi Yishmael. Morning prayer book.

500. Sefat Emet 5631 Melil 1 Passover: Haggadah.

501. Jared Diamond, "What's Your Consumption Factor?" *Pacific Ecologist*, January 2008, https://www.researchgate.net/publication/265024582_What's_Your _Consumption_Factor.

502. See University of Colorado at Boulder, "Parting the Waters: Computer Modeling Applies Physics to Red Sea Escape Route," Phys.org, September 21, 2010, https://phys.org/news/2010-09-physics-red-sea-route-video.html, and Carl Drews and Weiqing Han, "Dynamics of Wind Setdown at Suez and the Eastern Nile Delta," PLOS ONE 5, no. 8, August 3, 2010, https://doi.org/10.1371 /journal.pone.0012481.

503. Jean T. Ellis and Douglas J. Sherman, "Perspectives on Coastal and Marine Hazards and Disasters," in *Coastal and Marine Hazards, Risks, and Disasters*, John F. Shroder ed. (Amsterdam: Elsevier, 2015), 1–13.

504. Isaiah 40:26.

505. Rabbi Shlomo Wolbe, Letters 1:5, and Chafetz Chayim, Shmirat HaLashon, part 2 quoted in *The Environment in Jewish Thought and Law*, Rabbi Shilo Ben-David (Jerusalem: Sviva, 2018), 185.

506. This content was produced by Canfei Nesharim, a branch of Grow Torah. It is available at http://canfeinesharim.org/water-appreciating-a-limited -resource-longer-article-for-deeper-study/.

507. Babylonian Talmud, Ta'anit 10a, citing Job 5:10. Thus when rain is withheld in Israel, it is because of Divine intervention in response to Israel's actions, as the second paragraph of *Shema* makes clear.

508. "Climate: Israel," Country Studies, US Library of Congress, accessed February 6, 2020, http://countrystudies.us/israel/36.htm.

509. "Normals & Extremes Central Park, NY (1869 to Present)," National Weather Service Forecast Office, USA.gov, published April 1, 2006, https://www .weather.gov/media/okx/Climate/CentralPark/nycnormals.pdf.

510. "Sataf – Ancient Agriculture in Action," Jewish National Fund, https://www.kkl-jnf.org/tourism-and-recreation/forests-and-parks/sataf-site.aspx. The wheat and barley were planted during the winter rains. Fig and date trees survive near water sources, while olives trees, grapevines, and pomegranate trees are able to subsist without rain for six months based on the water they received in the winter.

511. "Wastewater: The Untapped Resource," UN World Water Development Report, UNESCO, 2017, https://reliefweb.int/report/world/2017-un-world-water-development-report-wastewater-untapped-resource.

512. "Progress on Sanitation and Drinking-Water: Joint Monitoring Programme 2010 Update" (Geneva: WHO and UNICEF, 2010), https://www.who.int/water_sanitation_health/publications/9789241563956/en/.

513. United Nations, "SDG 6 Synthesis Report 2018 on Water and Sanitation," 2018, https://www.unwater.org/publication_categories/sdg-6-synthesis-report-2018-on-water-and-sanitation/.

514. Mekhilta d'Rabbi Yishmael 15:25 (translation from Sefaria).

515. Nachmanides on Exodus 15:25.

516. Likutei Moharan 112.

517. Leslie P. Norton, "The No. 1 Company in Key Sectors of Barron's 100 Most Sustainable Companies," *Barron's*, February 13, 2020, https://www.barrons.com/articles/the-no-1-company-in-key-sectors-of-barrons-100-most-sustainable-companies-51581600600.

518. Tzvi Freeman, "The Horse Kid Returns," Chabad.org, accessed August 5, 2019, https://www.chabad.org/library/article_cdo/aid/1959506/jewish/The-Horse-Kid-Returns.htm.

519. Rabbi Shmuel Simenowitz, "Water Conservation: When the Wood Meets the Water," Canfei Nesharim, a branch of Grow Torah, December 31, 2013, http://canfeinesharim.org/parshat-beshalach-water-conservation-when-the-wood-meets-the-water/.

520. Rabbi Aryeh Trugman on his commentary to Beshalach.

521. Ivan Samarawira. "Date Palm, Potential Source for Refined Sugar," *Economic Botany* 37, no. 2 (April 1983), 181–186.

522. Mohamed E. El-Khouly, Eithar El-Mohsnawy, and Shunichi Fukuzumi, "Solar Energy Conversion: From Natural to Artificial Photosynthesis," *Journal of Photochemistry and Photobiology C: Photochemistry Reviews* 31, June 2017, 36–83, https://doi.org/10.1016/j.jphotochemrev.2017.02.001.

523. *Mind Over Matter: The Lubavitcher Rebbe on Science, Technology and Medicine*, comp. Rabbi Joseph Ginsburg and Professor Herman Branover, ed. trans. Dr. Arnie Gotfryd (Jerusalem: Shamir, 2000), under the Hebrew title *Mah Rabu Ma'asecha Hashem!* (p. 252–3).

524. See "Veg Rabbis," Jewish Veg, accessed February 6, 2020, https://www.jewishveg.org/veg-rabbis.

525. See Rabbi J. David Bleich, "Chapter VI," in *Contemporary Halakhic Problems* (New York: KTAV Publishing House, 1977–2005), and "Year 18", *Kovetz Bais Aharon veYisroel* 107, no. 5 (Sivan–Tammuz 5763, Spring 2003).
And *Ha-Be'er* 23, no. 1 (Tishri 5764, Fall 2004), Dov Ben Moshe Weiss ed., https://www.hebrewbooks.org/50589.

526. Ha'amek Davar on Exodus 16:14.

527. Megan A. McCrory et al., "Fast-Food Offerings in the United States in 1986, 1991, and 2016 Show Large Increases in Food Variety, Portion Size, Dietary Energy, and Selected Micronutrients," *Journal of the Academy of Nutrition and Dietetics* 119, no. 6, February 27, 2019, 923–933, https://doi.org/10.1016/j.jand.2018.12.004.

528. "US Obesity Levels by State," ProCon.org, accessed August 2018, https://obesity.procon.org/view.resource.php?resourceID=006026.

529. Oliver Milman, "Americans Waste 150,000 Tons of Food Each Day – Equal to a Pound per Person," *The Guardian*, April 18, 2018, https://www.theguardian.com/environment/2018/apr/18/americans-waste-food-fruit-vegetables-study.

530. Babylonian Talmud, Yoma 76a.

531. Rachel Widome, "Eating When There Is Not Enough to Eat: Eating Behaviors and Perceptions of Food among Food-Insecure Youths," *American Journal of Public Health* 99, no. 5, May 2009, 822–828, https://10.2105/AJPH.2008.139758\.

532. Paul Artiuch and Samuel Kornstein, "Sustainable Approaches to Reducing Food Waste in India" (Boston: MIT, 2012), http://web.mit.edu/colab/pdf/papers/Reducing_Food_Waste_India.pdf.

533. Ibid.

534. Shuai Yang, Yujie Xiao, and Yong-Hong Kuo, "The Supply Chain Design for Perishable Food with Stochastic Demand," *Sustainability* 9, no. 7, July 2017, 1195, https://doi.org/10.3390/su9071195.

535. Rashi on Exodus 16:21, citing Mekhilta (a midrash).

536. Quoting Ma'aseh Alfass, as quoted by Rabbi Prof. David Golinkin, "Why is Shabbat Shirah 'For the Birds'?" The Schechter Institutes, accessed June 1, 2020, http://www.schechter.edu/why-is-shabbat-shirah-for-the-birds-2/.

537. Josie A. Galbraith et al., "Supplementary Feeding Restructures Urban Bird Communities," *Proceedings of the National Academy of Sciences of the United States of America* 112, no. 20, May 2015, https://doi.org/10.1073/pnas.1501489112.

538. James Gorman, "It Could Be the Age of the Chicken, Geologically," *The New York Times*, December 11, 2018, https://www.nytimes.com/2018/12/11/science/chicken-anthropocene-archaeology.html.

539. Carys E. Bennett et al., "The Broiler Chicken as a Signal of a Human Reconfigured Biosphere," *The Royal Society* 5, no. 12, December 12, 2018, https://doi.org/10.1098/rsos.180325.

540. Malbim on Exodus 16:15.

541. Tur Ha'Arokh on Exodus 16:15.

542. Chizkuni to Numbers 11:8, based on the Midrash.

543. Joane Slavin and Beate Lloyd, "Health Benefits of Fruits and Vegetables," *Advances in Nutrition* 3, no. 4, July 2012, 506–516, https://doi.org/10.3945/an.112.002154.

544. T.H. Chan, "Processed Foods and Health," The Nutrition Source, accessed June 9, 2020, https://www.hsph.harvard.edu/nutritionsource/processed-foods/.

545. Maimonides, *Guide to the Perplexed* 3:22.

546. Bob Lee, Alan R. Graefe, and Robert Burns, "An Exploratory Study of the Outdoor Recreation Participation of Families Who Have a Child under Sixteen," in *Proceedings of the 2006 Northeastern Recreation Research Symposium* (Newtown Square: Northern Research Station, 2006).

547. https://bcorporation.net/.

548. Bekhor Shor on Exodus 18:21.

549. Kelvin S.H. Peh and Ofir Drori, "Fighting Corruption to Save the Environment: Cameroon's Experience," *AMBIO* 39, no. 4, May 13, 2010, 336–339, https://doi.org/https://dx.doi.org/10.1007%2Fs13280-010-0053-0.

550. Rabbi Jonathan Sacks, "Yitro (5774) – A Nation of Leaders," *Covenant and Conversation*, January 14, 2014, http://rabbisacks.org/yitro-5774-nation-leaders/.

551. Michael Cox, "The Pathology of Command and Control: a Formal Synthesis," *Ecology and Society* 21, no. 3, 2016, 33, http://dx.doi.org/10.5751/ES-08698-210333.

552. J. Stephen Lansing, *Priests & Programmers. Technologies of Power in the Engineered Landscape of Bali* (Princeton: Princeton University Press, 2007).

553. Mekhilta HaChodesh, section 1.

554. Deanne Stillman, *Desert Reckoning: A Town Sheriff, a Mojave Hermit, and the Biggest Manhunt in Modern California History* (Indiana: Bold Type Books, 2012).

555. Psalms 24:1.

556. Ibid., 115:16.

557. Babylonian Talmud, Berakhot 35a.

558. John Sean Doyle, "The Gratitude Diet:™ Savoring and Losing Weight," *Psychology Today*, December 31, 2016, https://www.psychologytoday.com/us/blog/luminous-things/201612/the-gratitude-diet.

559. This content was produced by Canfei Nesharim, a branch of Grow Torah. It is available at http://canfeinesharim.org/parshat-yitro-love-of-g-d-and-material-desire/.

560. HaKetav VeHaKabbalah on Parshat Yitro.

561. Deuteronomy 6:5.

562. Rabbi Elchanan Samet, "The Tenth Commandment: 'You Shall Not Covet,'" 2002, Yeshivat Har Etzion, https://www.etzion.org.il/en/tenth-commandment-you-shall-not-covet.

563. "How Big Is Your Ecological Footprint?" Center for Sustainable Economy, accessed March 2, 2019, http://myfootprint.org/en/.

564. Midrash Melekh Moshiach in Beit HaMidrash, Jellenik ed., quoted in *Torah Shelema* p. 124, Parshat Yitro #405.

565. Or HaChayim on Exodus 20:20.

566. Jared Diamond, *Collapse* (London: Penguin, 2005), 242.

567. "Giving USA 2019," Giving USA, June 18, 2019, https://givingusa.org/giving -usa-2019-americans-gave-427-71-billion-to-charity-in-2018-amid-complex -year-for-charitable-giving/.

568. Larry Kramer, "Philanthropy Must Stop Fiddling While the World Burns," *The Chronicle of Philanthropy*, January 7, 2020, https://www.philanthropy.com /article/Philanthropy-Must-Stop/247761.

569. Rashi on Exodus 21:24.

570. Sean Fleming, "How Much Is Nature Worth?" World Economic Forum, October 30, 2018, https://www.weforum.org/agenda/2018/10/this-is-why -putting-a-price-on-the-value-of-nature-could-help-the-environment/.

571. Mishnah Sanhedrin 1:4.

572. Mishnah Bava Kama 4:4.

573. Israel Rosenson, *Behold It Was Very Good* (Jerusalem: Hanoi Vehanetzach, 2001), 97.

574. Bernard E. Rollin, "Animal Rights as a Mainstream Phenomenon," MDPI 1, no, 1, January 2011, 102–115.

575. Rashi on Exodus 21:33.

576. Tosefta Bava Kama 2:12 as quoted in Israel Rosenson, *Behold It Was Very Good* (Jerusalem: Hanoi Vehanetzach, 2001), 110.

577. Global Terrorism Index 2017, Institute for Economics and Peace, November 15, 2017, https://reliefweb.int/report/world/global-terrorism-index-2017.

578. Olayinka Ajala, "Why Clashes Are on the Rise between Farmers and Herdsmen in the Sahel," *The Conversation*, May 2, 2018, https://theconversation .com/why-clashes-are-on-the-rise-between-farmers-and-herdsmen-in-the -sahel-95554.

579. Maharal, Netivot Olam, Netiv HaTzedaka 6:5.

580. Rabbi Matis Weinberg, *Frameworks: Exodus* (Boston: Foundation for Jewish Publications, 1999), 187.

581. Rabbi Daniel Kohn, lecture, Yeshivat Sulam Yaakov, Jerusalem, 2012.

582. Rashi on Exodus 22:24.

583. James R. Kahn and Judith A. McDonald, "Third-World Debt and Tropical Deforestation," *Ecological Economics* 12, no. 2, February 1995, 107–123, https:// www.sciencedirect.com/science/article/abs/pii/092180099400024P.

584. Pervaze A. Sheikh, *Debt-for-Nature Initiatives and the Tropical Forest Conservation Act: Status and Implementation* (Washington DC: Congressional Research Service, 2010).

585. Richard Schwartz, *Judaism and Vegetarianism* (New York: Lantern Books, 2001), 22.

586. Rabbi Elie Munk, *The Call of the Torah* (New York: ArtScroll, 1992), 268.

587. Proverbs 12:10.

588. Midrash Leviticus Rabbah 27:11.

589. Kathrin Wagner et al., "Effects of Mother versus Artificial Rearing during the First 12 Weeks of Life on Challenge Responses of Dairy Cows," *Applied Animal Behaviour Science* 164, March 2015, 1–11.

590. Rabbi David Rosen, "Jewish Ethics, Animal Welfare, and Veganism: A Panel of Rabbis and Experts," Jewish Eco Seminars, JES Productions, January 2018, https://www.youtube.com/watch?v=UHIyXrN1JAI.

591. Rabbi Samuel David Luzzatto (Shadal) on Exodus 23:5.

592. Rabbi Shmuly Yanklowitz, "How Kosher Is Your Milk?" *Jewish Journal*, June 7, 2012, https://jewishjournal.com/culture/food/104874/how-kosher-is -your-milk/.

593. Rashi on Exodus 23:12.

594. Malbim on Exodus 23:12.

595. Commentary to Exodus 32:12 in Samson Raphael Hirsch, *The Pentateuch*, vol. 2: Exodus, Isaac Levy trans. (Gateshead: Judaica Press, 1982).

596. Babylonian Talmud, Shabbat 88a.

597. Garrett Hardin, "The Tragedy of the Commons," *Science* 162, no. 3859, December 13, 1968, 1243–1248, DOI: 10.1126/science.162.3859.1243.

598. Elinor Ostrom, *Governing the Commons: The Evolution of Institutions for Collective Action* (Cambridge, UK: Cambridge University Press, 1990).

599. Silk emanates from the cocoon of a silkworm not the worm itself, and the rabbis point out that this is considered plant material, because, if not, the material would be from an impure insect and forbidden in the Tabernacle (see Rabbeinu Bachaya on Exodus 25:3).

600. Rabbi Yanki Tauber, "Wood Submerged in Stone: Joseph, Judah and the Servant-King," Chabad.org, accessed January 16, 2019, www.chabad.org /therebbe/article_cdo/aid/4032810/jewish/Avot-117-Wood-Submerged-in -Stone-Joseph-Judah-and-the-Servant-King.htm.

601. Pardes Rimonim, Sha'ar 12, ch. 2, f. 66a.

602. Batsheva Goldman-Ida, *Hasidic Art & Kabbalah* (Boston: Brill Academic Publisher, 2017), 85.

603. Rabbi Tuvia Aronson, commentary on the Torah portion of Terumah 5762 (2002), published on torathateva.org, accessed in 2005, citing Abarbanel commentary to Parshat Terumah, citing Josephus, *The Antiquities of the Jews* 43:11.

604. Rabbeinu Bachaya on Exodus 25:5, citing Babylonian Talmud, Shabbat 28b.

605. Odell Shepard, *The Lore of the Unicorn* (California: CreateSpace, 2011), 176.

606. Lloyd F. Lowry, Kristin L. Laidre, and Randall R. Reeves, "Monodon Monoceros," IUCN Red List of Threatened Species, July 3 2017, https://dx.doi .org/10.2305/IUCN.UK.2017-3.RLTS.T13704A50367651.en.

607. This content has been adapted from an article produced by Canfei Nesharim,

a branch of Grow Torah. The full article is available at http://canfeinesharim .org/trees_torah_caringfortheearth_longerarticle/.

608. Midrash Tanchuma (Warsaw edition), Parshat Terumah, §9.

609. Psalms 96:12–13, Artscroll translation. This chapter is read or sung every week during Kabbalat Shabbat.

610. James A. Duke, "Acacia Tortilis (Forsk) Hayne," Handbook of Energy Crops, Purdue University Center for New Crops and Plants Products, https:// hort.purdue.edu/newcrop/duke_energy/Acacia_tortilis.html.

611. Tanchuma Vayak-hel 9 and Midrash Exodus Rabbah Terumah 35.

612. Adam Startin, "Fact Check: Are There Really More Trees Today Than 100 Years Ago?," Tentree International, October 22, 2017, https://www.tentree.com /blogs/posts/fact-check-are-there-really-more-trees-today-than-100-years-ago.

613. Thomas W. Crowther, Henry B. Glick, and Kristofer Covey, "Mapping Tree Density at a Global Scale," Nature 525 (September 2015), 201–205, 10.1038/ nature14967.

614. Rabbi Joshua ibn Shuaib of medieval Spain, commentary on Terumah, cited in Torah Shelema, compiled by Rabbi Menachem Mendel Kasher (1895–1983), p. 14 of volume that includes Parshat Terumah to Exodus 25:6.

615. Exodus 25:8.

616. Rabbi Samson Raphael Hirsch, commentary on Exodus 25:10–11.

617. Psalms 128:3.

618. Eda Goldstein, "The Marvels of a 2000-Year-Old Olive Tree in Israel," accessed January 3, 2020, www.greenprophet.com/2009/03/olive-tree-ancient -israel/.

619. Luca Sebastiani, et al. The Olive Tree Genome (New York: Springer, 2016), 14.

620. Babylonian Talmud, Arakhin 16a.

621. Chomat Anakh on Exodus 28:15.

622. Rabbi Ovadia Bartenura on Exodus 28:15.

623. Babylonian Talmud, Shabbat 31a.

624. This content was produced by Canfei Nesharim, a branch of Grow Torah. It is available at http://canfeinesharim.org/parshat-tetzaveh-all-that-is-gold -does-not-glitter/.

625. William Shakespeare, The Merchant of Venice (Essex: Longman, 1994).

626. Exodus 25–28, and other verses.

627. Rashi on Exodus 28:5, explained in Exodus 39:1–5.

628. The EPA has identified 156 hardrock mining sites nationwide that have the potential to cost between $7 billion and $24 billion total to clean up. See "Who Should Pay for Mine Clean-Up: Industry or Taxpayers?" Financial Assurance and Superfund, Earthworks, accessed January 12, 2019, https://earthworks.org /issues/financial_assurance_bonding_and_cercla_108b/.

629. "How Gold Is Mined – Part 11: Heap Leach Mining," Ely Gold Royalties,

accessed January 12, 2019, https://elygoldinc.com/investors/articles/2019/gold-leaching-to-extract-gold.

630. R. Eisler and S.N. Wiemeyer, "Cyanide Hazards to Plants and Animals from Gold Mining and Related Water Issues," Reviews of Environmental Contamination and Toxicology 183, 2004, 21–54, https://doi.org/10.1007/978-1-4419-9100-3_2.

631. "New Toxic Spill Hits Eastern Europe," BBC News, March 10, 2000, http://news.bbc.co.uk/2/hi/europe/673544.stm.

632. "$180 Million Investment to Tackle the Hidden Cost of Gold," The Global Environment Facility, February 17, 2019, https://www.thegef.org/news/180-million-investment-tackle-hidden-cost-gold.

633. L.J. Esdaile, J.M. Chalker, "The Mercury Problem in Artisanal and Small-Scale Gold Mining," Chemistry Europe, January 3, 2018, https://chemistry-europe.onlinelibrary.wiley.com/doi/full/10.1002/chem.201704840.

634. "Artisanal and Small-Scale Gold Mining without Mercury," International Cooperation, US EPA, accessed February 9, 2020, https://www.epa.gov/international-cooperation/artisanal-and-small-scale-gold-mining-without-mercury.

635. Exodus 28:2.

636. There are a number of recycled jewelry companies emerging. See "25 Eco Jewelry Brands Making Stunning Pieces out of Up-Cycled and Fair-Mined Metals," Conscious Collective, Green Dreamer, accessed February 9, 2020, https://consciousfashion.co/guides/eco-jewelry-brands.

637. Orot HaKodesh II: 431. Quoted in: Rabbi Arthur Waskow, Torah of the Earth Vol 1: Exploring 4,000 Years of Ecology in Jewish Thought (Vermont: Jewish Lights, 2000), 28.

638. Kli Yakar on Exodus 28:31, based on Rabbi Meir in Babylonian Talmud, Menachot 43b.

639. Chenchen Peng, Kazuo Yamashita, and Eiichi Kobayashi, "Effects of the Coastal Environment on Well-Being," Journal of Coastal Zone Management 19, 2016, 421, https://doi.org/10.4172/2473-3350.1000421.

640. The Babylonian Talmud, Yoma 72b, explains that the High Priest's clothes could be reused by the temporary High Priest, appointed during a war.

641. Numbers 20:26.

642. Dana Thomas, "The High Price of Fast Fashion," The Wall Street Journal, August 29, 2019, citing a study by the British charity Barnado's https://www.wsj.com/articles/the-high-price-of-fast-fashion-11567096637.

643. "Barnardo's Calls for People to Think 'Pre-Loved' before Buying New Clothes," Barnado's, July 19, 2019, https://www.barnardos.org.uk/news/barnardos-calls-people-think-pre-loved-buying-new-clothes, based on a poll conducted by Censuswide.

644. *Apparel and Footwear in 2016: Trend, Developments and Prospects* (London: Euromonitor International, 2016).

645. "UN Helps Fashion Industry Shift to Low Carbon," *United Nations Climate Change News*, UNFCCC, September 6, 2018, https://unfccc.int/news/un-helps -fashion-industry-shift-to-low-carbon.

646. Laura Farrant, Stig Irving Olsen, and Arne Wangel, "Environmental Benefits from Reusing Clothes," *The International Journal of Life Cycle Assessment* 15, no. 7, August 2010, 726–736, https://doi.org/10.1007/s11367-010-0197-y.

647. Gemma Alexander, "How to Find Ethical Jewelry," Earth911, February 5, 2019, https://earth911.com/business-policy/how-to-find-ethical-jewelry/.

648. This commentary was adapted from content produced by Canfei Nesharim, a branch of Grow Torah. It is available at http://canfeinesharim.org/parshat -ki-tisa-material-wealth-the-coin-of-fire/.

649. Rashi on Exodus 30:15–16.

650. Rashi on Exodus 30:13.

651. Rabbi Noam Elimelech of Lizhensk, *Noam Elimelech* on Ki Tisa, p. 130 in edition of Yarid Hasefarim, Jerusalem, 1995.

652. David Segal, "Syrian Workers Toil on Turkey's Hazelnut Farms with Little to Show for It," *The New York Times*, April 29, 2019, https://www.nytimes.com /2019/04/29/business/syrian-refugees-turkey-hazelnut-farms.html.

653. Ecclesiastes 7:20.

654. Sefat Emet, Shekalim 5655.

655. "Why We Do It," Reducetarian Foundation, accessed February 9, 2020, https://www.reducetarian.org/why.

656. Babylonian Talmud, Berakhot 32a. Quoted by Rabbi Sharon Brous, www .ikar-la.org.

657. Rabbi Levi Yitzchok of Berditchev, Kedushat Levi, Noach, §18, quoting the Zohar.

658. Rabbi Sharon Brous, *The Climate Crisis Is Here. What We Do Now Matters,* September 2019, https://ikar-la.org/wp-content/uploads/RH1-Climate -WITH-LINKS.pdf, 5.

659. Citizen's Climate Lobby, https://citizensclimatelobby.org/energy-inno vation-and-carbon-dividend-act/.

660. "UK Parliament declares climate change emergency," BBC News, May 1, 2019, https://www.bbc.com/news/uk-politics-48126677.

661. Yonatan Neril, "Sustainability in Settling the Land of Israel," produced by Canfei Nesharim, a branch of Grow Torah. It is available at http://canfeinesharim .org/sustainability-in-settling-the-land-of-israel/.

662. Babylonian Talmud, Ketubot 111b.

663. Tosefta Beitza 4:11, Talmud Yerushalmi, Beitza ch. 5, Bablyonian Talmud, Beitza 40a.

664. *Toldot HaYehudim B'Eretz Yisrael B'Tkufat HaMishnah v'haTalmud*, 101–2.

665. Mishnah Bava Kama 7:7, and Maimonides, *Hilkhot Nizkei Mamon* 5:2. Forests and desert areas were exempt from this decree.

666. Babylonian Talmud, Bava Kama 80a, according to Rav Yehuda.

667. Babylonian Talmud, Sanhedrin 25b.

668. "Cattle Ranching in the Amazon Region," Yale School of Forestry and Environmental Studies, Global Forest Atlas, accessed June 15, 2020, https://globalforestatlas.yale.edu/amazon/land-use/cattle-ranching.

669. John Vidal, "Destroyed Habitat Creates the Perfect Conditions for Coronavirus to Emerge," *Scientific American*, Ensia, March 18, 2020, https://www.scientificamerican.com/article/destroyed-habitat-creates-the-perfect-conditions-for-coronavirus-to-emerge/.

670. J. Olivero, J.E. Fa, R. Real et al., "Recent Loss of Closed Forests Is Associated with Ebola Virus Disease Outbreaks," *Scientific Reports* 7, 14291 (2017), https://doi.org/10.1038/s41598-017-14727-9.

671. Nathan Rott, "Scientists Say the Coronavirus Pandemic Has Worsened Deforestation Worldwide," NPR, June 23, 2020, https://www.npr.org/2020/06/23/882481310/scientists-say-the-coronavirus-pandemic-has-worsened-deforestation-worldwide.

672. Numbers 12:3.

673. Abarbanel on Exodus 34:3.

674. Yehuda Shurpin, "What Is the Meaning of the 'Evil Eye'?" accessed March 29, 2020, https://www.chabad.org/library/article_cdo/aid/166909/jewish/What-Is-the-Meaning-of-the-Evil-Eye.htm?gclid=EAIaIQobChMIlKXPvZ-_6AIVkkDTCh3OiQGgEAAYASAAEgLpMvD_BwE.

675. Philip Landrigan et al., "Chemical Contaminants in Breast Milk and Their Impacts on Children's Health: An Overview," Environmental Health Perspectives, June 1, 2002, https://doi.org/10.1289/ehp.021100313.

676. Calum Neill, Janelle Gerard, and Katherine D. Arbuthnott, "Nature Contact and Mood Benefits: Contact Duration and Mood Type," *The Journal of Positive Psychology* 14, no. 6, December 2018, https://doi.org/10.1080/17439760.2018.1557242.

677. This is adapted from content produced by Canfei Nesharim, a branch of Grow Torah. The original content is available at http://canfeinesharim.org/parshat-vayakhel-an-ecological-message-in-shabbat/.

678. Rabbi Norman Lamm, "Ecology in Jewish Law and Theology" in *Faith and Doubt: Studies in Traditional Jewish Thought; Third Augmented Edition*, Bernard Scharfstein ed. (New Jersey: KTAV Publishing House, 2006), 163–164.

679. Exodus 20:10.

680. There are 39 categories of creative work forbidden on Shabbat. Some examples are cooking and other constructive uses of fire, sewing, and building.

681. Rabbi Abraham Joshua Heschel, *Between Man and God* (New York: Simon and Schuster, 1959), 221–22.

682. Rabbi Samson Raphael Hirsch, "The Jewish Sabbath," in *Judaism Eternal: Selected Essays from the Writings of Rabbi Samson Raphael Hirsch*, 1st ed., Dayan Isidore Grunfeld ed. (London: The Soncino Press, 1956), 30.

683. Genesis 2:15.

684. Rabbi Eliyahu Dessler, Mikhtav Me'Eliyahu vol. 1, Kuntres HaChesed, 35–38.

685. Michael I. Norton, Daniel Mochon, and Dan Ariely, "The IKEA Effect: When Labor Leads to Love," *Journal of Consumer Psychology* 22, no. 3, July 2012, 453–60.

686. Selin Kesebir and Pelin Kesebir, "A Growing Disconnection from Nature Is Evident in Cultural Products," *Perspectives on Psychological Science* 12, no. 2, March 27, 2017, 258–69, https://doi.org/10.1177%2F1745691616662473.

687. Ezekiel 47:7–12.

688. Rabbi Ellen Bernstein, "Vayikra, The Culture of Giving Back," forthcoming article.

689. Numbers 21:8.

690. Marin Vincent, et al., "Contact Killing and Antimicrobial Properties of Copper," *Journal of Applied Microbiology* 124, no. 5, May 2018, 1032–1046, https://doi.org/10.1111/jam.13681.

691. Rabbi David Seidenberg, "'And He Made the Copper Basin for Washing': Our New Normal," March 20, 2020, https://blogs.timesofisrael.com/and-he-made-the-copper-basin-for-washing-our-new-normal/.

692. Neeltje van Doremalen et al., "Aerosol and Surface Stability of SARS-CoV-2 as Compared with SARS-CoV-1," April 16, 2020, *New England Journal of Medicine 2020*, 382:1564-1567 DOI: 10.1056/NEJMc2004973.

693. This content was produced by Canfei Nesharim, a branch of Grow Torah. It is available at http://canfeinesharim.org/wp-content/uploads/2014/05/Parsha-pekudey-dvartorah-God-is-in-the-details.pdf.

694. See Rashi on Exodus 38:21: "In the Torah portion of Pekudei, the weight of all the silver, gold, and copper gifts to the Tabernacle is weighed, and all the utensils for every ritual are counted."

695. Between these two descriptions is a short section detailing the manufacturing of the priestly garments.

696. As the Mishnah in Chagigah 1:8 states, many laws are like "mountains hanging on a single thread of verses."

697. Midrash Numbers Rabbah 12:13.

698. John Javna, Sophie Javna, and Jesse Javna, *50 Simple Things You Can Do to Save the Earth* (New York: Hyperion Books, 2008).

699. Marjorie Lamb, *Two Minutes a Day for a Greener Planet: Quick and Simple Things You Can Do to Save the Earth* (Toronto: Harpercollins, 1990), and B. Fleishhacker, *101 Ways to Save Money and Save Our Planet* (Los Angeles: Paper Chase Press, 1992).

700. Rick LeBlanc, "Plastic Recycling Facts and Figures," The Balance Small Business, updated October 10, 2019, https://www.thebalancesmb.com/plastic -recycling-facts-and-figures-2877886.

701. Even paper bags do not always decompose in landfills. The most ecological option appears to be the reuse of bags you already have as much as possible. See Zoë Schlanger, "Your Cotton Tote Is Pretty Much the Worst Replacement for a Plastic Bag," *Quartz*, April 1, 2019, https://qz.com/1585027/when-it-comes-to -climate-change-cotton-totes-might-be-worse-than-plastic/.

702. Morgan O'Mara, "How Much Paper Is Used in One Day?", Record Nations, January 3, 2020, https://www.recordnations.com/2016/02/how-much-paper -is-used-in-one-day/.

703. Maimonides, Mishneh Torah, Laws of Repentance 3:4.

704. Rashi on Exodus 38:21.

705. Jonathan Wentworth, *Biodiversity Auditing – Postnote 490* (London: Parliamentary Office of Science and Technology, Houses of Parliament, March 2015).

706. Resource Guide on National Greenhouse Gas Inventories, UNFCCC, 2009, http://unfccc.int/resource/docs/publications/09_resource_guide3.pdf.

707. Kli Yakar on Exodus 39:43, citing Genesis 1:31.

708. Tehrene Firman, "8 Eco-Friendly Clothing Brands to Give Your Wardrobe a Totally Chic (and Sustainable) Makeover," Well+Good, July 1, 2019, https:// www.wellandgood.com/good-looks/eco-friendly-clothing/.

Index

If you liked *Eco Bible*, please write a short review on www.amazon.com.

Type "Eco Bible Neril Dee" to find this book.

Thank you so much!